19·11·76

edited by I.Masser · London papers in regional science 6 · a pion publication

theory and practice in regional science

Pion Limited, 207 Brondesbury Park, London NW2 5JN

Printed in Great Britain by J.W.Arrowsmith Limited, Bristol.

Preface

This volume contains most of the papers that were presented at the seventh Annual Conference of the British section of the Regional Science Association, held in London on August 22nd and 23rd 1974. These papers review aspects of urban and regional theory and consider the application in policy making of methods based on regional science. The relevance of these issues to the future development of regional science is evident not only in the papers themselves but also by the large number of British section members attending the meeting who were engaged in local- and central-government planning agencies. An important consequence of this meeting was the decision of the British section to set up workshop groups to review recent developments in the field and to promote original research on topics of common interest.

The tone of the meeting and of the papers contained in this volume is captured by Isard in the last section of his paper. He suggests that the real and positive advances that have been made in regional science during the last ten years must be viewed in the context of an even greater expansion in peoples' perception of what needs to be done in terms of the theory of, the methodology for, and the application to planning problems. Some of the implications of this theme for urban and regional theory are considered in greater detail in the other papers contained in the first section of this volume, especially in the paper by Carney and his colleagues which points to some of the limitations of current theories and argues that a critique of the ideology of regional underdevelopment is required before long-term technical solutions to this kind of problem can be formulated.

The second section of the collection contains papers largely concerned with methodology and possible application of some recent developments in mathematics to regional science, while the last section is devoted to the application of regional science methods to the clarification of policy issues. The need to combine theoretical elegance with practical relevance is particularly well illustrated in the paper by Rosing and Odell, which describes the results of their simulation of the development of the North Sea Oil Province. The findings of this research project draw attention to a number of important policy issues, and demonstrate the practical as well as the theoretical value of regional science as a field of study.

IM
Instituut voor Planologie, Rijksuniversiteit Utrecht

Contributors

R. H. Atkin   *Department of Mathematics, University of Essex, Wivenhoe Park, Colchester CO4 3SQ*

T. B. Boffey   *Department of Computational and Statistical Science, University of Liverpool, Liverpool L69 3BX*

J. Carney   *North East Area Study, University of Durham, Durham DH1 3LE*

M. E. Frost   *Department of Geography, Kings College, University of London, London WC2R 2LS*

L. W. Hepple   *Department of Geography, University of Bristol, Bristol BS8 1SS*

R. Hudson   *Department of Geography, University of Durham, Durham DH1 3LE*

W. Isard   *Department of Regional Science, University of Pennsylvania, Philadelphia, Pennsylvania 19174*

G. Ive   *Department of Surveying, Liverpool Polytechnic, Liverpool L3 3AF*

J. Lewis   *Department of Geography, University of Cambridge, Cambridge CB2 3EN*

S. M. Macgill   *Department of Geography, University of Leeds, Leeds LS2 9JT*

P. R. Odell   *Economische Geografisch Instituut, Erasmus Universiteit, Postbus 1738, Rotterdam*

K. E. Rosing   *Economische Geografisch Instituut, Erasmus Universiteit, Postbus 1738, Rotterdam*

G. R. Walter   *Department of Economics, University of Victoria, Victoria, British Columbia*

A. G. Wilson   *Department of Geography, University of Leeds, Leeds LS2 9JT*

Contents

Some Directions for the Extension of Dynamic Spatial Analysis

W.ISARD
University of Pennsylvania

In the papers which I have presented in past years to the British section of the Regional Science Association, I have been exploring several new directions for the development of a proper dynamics for regional science. Still other directions need to be probed, and in this paper I wish to begin to attack one of them. To do so, however, leads me to present a rather wild background of ideas, for which I must ask tolerance.

Let me build upon several of the papers already presented. Last year I spoke about micro- and macro-trading behaviour in the context of an optimal space–time development model (Isard and Liossatos, 1975a). I presented the basic local income identity or 'supply = demand' equation:

$$\dot{K}(x, t) = Y(x, t) - C(x, t) - \overset{x}{U}(x, t) - \sigma U(x, t) , \tag{1}$$

where at space–time point (x, t)
$K(x, t)$ is the capital stock per unit length,
$\dot{K}(x, t)$ is the time rate of change of capital stock, that is the investment or increase in capital stock per unit length per unit time,
$Y(x, t)$ is the production per unit length per unit time,
$C(x, t)$ is the consumption per unit length per unit time,
σ is the transport rate in terms of goods used up per unit flow of goods, with dimensions of $(\text{length})^{-1}$,
$U(x, t)$ is the flow of goods, through any point x at time t, per unit time,
σU is the transport cost of the flow U in terms of goods used up per unit length and per unit time, and
$\overset{x}{U}(x, t)$ is the space rate of change of the flow U (that is net exports when positive, and net imports when negative) of goods per unit length and per unit time.

In equation (1), supply is represented by Y, and demand by the sum of $\dot{K}$, C, $\overset{x}{U}$, and σU.

During the last year I have been able to extend this model to draw upon classical field-theoretical models of physical phenomena, including the model of the motion of a spring (a simple harmonic oscillator), transverse motion of a string, electrical transmission phenomena, electro-magnetic wave propagation, and wave propagation in a fluid. Thereby it becomes possible to demonstrate a basic unity of our social space–time development model and basic physical phenomena. In doing so, I need to add another equation to the model, namely

$$l\dot{U}(x, t) = -\xi\overset{x}{K}(x, t) - \sigma U(x, t) , \tag{2}$$

where $-\xi\overset{x}{K}$ represents a driving force for capital diffusion. Differences in the stock of capital $K(x, t)$ and $K(x + dx, t)$ at neighbouring points x and $x + dx$ lead to differences in the marginal productivity of capital and thus to differences in 'profitability' of capital at these points. Deleting the term σU in equation (1) and putting it in equation (2), we see that in equation (2) σU, which represents transport costs on the flow U through x at time t, diminishes the driving force $-\xi\overset{x}{K}$ just as resistance in a transmission line diminishes the driving force there. The driving force diminished by the transport cost is then balanced by an inertial-type force $l\dot{U}$, which resists any change in U, where the coefficient l represents a propensity (a force per unit of $\dot{U}$) for the system to resist change in U. I do not have time to dwell on these parallels with physical phenomena. They are making it possible to gain many new insights for the construction of more meaningful space–time development models (Isard and Liossatos, 1975b, 1975c).

In addition to space–time development models, I have discussed another major topic at British sections meetings, namely, *general interregional equilibrium*. In a paper which drew heavily upon material in my book (Isard *et al.*, 1969, chapters 11, 13, 14), I presented a framework which involves U regions, each embodying l economic commodities, m consumers, n producers, and f traders. The givens of the system are the stock of each of the l goods which each consumer in each region initially holds, the utility function of each consumer, and the transformation function of each producer. The unknowns of the system are the Uml demands of consumers, the Unl inputs and outputs of producers, the $Ul - 1$ prices, and the $U(U - 1)fl$ interregional shipments. We then showed that the first-order conditions on consumption to maximize utility of each consumer, the first-order conditions on production to maximize profits of each producer, the no-gains-from-trade conditions for each trader, plus the 'supply = demand' equation for each commodity in each region, plus the budget constraint on each consumer, and the production constraint on each producer as embodied in his transformation function, were sufficient in number theoretically to solve for the unknowns of the systems.

I can now report that we have been able to fuse this general interregional equilibrium framework with our optimal space–time development model (Isard and Liossatos, 1975d). That is we are able to combine laws of motion with general equilibrium conditions.

In another paper presented at the second British section meeting (Isard, 1968) I was concerned with extending the economic system to incorporate basic variables of the ecosystem—in fact to fuse the economic and ecosystems into one framework. I can now state that to some extent we are able to do this operation successfully.

We are able to extend the interregional input–output framework, which is a derivative of a general interregional equilibrium one, to incorporate both numerous air, water, and solid-waste pollutants as ecological commodities, and numerous treatment (depollution) activities designed to reduce the amount of pollutants imposed on the environment (Isard *et al.*, 1975). Even further, we are able to extend the input–output framework to incorporate basic natural production processes like those in food chains, photosynthesis, and the phosphorous cycle so that there is full interplay between the ecological and economic systems; but here the problem of developing an operational model for policy purposes is much more difficult (Isard, 1974). We can also conceptually add in all the diverse activities of noneconomic organisations such as government agencies, religious institutions, educational units, political parties, social groups, cultural entities, and so forth, consider each organisation as well as each individual to have more than one role, embrace legislative, election, and other nonmarket processes (both in noncooperative and cooperative contexts), and introduce my $(\phi - l)$ noneconomic commodities, such as c-power, c-respect, c-rectitude, and c-sociality.

Although we have made important advances in synthesis along the lines noted, I am still dissatisfied, both conceptually and operationally, with what we have. There are many basic shortcomings. Many developments are needed. To give you some idea of these, I very hesitantly present a confusing and relatively disorganised figure 1, only part of which can be reproduced on the following page. It presents notations on all the important areas which I feel should be probed and fused into a single model and framework. I am including it here because some of my students find it useful for obtaining some notion of the large number and complexity of the developments required.

I have outlined boldly the box in the centre which refers to the $(K, U, C, Y, \sigma, l, \xi)$ model already mentioned. Above is another large box which refers to the general interregional equilibrium system that I have just talked about, extended to include many species and habitats as well as regions and the ecosystem. Below the $(K, U, C, Y, \sigma, l, \xi)$ box is a tree-like diagram designated *hierarchy*. This diagram refers to a third basic field of knowledge which must be further developed and fused into the synthetic framework we already have. In the rest of this paper I want to talk about this needed development. However, I want to do so bearing in mind that there are numerous other areas which must be probed and incorporated into our model's conceptual framework.

Now how do we incorporate our work on the changing hierarchical organisation? I believe that the simplest and most effective way to do it is to develop a dynamic model for a central place system, starting from scratch and for the simplest type of region that we can conceive.

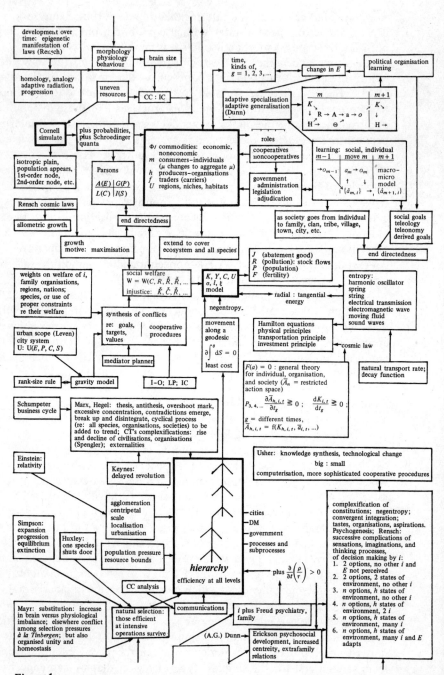

Figure 1

In work under way Isard and Kanemoto (1976) take a river valley hemmed in on both sides by mountain ranges. Let this valley be approximated by a line or a band of width very small compared to its length—that is, it is a line region. Let us assume that the fertility of the soil is the same throughout, although this assumption can be dropped at a later stage. Also we shall assume that the valley is fully settled with self-subsistent farmsteads, all of the same efficient size. This assumption, too, can be dropped later so that the valley can be partially settled when the first industrial development takes place. We posit that information and technology is fully diffused and thus that all farmers have the same production function:

$$G(x, t) = G[N(x, t), L(x, t), T(t)] , \tag{3}$$

where
$G(x, t)$ is a production density at x at time t,
$N(x, t)$ is a labour force density,
$L(x, t)$ is the land per unit distance devoted to the farm production,
$T(t)$ is the level of technology.
We shall assume diminishing returns to scale for each farming enterprise such that

$$\frac{\partial G}{\partial N}, \frac{\partial G}{\partial L} > 0 ; \quad \text{and} \quad \frac{\partial^2 G}{\partial N^2}, \frac{\partial^2 G}{\partial L^2} < 0 .$$

We take land to be a free good. In this case our society is a simple summation of farm households, none of whom engages in trade. Society's welfare is a simple summation of welfare of these households. A utility density function corresponds to each household:

$$u(x) = u[g(x)] , \tag{4}$$

where
$g(x)$ is the consumption density of the good by the household located at x, with
$\dfrac{\partial u}{\partial g} > 0$ representing a condition of positive marginal utility, and

$\dfrac{\partial^2 u}{\partial g^2} < 0$ representing a condition of diminishing marginal utility.

In maximising its utility each farmstead, with its fixed amount of labour, increases its land input until $\partial G/\partial L = 0$ (because we take land as a free good). This then defines $L(x, t)$ in equation (3) and, with $N(x, t)$ and $T(t)$ specified, we obtain the output $G(x, t)$. Since each farmstead consumes what it produces, we have $g(x, t) = G(x, t)$ which then yields the maximum utility levels $u^*[g(x, t)]$ and $\int_0^B u^*[g(x, t)]dx$. At each location there is an implicit social welfare price, $\partial u^*/\partial g(x)$, for the agricultural good.

Technology is taken to increase with time, that is $(\partial T/\partial t) > 0$. Since $\partial G/\partial T > 0$, then

$$\frac{\partial g}{\partial t} > 0 \,,$$

and consequently

$$\frac{\mathrm{d}u^*}{\mathrm{d}t} > 0 \,, \qquad \frac{\mathrm{d}}{\mathrm{d}t}\int_0^B u^*(x)\mathrm{d}x > 0 \,.$$

As has occurred historically, at some time, $t = t'$, technology advances to the stage where it becomes profitable or socially desirable for some entrepreneur to engage in the production of a commodity for more than one farm household. Put another way, a situation arises where increasing returns to scale in the production of a commodity with a new technique offsets the transport costs that are involved in distributing the commodity to one or more neighbouring farm households, and some enterprising (maximising) individual becomes aware of this[1]. He decides to produce the commodity. If his optimal operations require only a fraction of the total farm population as a market, then the optimal location of these operations will be indeterminate. However, we may posit that continuing advance of production technology extends the range of increasing returns to the point where eventually the single manufacturing operation serves the entire set of farms in the region. Accordingly, under the assumption of zero costs of relocation, the entrepreneur would come to locate at the center of the region, provided that technological know-how was fully diffused. However, we wish to adopt the further assumption that technological advance takes place or becomes known at some gateway point of the region and spreads only gradually over the line region. That is

$$T(x, t) = T(0, t)\exp(-\gamma x) \,, \tag{5}$$

where γ is a positive constant. Hence, at time point t, the production function for our single firm for any location x' is:

$$M(x', t) = M[N(x', t), T(x', t)] \,. \tag{6}$$

At the start we assume that there is no land requirement for manufacturing (and that the city population requires a negligible amount of land for residential and other purposes).

Since there now exists a second good, the preference structure or utility function of the farmstead now relates to different possible bundles of the two goods, that is

$$u(x, t) = u[g(x, t), f(x, t)] \,, \tag{7}$$

[1] Before this, many new techniques may have been devised but found to be unprofitable.

where $f(x, t)$ is the consumption density of the second good, say, manufactures by the household located at x at time t. This then leads to exchange of the two goods. If we assume that exchange takes place at x', the location of the factory (the site of an emerging city), and further that each farmer bears the transport cost, such that the total transport cost in bringing both agricultural goods to the market and transporting manufactures to the farmstead are explicitly considered in terms of dissipation of his holdings of manufactured goods (or are paid for with manufactured goods), we have

$$\int_0^B g(x, t)\phi(x, t)dx + g(x', t)\overline{\phi}(x', t) = \int_0^B G(x, t)dx \; ; \qquad (8)$$

a 'demand = supply' equation for agricultural goods, where
$g(x, t)$ is the *per capita* consumption density of agricultural goods at
    location x at time t,
$\phi(x, t)$ is the agricultural population density corresponding to $N(x)$ at
    location x,
$g(x', t)$ is the *per capita* consumption density of city (factory) population
    at x', and
$\overline{\phi}(x', t)$ is the city (factory) population density corresponding to $N(x')$ at x'.
The left-hand side of equation (8) represents system demand; the right-hand side system supply.
    We also have

$$\int_0^B m(x, t)\phi(x, t)(1 + \tau|x - x'|)dx + m(x', t)\overline{\phi}(x', t) = M(x', t) , \qquad (9)$$

a 'supply = demand' equation for manufactured goods, where
$m(x, t)$ and $m(x', t)$ are the *per capita* consumption densities of
    manufactured goods by populations at agricultural location x
    and city location x' respectively, and
$\tau|x - x'|$ is the total transport costs involved in exchange per unit
    manufactured good received at x.
Given the two 'supply = demand' constraints and the two production functions, we seek at any time t to maximise system welfare. This may be taken to be the unweighted sum of utility densities at all points. That is, we seek to

$$\text{maximise} \int_0^B u(x, t)\phi(x, t)dx + u(x', t)\overline{\phi}(x', t) , \qquad (10)$$

subject to equations (3), (6), (8), and (9).

Thus for any time t we may set up the Lagrangian

$$\mathcal{L} = \int_0^B u[g(x), m(x)]\phi(x)\mathrm{d}x + u[g(x'), m(x')]\overline{\phi}(x')$$

$$+ \delta \int_0^B m(x)\phi(x)(1 + \tau|x - x'|)\mathrm{d}x + m(x')\overline{\phi}(x') - M[N(x'), T(0)\exp(-\gamma x')]$$

$$+ \lambda \int_0^B g(x)\phi(x)\mathrm{d}x + g(x')\overline{\phi}(x') - \int_0^B G[N(x), L(x), T]\mathrm{d}x \ ,$$

where δ, λ are undetermined Lagrangian multipliers. We then can determine the conditions for maximisation. These turn out to be usual first-order conditions; for example, at any location the ratio of marginal utility of the two goods should be equal to the ratio of their prices (in this context these are Lagrangian multipliers).

We have sketched the first stage of our model, an economy which consists of self-subsistent farmsteads, and the second stage of our model, which is the same plus a single city which produces manufactured goods and serving all farmsteads. We can now move on to the third stage.

The third stage begins when, as a result of the growth of demands due to technological advance over time [recall $(\partial T/\partial t) > 0$], a second location (city) for manufacturing emerges. Such emergence is justified because as the first city grows, the advantages of growth from further scale economies diminish steadily while at the same time the mounting demand by all farmsteads comes to make possible greater transport cost savings from serving the most distant farmsteads from a manufacturing location closer to them. So in this third stage, which is reached when possible transport-cost savings come to offset the additional gains from increasing returns to scale, a second city emerges. Further, if we assume zero relocation costs, the first city will relocate. However, we keep in mind the fact that the technology diffuses only with time (that is, there is spatial friction in diffusion) so that the city located closer to the gateway point (presumably the first city) is, and continues to be, larger than the second.

During the third stage, growth continues. The cities constantly relocate because of relative changes in transport-cost savings and scale economies. In time a third city emerges, and then a fourth city. At some point a third category of commodities appears, which we find it convenient to designate *services*. Initially, because of the very high cost of production of services and because of the necessity for food and manufactured products, such as textiles and beer, there is no effective demand for the output of service activities. But ultimately affluence appears, and demand for services becomes effective. We shall assume that service activities take place in a city, and that their presence there leads to agglomeration economies for all firms.

With the emergence of service commodities, and the urbanisation type of agglomeration economies they make possible, a fourth stage begins. Associated with it is another, higher order of nodes.

I could set down production functions for service activities, reformulate all production functions to take into account agglomeration economies, state conditions for optimum location, the size of each city, and so forth, but I do not have the time and space to do so. The important thing is that I give an idea of how we can depict and analyse a changing hierarchical structure of nodes in a way which will permit it to be synthesised into a general equilibrium system and a general space–time development model. Obviously, I shall need to present the formal details in future manuscript, at which I am now busy with Y. Kanemoto and others.

However hard we work, it is clear that it will be some time before we will have an operational model which then can be used to project the basic characteristics of a hierarchy of central places (or nodes) for a system of regions, for example the Philadelphia region in the USA, or the Northern region in Britain. It will be a longer time still before we will have reached the stage where we are able effectively to introduce into our frameworks and operational models other important and basic advances (see figure 1)—such as social learning or *adaptive generalisation* as my former student Dunn would call it—and before we achieve increased organised unification with increased diversity (as Teilhard puts it). It is also clear that as society progresses and becomes more complex, social homeostasis grows in importance relative to individual homeostasis. Put another way, the need for efficient joint actions (behaviour) becomes increasingly intense relative to the need for efficient individual actions (behaviour). This means that our models must increasingly come to embrace efficient joint actions, or to maximise joint actions in place of maximising individual actions. None of the models contemplated really embrace this feature although I have begun to explore this direction in my *General Theory* (Isard *et al.*, 1969, chapter 14). This opens up tremendous areas for further research.

I must close by indicating that we have been able to achieve a number of important advances in developing relevant models and in synthesising them. Our awareness and perception of what needs to be done to simulate or understand the space–time development of a system of regions has also increased tremendously; so we are no further ahead than we were 10 years ago. While this may be a discouraging note for those of us in the older generation, it should be very encouraging for British regional scientists who are mostly in the younger generation and thus have more territory than ever to conquer.

Acknowledgement. This research was supported by National Science Foundation grant P251018. It draws heavily upon current work with Y. Kanemoto.

References

Isard, W., 1968, "Some notes on the linkage of the ecologic and economic systems", *Papers of the Regional Science Association*, **22**.

Isard, W., 1974, *Ecologic-Economic Analysis for Regional Planning* (Free Press, New York).

Isard, W., Cesario, F., Reiner, T., 1975, "Marginal pollution analysis for the management of the urban environment", *Regional Science Monograph and Dissertation Series*, number 4, Center for Urban Development Research, Cornell University, Ithaca, NY.

Isard, W., Kanemoto, Y., 1976, "Dynamics of Urban System Development", forthcoming.

Isard, W., Liossatos, P., 1975a, "Trading behavior (transport), macro and micro, in an optimal space-time development model", *London Papers in Regional Science 5: Regional Science—New Concepts and Old Problems,* Ed. E. L. Cripps (Pion, London), pp.1-17.

Isard, W., Liossatos, P., 1975b, "Parallels from physics for space-time development models, part I", *Regional Science and Urban Economics*, **5** (1), 5-40.

Isard, W., Liossatos, P., 1975c, "Parallels from physics for space-time development models, part II: Interpretation and extensions of the basic model", *Papers of the Regional Science Association*, **35**.

Isard, W., Liossatos, P., 1975d, "General micro behavior and optimal macro space-time planning, *Regional Science and Urban Economics*, **5** (4).

Isard, W., and others, 1969, *General Theory: Social, Political, Economic and Regional* (MIT Press, Cambridge, Mass.).

Regional Underdevelopment in Late Capitalism: A Study of the Northeast of England

J.CARNEY
North East Area Study, Durham
R.HUDSON
University of Durham
G.IVE
Liverpool Polytechnic
J.LEWIS
University of Cambridge

1 Introduction

The aim of this paper is to explore a new approach to the conceptualisation of 'regional problems' in late capitalist societies. We have drawn on two sources simultaneously for our approach, and the structure of the paper reflects this. Our first source is underdevelopment theory, which has been formulated, almost entirely, to analyse the relationships between advanced capitalist and backward dependent colonial countries in the global space economy of capitalism. The key concepts from this are presented in section 2. Section 3 is a study of the history of the Northeast of England since the industrial revolution. It is an interpretative sketch based on the categories and concepts touched on in the first section of the paper. It must be stressed that in attempting this kind of project it is difficult to strike a correct balance between theoretical sophistication and attention to empirical detail, so we would prefer to think of what follows as a set of perspectives that illuminate new aspects of the problem rather than a series of clear-cut answers.

To introduce the kind of theoretical positions that are put forward within underdevelopment theory as it could be applied to the regions of late capitalist countries rather than to dependent colonial ones, we would like to take a passage by Henri Lefebvre, one of the most influential of the French Marxists currently working on the urban and regional problem (see Castells, 1972; 1973; Lefebvre, 1970; 1972a; 1972b; and collections such as C.E.R.M., 1974). In his essay "La bourgeoisie et l'espace" Lefebvre describes contemporary France thus:

"France is also an imperial nation, though not the most powerful. Since the beginning of the twentieth century, French imperialism has been the prey of greater imperialisms: English, German, American. The most characteristic feature of France is a set of contradictions which re-emerged in 1968. On the one hand we have the doctrine of the 'rights of man'; a product of the democratic revolution—the French Revolution. On the other hand, the realities of imperialism; the bourgeoisie as an artful and very resilient ruling class; the state's performance of a directive role; exploitation of French workers; the the superexploitation of aliens—three and a half million of them in

France itself. Nevertheless France has other aspects: the capital is
huge and too large for the country. Paris draws everything to it: men,
brains, and wealth. A centre of decision and debate, Paris is surrounded
by subordinated and hierarchically organised areas which it at once
dominates and exploits. Imperial France has lost her colonies, but an
internal neocolonialism has become established. Contemporary France
is made up of overdeveloped, overindustrialised, and overurbanised
areas, together with areas of increasing underdevelopment, particularly
in Brittany and the Midi" (Lefebvre, 1972b, pp.257, 258, our
translation).

What is of interest to us in this passage is not so much the ideas about
the contradiction between the ideology of the social order and its economic
basis, but rather those ideas concerning contradictions within that basis.
At the level of appearances, the similarities between the French situation
which has been described in this way, and the British, are obvious and
striking. What we wish to establish is a deeper similarity, expressed in the
conceptualisation of both countries as late capitalist societies. Within such
a context they are both declining imperial powers, under the shadow of
the more powerful, vigorous, and still rising imperialisms of the United
States and Japan; both attempting to internalise their lost empires by the
importation of alien labour and regional underdevelopment; both heavily
dependent on the State as an economic and social regulator; both with
oversized capitals performing an important hegemonic role[1]. The
significance of these similarities will become clearer as we introduce the
key concepts for our understanding of the space-economy of late
capitalism by an examination of three terms used above; exploitation,
imperialism, and underdevelopment.

2 Exploitation, imperialism, underdevelopment
Exploitation can best be understood by an examination of the relationship
between the capitalist and the worker in a system of commodity production
[for a fuller explanation of exploitation see Marx, 1970, pp.167–230.
A recent treatment of this question using the notation employed in this
paper is contained in Hodgson (1974)]. Commodities, in general, are the
embodiment of 'dead' labour. An exchange of these is of a commodity
which embodies a given amount of 'dead' labour—or value—for another
which embodies an equal amount: hence exchange of equivalents. However,
when living labour itself is treated as a commodity, what is exchanged for the
money wage—the ability to buy wage goods of a certain value—is not a
given amount of value, but the ability to labour and thus create further
value. The difference between the value represented by the wage and the net
value of the commodity after labour has been applied to it is termed surplus

[1] The concept of hegemony was developed by Gramsci to explain how cultural
supremacy could legitimate a social authority; see Gramsci (1971, p.104) for its use
in the analysis of regional leadership.

value and is taken by the person who buys labour power as a commodity and sets it to work—the capitalist. One can express an aspect of this exploitative relationship, its intensity, by calculating the rate of exploitation. This is given by the ratio of surplus value created to the value of the wage. Algebraically this can be expressed thus:

$$e = \frac{s}{v},$$ (1)

where e is the rate of exploitation; s is the surplus value; v is the variable capital (wages).

The connection between this rate and the rate of profit for a single period of production is simple once one introduces the value of the constant capital flow (that is the raw materials and replacement of the means of production) and the value of the constant capital stock. The rate of profit can then be expressed as the ratio of the surplus value created to the total capital advanced. Extending the notation above, this is given by

$$p' = \frac{s}{k+c+v},$$ (2)

where p' is the rate of profit; k is the constant capital stock; c is the constant capital flow.

Exploitation, then, refers to the way in which surplus value is produced by labour and taken by the capitalist as the basis for his profit. However, this explanation does not immediately appear to illuminate Lefebvre's use of the term to describe the relationship between Paris and the surrounding areas. To see that it is in fact consistent, it is necessary to penetrate the fetishism of areas, which can be seen as a parallel to the fetishism of commodities. In a famous passage on the fetishism of commodities, Marx wrote:

"There is a definite social relation between men, that assumes, in their eyes, the fantastic form of a relationship between things" (Marx, 1970, p.72).

While the fetishism of commodities mystifies the true nature of the social relationships of capitalist production, the fetishism of areas threatens to mystify those same social relations in space. Hence the exploitation of one area by another is only another expression of the relationship between classes in any class society, so long as we accept that these classes exist in space. To understand the spatial expression of any social relation, such as the movement of surplus value, one must destroy the myth that areas, *qua* areas, can interact.

There is, of course, a second strand to this argument in that while man–man relationships have a spatial expression, so too do man–nature relationships. It is common to speak of the exploitation of natural resources. More correctly, production involves the appropriation of the products of nature—exploitation being reserved for those cases where this is done without regard to the capacity to reproduce these resources, and/or the social division of labour resting on the process of appropriation. Thus in addition to the process of exploitation through the production process, there may be exploitation of the natural wealth of an area.

Given this usage of the term exploitation it is easy to understand an elementary explanation of imperialism. [The classic work on imperialism is Lenin (1971), but see also Hobson (1902), Luxemburg and Bukharin (1972), the masterly summary of Lichtheim (1971), and Baran (1973). Bernstein (1973) is also useful.] As the home economy of a capitalist country reaches a state of full employment it is possible for wages to be raised by the victories of labour in the class struggle, and the rate of exploitation—and thus the rate of profit—reduced, unless another source of labour which is willing to exchange its labour power for the existing wage can be found. The British economy has drawn on three such sources since 1800: Irish immigrants, Third World labour in both the formal and informal empires and, most recently, Third World immigrants. If the rate of exploitation can thus be held constant, or increased, then there would be no reduction in the rate of profit, were it not for two other important qualitative changes in the economy which affect the rate of profit, and the realisation of profit, respectively.

The first of these is a rise in the organic composition of capital over time. This is most easily explained by returning to our algebraic shorthand, for the organic composition of capital is given by the ratio of constant capital $(k + c)$ to variable capital (v) thus:

$$o = \frac{k+c}{v},$$
(3)

where o is the organic composition of capital.

As a result of technical progress, the reinvestment of realised surplus value tends to be in constant capital-using, or capital-intensive, techniques, which finds its expression in a rising value of this ratio. To see how this affects the rate of profit, let us return to our expression for this and divide both top and bottom by (v). This gives

$$p' = \frac{s/v}{(k+c)/v + 1}, \qquad \text{or } p' = \frac{e}{o+1}.$$
(4)

Clearly, with a constant rate of exploitation, any rise in organic composition will reduce the rate of profit. The only way in which this can be counteracted is by incorporating new sectors of the economy, with a lower than average organic composition, whether at home or overseas, in the orbit of national capitalist investment.

The tendency of the rate of profit to fall because of increasing organic composition of capital is put forward here not in the sense of a neoclassical technical determination of the rate of profit by aggregate functions.

Indeed the problem of what determines the rate of profit is an extremely complex one. What we wish to draw attention to here are the problems which dynamic capital accumulation over long periods of time inevitably confronts, emphasising differences in the rate of profit as the mechanism associated with shifts in capital flows. [The theory of the rate of profit is well discussed by Kregel (1971) and in Harcourt and Laing (1971). The law of the falling rate of profit is expounded in Marx (1972, pp.211–337), and its status as a law is examined by Hodgson (1974).]

The second important change in the economy results from the tendencies of capital both to concentrate and centralise, for as the home market becomes partitioned between monopolists and/or saturated, the inability of capitalists to sell their commodities and thereby realise the surplus value they have appropriated leads to a search for fresh markets overseas. Overcapacity in developing capitalist economies, as it becomes endemic and apparent even at the peak of booms in the trade cycle, expresses this problem in another way. By overcapacity we mean a stock of capital which, at the real wage corresponding to the full employment of labour, is more than sufficient to employ that labour at the optimum level of utilisation—that is at minimum cost. It is thus, in principle, distinguishable from underutilisation of labour and the means of production, which results from insufficient effective demand in slumps.

However, both these problems are associated with what may be called overproduction. This means that productive potential is in excess of the marketable amount of production. This arises because of the chronic limitations on expansion of the home market under capitalism. The rise of monopolies with price-fixing policies can be seen both as a response to, and cause of, overproduction and the realisation problem.

There is thus a powerful drive to expand markets abroad by exporting both goods and capital. The export of goods helps solve the problems of overproduction and realisation at home. [See Robinson (1973), and the debate between Gallagher and Robinson (1953) and Macdonagh (1962), both reprinted in Shaw (1970).] The export of capital performs the triple function of helping expand markets for these goods, absorbing part of the excess capital in the home economy, and increasing the average rate of profit by incorporating areas where the rate of exploitation is higher and/or the organic composition of capital is lower than at home. It is thus not surprising that the export of capital has come to be regarded as a distinctive characteristic of the stage of monopoly capitalism.

It is within the context of this economic basis for imperialism that we can begin to understand the emergence of state intervention in the economy. On the one hand, interimperialist rivalries for new markets led to the need for formal political empires—as opposed to the informal economic empires which had characterised, say, British involvement in Latin America; and later led to the international interimperialist wars. On the other hand, the need to maintain effective demand at home became apparent in the 1930s and state rearmament proved to be the forerunner of the Keynesian policies used by the state to maintain the system after the Second World War.

Obviously, this explanation of imperialism, by stressing its economic aspects and effect on the state, has played down other important features —such as the drive to secure raw-material sources, the largely strategic role of certain colonies, and the conflicts which developed between capitalists in the metropolis and those emerging in the colonies. Nevertheless, it provides a sufficient basis for a brief analysis of underdevelopment theory.

If imperialism describes the system by which the internal contradictions of a monopoly capitalist economy can be reduced temporarily, then underdevelopment is best seen as the impact of imperialism on the Third World. By this we mean primarily the appropriation of surplus value created by labour abroad by capitalists in the metropolis. However, other aspects of the process which are usually emphasised are the effect of the ownership of the means of production by metropolitan capitalists on the class structure of the country; the inevitable intensification of the process which results from the difficulty of repatriating profits without either intensifying the realisation problem at home or creating one abroad by restricting market expansion; and the higher rates of profit which capital export allows.

These themes receive different emphasis in the works of the major contemporary underdevelopment theorists, and it will help us clarify the term underdevelopment to see how these emphases arise from two alternative explanations of imperialism. Those who see the major cause of imperialism as the realisation problem—that is, they see capitalism as inherently overproductive—stress the circulation of surplus value. Frank (1969b) is the best known example of this approach, and in his analysis of underdevelopment in Latin America draws attention to the increasing magnitude of foreign investment to show that relations of dependence intensify because of the difficulty of repatriating profits. The same kind of emphasis in argument is evident in Rodney's work on underdevelopment in Africa (Rodney, 1972). This approach leads both of them to consider the effect of the increasing ownership of the means of production by metropolitan capitalists on the economic, social, and political structures of the dependent countries. They also develop some interesting ideas on the internal circulation of surplus value in urban 'chains of exploitation' which are taken up by Harvey (1973).

The second emphasis is evident in Laclau's critique of Frank (Laclau, 1971). For him the production of surplus value is more important than its circulation, and so he sees the process of underdevelopment as depending far more on superexploitation and lower organic composition of capital than on any market-expanding function that capital export may perform. From this point of view imperialist development of colonial countries is held to take the form of limited 'enclave growth', in a situation of 'unlimited labour forever' (this approach to the determination of wage rates is elaborated in Turner and Jackson, 1970) which acts to keep down wage levels in the enclave. Only if it is possible to keep the organic composition of the capital low in an extensive expansion of the economy from the enclave will wage levels be kept down.

Drawing on this body of theory[2] it is possible to suggest certain characteristic features of underdeveloped regions in the way Szentes (1971) has done for countries, and 'test' them against our British case study—the Northeast. The problems of doing this with underdevelopment theory in general are well brought out by Vickery in her comments on the correct use of Frank's work:

"... we have to be careful not to treat a specific study such as Frank's as though it were just another abstract functionalist model that can be applied to any society that comes along. Frank's account of the development of underdevelopment is the result of a concrete historical study of a pair of countries, Chile and Brazil, and should not be dogmatically extended to African and Asian countries without equally concrete analysis" (Vickery, 1972).

3 Underdevelopment: the Northeast in historical perspective

The origins of the industrial development of the Northeast are to be found in the coal industry and its trade with London. Coal was, from the first, dominated by the great cartels of large local landowners who found the exploitation of coal resources to be a plentiful alternative source of surplus value to their ground rents. The development of coal mining soon became more important than landowning in terms of surplus value created. The fact that this surplus value remained in the hands of an essentially precapitalist class had important consequences later on (Sweezy, 1938).

Under the highly competitive conditions prevalent elsewhere in the economy at this time (see Thompson, 1963) capitalists were constantly forced by pressure on their profits to innovate and/or expand to obtain scale economies in order to remain active. The monopolists of the Grand Alliance in the Northeast, however, were in a very different position. Much of their effort went into the control of aggregate supply and the maintenance of barriers to entry—such as the purchase of negative wayleaves—since for them profit margins could be manipulated. Despite this nonreproductive use of their capital, the magnitude of the monopolists' realised surplus value, relative to the base which produced it, still allowed

[2] We have excluded the work of Emmanuel (1972) from consideration here not simply because of the numerous theoretical errors in it which Bettelheim (1972) and Pilling (1973) have pointed out, but because we feel that the most useful elements in it have yet to be formulated in their most productive manner. We do not have the space here to transfer his explanation of 'unequal exchange' into the framework of the transformation problem where we feel it belongs.

a rapid rate of industrialisation marked by the development of the
railways and embryonic engineering and iron industries.

However, possession of an investible surplus is by no means the only
necessary condition for continued capitalist accumulation, as the emergence
of problems for further accumulation in the coal industry after 1840 shows.

First, the rapid accumulation of the early period had been based on the
exploitation of readily accessible coal seams. As mining activity moved
south from the Tyne to the concealed coalfields, the amount of capital
stock necessary for resource exploitation rose sharply, and so not only
reduced the rate of profit, but also reduced the amount of already
accumulated capital available for investment in other industries.

The second problem was the availability of labour at the existing wage
levels, which had two aspects. The first was the need for an expansion of
the labour force by immigration, but wage levels were not high enough to
attract much labour from further than the immediate rural fringe of the
region. Intimately related to this was the start of unionisation in the
mines which was marked by the great strike of 1844; an historic moment
in the development of the British labour movement. All 40000 men
employed on the Northumberland and Durham coalfield came out in an
attempt to end the petty cheating by their employers through the truck
system and underpayment by weight. The coal owners, refusing to
recognise the union, responded first by evicting the miners and their
families from their cottages, then prosecuting those who camped out for
trespassing. Lord Londonderry, a major coal owner, tried to force the
men at Seaham back to work by forbidding local traders to give the strikers
credit, but the strike was finally ended after five months. when the coal
owners began to import nonunionised labour from Ireland (this strike
is described by Engels, 1969, pp.290–294).

The third problem was that the essentially noncompetitive nature of the
Northeast's massive involvement in the London coal market had led to
overcapacity. While in a monopolistic position, the suppliers were able to
minimise the effect of slumps, but as competition from other coal
producers with less overcapacity grew in the 1850s and 1860s, they not
only felt the effect of any slumps, but also felt it more acutely than
elsewhere. Thus the depression of the 1870s saw the attempts to cut
wages [described by Allen (1971)] thereby increasing the rate of
exploitation.

At the same time as these problems were emerging to slow down the
rate of accumulation in the coal export trade, the iron and steel industry
was developing to an important position in the economy of the Northeast.
The production of wrought iron had been increasing since the 1830s, with
works at Newcastle, Tow Law, Consett, and later Middlesborough; but it
was the discovery of the main Cleveland ore seam in 1850 that allowed
the expansion of Teesside production, which in turn enabled the Teesside

Ironmasters to dominate the national market. This meant an expansion of coal output, which was to continue until 1911, and important changes in ownership patterns. These resulted from the switch from national to local markets for coal, for as the local market for iron and steel production became, in turn, dependent on the local market of shipbuilding, vertical integration took place. To understand these changes a brief reference to the evolution of the steel industry is necessary (Bell, 1969).

Its origins were in the 1870s when the Ironmasters' response to the depression was diversification. The Gilchrist-Thomas process was the critical innovation in this, for it enabled the Ironmasters to compete internationally using the local ore. During the following 30 years, mergers during recessions increased the monopolistic positions of firms such as Dorman Long and Bolckow and Vaughan, leading to chronic overcapacity, given their increasingly uncompetitive position in the national and imperial markets, but growing demand from local shipbuilding was to prevent a dramatic collapse (Dougan, 1968; Cousins and Brown, 1970). Shipbuilding had always been important in the economy of the Northeast, but with the surge in global demand, resulting from imperial expansion, its output grew dramatically after 1880. The rate of accumulation in shipbuilding was so rapid that firms were soon able to integrate their raw-materials suppliers, as shown by the case of Furness Withy who formed the South Durham Steel and Iron Company, and then took over Weardale Steel, Coal and Coke Company, and other firms in the mid 1890s. In this way the economy of the Northeast became increasingly dependent on the fortunes of shipbuilding (Bowden and Gibb, 1970).

The Northeast at the turn of the century was thus not obviously stagnating. However, the signs of impending decline were already there: recessions marked by 'rationalisation' in the steel and shipbuilding industries; the start of a net outward-migration of labour, which was to rise from 33 000 in the first decade of the 20th century to 141 000 in the second; the reduced profitability of coal mining as the exploitable seams were now narrower and deeper. These trends were made all the more significant by the continued advance of the productive forces in other regions and industrialising countries, which was undermining the competitive position of the Northeast. Hence the influx of capital necessary for any further advances in the Northeast went instead to the growing consumption-goods industries of the Southeast, or was exported in the opening up of the African empire. The survival of the Northeast's economy until the First World War depended more on the production of armaments in the shipbuilding and engineering industries, than on the development of any longer-term commercial production.

When the British economy after the First World War plunged into an unparallelled overproduction crisis which the newly expanded empire was incapable of averting, it was the relatively unprofitable firms of the

Northeast which were amongst the first to collapse. The immediate result
of these collapses was to lower effective demand in the region and to
raise the percentage of the insured population who were unemployed to
~13% (Bowden and Gibb, 1970).

Although the regional economy had in a sense adjusted to slump
conditions, the depression of the 1930s still strongly affected regional
output, employment, working-class living conditions, and profitability.
The slump in the UK was led by the reduction in both investment and
export demand, which had its first impact on the sector of the economy
producing investment goods for home and overseas markets. In this sector
the immediate effect was unemployment as demand for its output vanished,
while the consumption-goods sector initially suffered only to the extent
that its demand was reduced by the loss of a market amongst the
unemployed investment-sector workers. Since the Northeast's industrial
structure was dominated by the investment-goods sector, unemployment
levels soon reached an average of 35%, while the falling price levels for
consumption goods meant that those in employment maintained, or
increased their real wages, so that production in the Southeast continued
more or less unabated (see Aldcroft and Richardson, 1969). The effect of
the depression on the Northeast was thus not simply due to its relative
inefficiency in production but also to its lack of diversification into the
consumption-goods sector.

Poulantzas (1969) wrote that the state in modern society is "... the
factor of cohesion in a social formation and the factor of reproduction of
the conditions of production". It was during the period from 1914 to
1945 that the first experiments in state intervention in the region occurred,
for example through subsidy of coal production. Direct social intervention
occurred in 1926 (Mason, 1970). This involved a whole range of state
tactics including the use of police against sections of the working class
who were resisting wage cuts in the coal industry—cuts imposed by owners
to attempt to restore profitability in the face of increasing international
competition for markets. Other forms of state social control thrown up
in the most acute phases of the depression in the region involved the
co-option of mass protest into harmless reformist channels. (This involved
the destruction of syndicalist movements: see Mason, 1970; Wilkinson,
1939; Douglass, 1972.)

Recovery of effective demand for the major components of regional
production output and restoration of a certain level of working-class
consumer demand in the region occurred through (a) rearmament demand
in the late 1930s; (b) demand created during both the Second World War
and the Korean war; and crucially (c) through increasing state intervention,
with the state acting both as the final-demand sector and as producer. Under
recent conditions the problem posed by the historic underdevelopment of
the Northeast, and of similar regions, to a late capitalist system is this:
the basis of such a system lies in high real wages and high demand for

consumer goods within the domestic market, and on capitalist consumption and state expenditure to prevent realisation crises re-emerging, whilst allowing continued capital accumulation. Now the basis of profitability in the Northeast historically has involved depression of wages as they enter into costs of production, and/or the reproduction of a large reserve army of unemployed. Moreover, a high proportion of realised surplus has typically been exported or consumed, not reinvested. Finally, the class structure thrown up in such conditions has not involved strata with the necessary real wages required to firmly establish mass consumption, or microsocial structures that make the penetration of consumerist values a rapid process. In a sense then, such a social formation is a barrier to the rapid expansion of the sorts of structures necessary for the stability and growth of state monopoly capitalism.

The state has therefore sought, in a sense, to reintegrate the region, or parts of it, into the mainstream of modern capitalism. This has involved intervention in the ownership of the means of production to restore profitability and to subsidise private-sector production and in the transfer of 'aid' to sustain effective consumer demand for products produced in the national consumption-goods industry. Further, public policy has sought to reinforce those trends in private-sector location-allocation which have been seen to be capable of 'modernising' not only the economic structure (through increases in organic composition and labour productivity) but also the consciousness of segments of the working class (see Carney and Hudson, 1974).

Seen as a space economy of empire, the UK space economy has had to attempt to undergo various historical transformations. Although their work is somewhat contentious (see Yaffe, 1973), Glyn and Sutcliffe (1972) have pointed out that at the core of imperial problems is the question of long-term declining profitability in manufacturing. This has intermeshed with other problems to do with the share of wages in national income (and hence the share of profits), with low rates of domestic investment, and with increasing international competition from other national capitalisms. State intervention in conditions of falling overall profitability has become crucial and clearly, because of the location-allocations attendant on the structuring of the means of production, will have regional expressions, since it is in regions like the Northeast that profitability crises will be most acute for some of the reasons we have touched on here. There is, however, another point.

In some parts of an emerging state capitalism which has shed its formal colonial empire, a successful transformation of economic and social structures towards high-productivity mass consumerism was structurally relatively easy. In these regions there are problems to do with the realisation of surplus: overproduction tendencies exist in these regions which make it important that capital somehow be transferred into colonial territories or that new markets for production, especially consumption goods, be opened up.

The combination of the need to restore profitability in sections of industry and to solve realisation problems, has typically been at the centre of the modern attempts to transform the internal structure of the Northeast. This, as well as the neocolonial export of surplus and the importation of colonial labour, is an expression of the internalisation of empire under conditions where, in a sense, the whole UK economy is becoming more peripheral in relation to the core national and international capitalist systems.

4 Categories and concepts
Although we have not tried to set out detailed theses about the Northeast, the remaining sections of this paper summarise the more important points.

It is possible to begin to reinterpret the economic and social history of the Northeast using the concepts of rate of exploitation; organic composition of capital; rate of profit; the import and export of surplus; the shares of wages and profits in the value of output; effective demand; accumulation and realisation problems.

5 Features of underdevelopment
The Northeast exhibits some of the features, both historically and contemporarily, of an underdeveloped social formation. [Carter (1974) uses some of these concepts in his study of the Highlands of Scotland.] These are connected with the following features.

5.1 Dependence mechanisms
5.1.1 *Direct economic dependence*
Ownership and control of substantial parts of the means of production have now passed outside the region. Garside (1971) points to an early start to this process which was accelerated during the depression years and became rapid with the introduction of nationalised industry organisation and the penetration into the region of units controlled by national and multinational corporations. Retailing and land markets, particularly commercial property markets are also now increasingly subordinated to the control of interests outside the region.

5.1.2 *Trade dependence*
The region is dependent on a relatively few markets for output and shows a heavy reliance on exports as a proportion of regional income. In addition, it acts as a market for the output of the national and, increasingly, the EEC consumption-goods sector. This trade system, both historically and contemporarily, results in a high sensitivity of the regional economy to fluctuations in national and international markets. Conditions of falling demand for regional output have recently produced increasing dependence on state transfers of surplus into the region.

5.1.3 *Other forms of dependence*

Szentes (1971) discusses other forms of dependence—financial, technical, political, and cultural—in a Third World context. Because we are dealing with an intranational situation, financial dependence, at least as regards currency mechanisms, is ruled out. State and finance market loan mechanisms, however, have yet to be investigated. Technical dependence refers to the subordination of local production to outside interests which have a monopoly of technical knowledge. Mandel (1970) points out the increasing national subordination of the UK economy to technological monopolies located particularly in the USA. It is not clear whether regional technological dependence in this context is a meaningful concept. We would point out, however, that in the technology of electronic computing system engineering and the whole area of cybernetics, the region has been unable to establish any kind of production capacity. This is surprising in light of the long established engineering capacity in the Northeast, that is until we consider the monopolistic arrangements in this sector of production which do not allow for the establishment of such production in the region.

We have only just begun to examine the history of working-class political institutions and political culture in the region. We see this work as paralleling Hindess' study of the decline of working-class politics (Hindess, 1972) and as drawing on the theses put forward by Miliband (1969; 1973). At the moment unfortunately, there is very little critical writing on either the region's working-class political culture or on the politics of other strata like the indigenous bourgeoisie. We feel, however, that notions on political underdevelopment (Cockroft *et al.*, 1972), cultural underdevelopment, and hegemony might be of equal importance to theses on economic underdevelopment.

Again, it is unfortunate that some recent and detailed studies of working-class culture in the region (Townsend and Taylor, 1974; Bulmer, 1970) do not have any consistent theoretical orientation of the sort we are trying to establish. Cousins (1973) (see also Cousins *et al.*, 1974) has described aspects of the ideology, if not the life-styles, of a regional elite of technocrats, working-class politicians, and local bourgeoisie. This work does provide a starting point for testing out theses about the role of local elites in an ongoing underdevelopment process (see Frank, 1972).

We feel that the structural process of state-initiated attempts at modernisation, including the penetration of elements of mass consumerism, is central. In addition, the operations of local education systems and media (see Bernstein, 1970; Murdock and Golding, 1974) are clearly crucial in the transformation of working-class culture. Propositions on class consciousness necessarily must eventually form a key element of regional underdevelopment theory.

5.2 Income drain

The crucial process involved in systematic income drain is the 'repatriation' out of the region of surplus value created during production, but income is also drained through monopoly pricing and payments of rent or interest. The state is heavily involved in this process through nationalised industries and through transfers of interest payments out of the region to finance capitalists. We are currently examining the details of income drain in private and public sectors through empirical work based on the census of production (for 1963 and 1968) and on company accounts. In addition we are devising a general simulation model for the key ratios identified in this paper which in the first intance will be based on a two-sector, two-region simulation, which will deal both with falling rates of profit and with realisation questions.

5.3 Internal class structure

Even simple models which show how wages and employment in sectors are dependent not only on output but also on a class struggle over the relative shares of capital and labour in that output, and which are additionally dependent on organic composition of capital and reinvestment processes, go some way to explaining observable features of the region's social history. If we also have a notion about how it has become structurally necessary for state capitalism to attempt to modernise the social structure of the region (see Carney and Hudson, 1974; Robinson, 1974), then it begins to be possible to interpret not only alterations in working-class living conditions, culture, and political institutions, such as trade unions, but also the position of other strata such as managers, the petty bourgeoisie, and the local bourgeoisie itself. Indeed Frank's theses (Frank, 1972) on the position of indigenous bourgeoisie in an underdeveloped society can be drawn on to explain how the local bourgeoisie in the region have become progressively controlled from outside the region. In this context the role of ideology in maintaining existing class structures can be studied (see Cousins, 1973).

6 The state and regional underdevelopment

In the internalised empire of late capitalism it is the state which figures largely in reallocating appropriated surplus value from the capitalists in the metropolis to workers in the satellites. This is a different situation to that of international capital export which has usually been performed by capitalists as a class rather than by the state. The involvement of the state in the production of surplus value through the process of capital export into the nationalised industries, and thus the deepening of the underdevelopment relationship, implies that further state intervention in areas like the Northeast is likely to occur. This is because modernisation drives initiated by the state in such regions tend to involve the alteration of the organic composition of capital through rationalisation of the labour force, and higher rates of exploitation, together with the production at a high rate, of an 'unemployable' stratum in the working class. Clearly this stratum has to be controlled. This control has to come through state social-policy measures. Modernisation intervention is also connected with attempts to increase effective demand in the region for output from the consumption-goods industries of the national economy and again is likely to deepen the underdevelopment relationship. Finally, because the state does not have unlimited powers for regional reconstruction, particularly when the whole economy is subject to increasing penetration from other state capitalisms, the modernisation of the region tends to remain incomplete. Hence conditions of incomplete reintegration seem to characterise the region: conditions readily discoverable in terms of internal economic and locational dualities. (See Carney *et al.,* 1975, for exemplification of this and further discussion of state regional policies.)

7 Quantity and quality
Small quantitative differences between areas in the rate of exploitation and the organic composition of capital are of much greater importance in the understanding of capital flows in regional underdevelopment than in understanding national underdevelopment because these rates are initially much closer together in the case of regional underdevelopment. While this means that the direction of these flows could have been changed more readily in an interregional context, the fact that this has not happened forces attention onto those qualitative differences which may explain this. The most obvious of these differences are related to social structure, degree of development of the productive forces, and the balance of advantage in the class struggle.

8 Fetishism of areas
We stress that theses about regional underdevelopment must not be framed simply in spatial terms, however appealing such formulations may appear.

9 Alternative approaches to regional science theory
The differences between our approach in this paper and those more frequently found in regional science raise important questions about the kind of theories which are most useful in studying the problem of regional underdevelopment and the way in which such theory can be produced. As regards the existing theory which can be drawn on for interpretative categories (see section 4) we feel that political economy in both its classical and neo-Keynesian forms (Sraffa, 1960; Dobb, 1973; Kregel, 1973; Meek, 1973; Robinson and Eatwell, 1973) has more to offer than neoclassical economics or Parsonian sociology.

   We have already stressed the need to blend existing theory and the historical study of concrete situations in constructing theory, but there is another aspect to the problem of producing theory—the cognitive interest

associated with any process of inquiry. It is in adopting the approach of
critical social science that we depart most radically from mainstream
regional science. To understand why we have done so it is necessary to
explain our dissatisfaction with the way in which the theories of regional
science disclose reality. A useful starting point for this is Engels' observation
on economics:

> "the laws of economics confront men in all ... unplanned and incoherent
> production as objective laws over which they have no power, therefore
> in the form of the laws of nature" (Engels, Anti-Duhring, quoted in
> Schmidt, 1971),

for this is also the way in which regional science presents its laws. The
reason for this lies in the cognitive interest connected with the empirical–
analytic sciences, which regional science has inherited by accepting their
logical–methodological rules. As Habermas argues this is an interest in
'technical control over objectified processes' (Habermas, 1972, p.309)[3].
Because the processes studied are objectified the possibility that the
production of laws could in any way affect the processes being studied
cannot be considered. While this is reasonable in the study of nature,
it is hard to justify in the study of social relations, for the knowledge of
laws by those whom the laws are about can render them inapplicable. In
so far as this leads to the removal of institutions based on force, this
represents emancipation from the compulsion of internal nature, which is
the cognitive interest of critical social science, especially in the form of
the critique of ideology. Habermas distinguishes critical social science by
the way in which it treats the goal of sciences of social action, such as
regional science—the production of nomological knowledge—thus

> "It [critical social science] is concerned with going beyond this goal to
> determine when theoretical statements grasp invariant regularities of
> social action as such and when they express ideologically frozen
> relations of dependence that can in principle be transformed"
> (Habermas, 1972, p.310).

We believe that this concern is a necessary one in studying many of the
problems that regional science is, or should be, concerned with, and to
achieve it will require a serious consideration of the limitations of its
existing methodology.

10 Regional science and regional underdevelopment

Finally, we repeat that the temporary externalisations of economic
contradictions that characterised an imperial phase of capitalist development
are, in some capitalist societies, and especially France and the UK, being
replaced, in part, by attempts to contain them internally. The latter, as a

---

[3] This discussion draws heavily on Habermas (1972). A useful introduction to his work
for those unfamiliar with Critical theory and the Frankfurt school is Wellmer (1971).

solution to structural contradictions may well be even more temporary than was the formal empire building phase.

If this is the case, the need to construct a theoretical approach which can lead to a long-term solution of the problems of regional underdevelopment becomes an urgent one. We believe that such an approach is possible, and that regional science can play a fundamental role in its discovery, that is, if its appreciation of the problems of late capitalism can be increased and improved.

Acknowledgements. We would like to thank Diana Carney, Graham Chapman, Dave Hughes, Jenny Pike, and Fred Robinson for their helpful comments on an earlier draft of this paper. The earlier draft appeared as working paper 9 in the Northeast Area Study Working Papers Series, University of Durham. It was published in August 1974. The authors alone are responsible for the views expressed here.

References
Aldcroft, D. H., Richardson, H. W., 1969, *The British Economy 1870-1939* (Macmillan, London).
Allen, V. L., 1971, *The Sociology of Industrial Relations* (Longman, London).
Baran, P. A., 1973, *The Political Economy of Growth* (Penguin, Harmondsworth).
Bell, Lady, 1969, *At the Works* (David and Charles, London), reprint.
Bernstein, B., 1970, "A critique of the concept of 'compensatory education'", in *Education for Democracy,* Eds D. Rubenstein, C. Stoneman (Penguin, Harmondsworth).
Bernstein, H. (Ed.), 1973, *Underdevelopment and Development* (Penguin, Harmondsworth).
Bettelheim, C., 1972, Appendices I and III, in *Unequal Exchange,* A. Emmanuel (New Left Books, London).
Blackburn, R. (Ed.), 1972, *Ideology in Social Science* (Fontana, London).
Bowden, P. J., Gibb, A. A., 1970, "Economic development in the twentieth century", in *Durham County and City with Teesside* (British Association, London), chapter 18.
Bulmer, M. I., 1970, "Collectivities in change" (University of Durham, England) mimeo.
Carney, J. G., Hudson, R., 1974, "Ideology, public policy and underdevelopment in the North-East", Northeast Area Study WP-6, University of Durham, England.
Carney, J. G., Taylor, C., Hudson, R., 1975, *Studies in the Political Economy of Regional Underdevelopment: the Case of the North-East,* forthcoming.
Carter, I., 1974, "The Highlands of Scotland as an underdeveloped region", in *Sociology and Development,* Eds E. de Kadt, G. Williams (Tavistock Publications, London).
Castells, M., 1972, *La Question Urbaine* (Maspero, Paris).
Castells, M., 1973, *Luttes Urbaines et Pouvoir Politique* (Maspero, Paris).
C.E.R.M., 1974, *Urbanisme Monopoliste; Urbanisme Democratique* (Cahiers du Centre d'Etudes et Recherches Marxiste, Paris).
Cockroft, J., Frank, A. G., Johnson, D. L., 1972, *Dependence and Underdevelopment* (Doubleday, Garden City, NJ).
Cousins, J., 1973, "The sociology of regionalism", Department of Sociology, University of Durham, England, mimeo.
Cousins, J., Davis, R. L., Paddon, M. J., Waton, A., 1974, "Aspects of contradiction in regional policy: the case of North East England", *Regional Studies,* 8, 133-144.
Cousins, J., Brown, R. K., 1970, "Shipbuilding", in *Durham County and City with Teesside* (British Association, London), chapter 21.
Dobb, M., 1973, *Theories of Value and Distribution since Adam Smith* (Cambridge University Press, Cambridge).

Dougan, D., 1968, *The History of North East Shipbuilding* (Allen and Unwin, London).
Douglass, D., 1972, *Pit Life in County Durham,* pamphlet (History Workshop, Oxford).
Emmanuel, A., 1972, *Unequal Exchange* (New Left Books, London).
Engels, F., 1969, *The Condition of the Working Class in England* (Panther, London).
Frank, A. G., 1969a, *Capitalism and Underdevelopment in Latin America* (Penguin, Harmondsworth).
Frank, A. G., 1969b, *Latin America: Underdevelopment or Revolution?* (Monthly Review Press, New York).
Frank, A. G., 1972, Lumpenbourgoisie: Lumpendevelopment (Monthly Review Press, New York).
Gallagher, J., Robinson, R., 1953, The Imperialism of Free Trade, *Economic History Review,* VI. Second series, pp.1-15.
Garside, W. R., 1971, *The Durham Miners 1919-1960* (Allen and Unwin, London).
Glyn, A., Sutcliffe, B., 1972, *British Capitalism, Workers and the Profits Squeeze* (Penguin, Harmondsworth).
Gramsci, A., 1971, *Selections from the Prison Notebooks* (Lawrence and Wishart, London).
Habermas, J., 1972, *Knowledge and Human Interests* (Heinemann, London).
Harcourt, G. C., Laing, N. F., 1971, *Capital and Growth* (Penguin, Harmondsworth).
Harvey, D. W., 1973, *Social Justice and the City* (Edward Arnold, London).
Hindess, B., 1972, *The Decline of Working Class Politics* (Paladin, London).
Hobson, J. A., 1902 (reprinted 1968), *Imperialism* (Allen and Unwin, London).
Hodgson, G., 1974, "The theory of the falling rate of profit", *New Left Review,* **84,** 55-82.
Kregel, J. A., 1971, *Rate of Profit, Distribution and Growth: Two Views* (Macmillan, London).
Kregel, J. A., 1973, *The Reconstruction of Political Economy* (Macmillan, London).
Laclau, E., 1971, "Feudalism and capitalism in Latin America", *New Left Review,* **67,** 19-38.
Lefebvre, H., 1970, *La Revolution Urbaine* (Gallimard, Paris).
Lefebvre, H., 1972a, *La Pensée Marxiste et la Ville* (Casterman, Paris).
Lefebvre, H., 1972b, *Le Droit à la Ville* (Anthropos, Paris).
Lichtheim, G., 1971, *Imperialism* (Penguin, Harmondsworth).
Lenin, V. I., 1971, *Imperialism: the Highest Stage of Capitalism* (Foreign Languages Press, Peking).
Luxemburg, R., Bukharin, N., 1972, *Imperialism and the Accumulation of Capital* (Allen Lane, London).
Mandel, E., 1970, *Europe versus America? Contradictions of Imperialism* (New Left Books, London).
Marx, K., 1970, *Capital, Volume 1* (Lawrence and Wishart, London).
Marx, K., 1972, *Capital, Volume 3* (Lawrence and Wishart, London).
Mason, A., 1970, *The General Strike in the North East* (Hull University Press, Hull).
Macdonagh, O., 1962, The Anti-Imperialism of Free Trade, *Economic History Review,* **14,** 489-501.
Meek, R. L., 1973, *Studies in the Labour Theory of Value,* 2nd edition (Lawrence and Wishart, London).
Miliband, R., 1969, *The State in Capitalist Society* (Weidenfield and Nicholson, London).
Miliband, R., 1973, *Parliamentary Socialism* (Merlin Press, London).
Murdock, G., Golding, P., 1974, "For a political economy of mass communications", in *The Socialist Register, 1973,* Eds R. Miliband, J. Saville (Merlin Press, London).
Pilling, G., 1973, "Imperialism, trade and 'unequal exchange': the work of Arghiri Emmanuel", *Economy and Society,* **2,** 164-185.

Poulantzas, N., 1969, "The problem of the capitalist state", *New Left Review*, **58**, 67-78. Also in *Ideology in Social Science*, 1972, Ed. R. Blackburn (Fontana, London).

Robinson, J., 1973, "The new mercantilism", in *Collected Economic Papers*, volume **4** (Blackwell, Oxford).

Robinson, J., Eatwell, J., 1973, *Introduction to Modern Economics* (McGraw-Hill, New York).

Robinson, J. F. F., 1974, "New town ideologies", Northeast Area Study WP-7, University of Durham, England.

Rodney, W., 1972, *How Europe Underdeveloped Africa* (Bogle L'Ouverture, Paris).

Schmidt, A., 1971, *The Concept of Nature in Marx* (New Left Books, London).

Shaw, A. G. L., 1970, *Great Britain and the Colonies 1815-1865* (Methuen, London).

Sraffa, P., 1960, *Production of Commodities by Means of Commodities* (Cambridge University Press, Cambridge).

Sweezy, P. M., 1938, *Monopoly and Competition in the English Coal Trade, 1550-1850* (Harvard University Press, Harvard).

Szentes, T., 1971, *The Political Economy of Underdevelopment* (Akademiai Kiado, Budapest).

Thompson, E. P., 1963, *The Making of the English Working Class* (Gollancz, London).

Townsend, A. R., Taylor, C., 1974, "Sense of place and local identity", Northeast Area Study WP-4, University of Durham, England.

Turner, H. A., Jackson, D., 1970, "On the determination of the general wage level, or 'unlimited labour forever' ", *Economic Journal*, **80**, 827-849.

Vickery, S., 1972, "An analysis of the military in underdeveloped countries: a case study in ruling class sociology", in *Counter Course*, Ed. T. Pateman (Penguin, Harmondsworth).

Wellmer, A., 1971, *Critical Theory of Society* (Herder, London).

Wilkinson, E., 1939, *The Town that was Murdered* (Left Book Club, London).

Yaffe, D., 1973, "The crisis of profitability: a critique of the Glyn-Sutcliffe thesis", *New Left Review*, **80**, 45-62.

Urban Growth, Rent, and Quasi-rent

G.R.WALTER
University of Victoria, Canada

Introduction

The concepts of rent and competition have retained a strong prescriptive role in the discussion of urban industrialism over the years. Early in the industrial revolution Ricardo made rent the centrepiece of his advocacy of urban industry over rural virtue, associating rent with competition for a fixed resource. The subsequent triumph of industrialism, facilitated by widespread acceptance of the classical economist's ideas, accelerated urban development and provided new areas for the application of rent doctrine. Dispute about urban rent was very much alive at the end of the 19th century, as demonstrated by the Marshall–George Cambridge debates recently unearthed by Professor Stigler (1969) and by Marshall's (1966) devoting a chapter of his *Principles of Economics* to "Marginal costs in relation to urban values".

In the postwar period Wingo (1961) made urban-transportation cost differentials paramount in his theory of urban land. He gave an exactitude to the concept of an urban differential or position rent in the Ricardian sense, but did not follow on to analyse the role of aggregate position rents in urban growth—although the role of residential competition in establishing the rent surface was explicitly brought out. Wingo's monocentric urban rent surface approach has had great currency, being visible in the work of Muth (1969), Mills (1967), and Angel and Hyman (1970) to name a few.

Alonso (1970) has addressed the problem of urban size, and has borrowed for this purpose the marginalist approach of microeconomic theory. He has not, however, interested himself in the role of competition as it might illuminate the problem of urban size.

The role of competition as a promoter of growth and form has not often been considered in the urban context. However, Jacobs (1970) has recently and forcefully advocated the fertile "inefficient" *laissez-faire* city; by contrast with the infertile "efficient" *civis corpus* of Detroit, reasserting the liberal philosophy of Adam Smith.

It would seem that we are in possession of some important fragments of a theory of urban vitality. Jacobs' reassertion of the liberal position, taken in juxtaposition with the "gigantism" at least initially arising out of French regional theory, provides a dichotomy out of which a useful synthesis may be made. This paper attempts to build on the Ricardian tradition as brought forward by Wingo, the liberal tradition as popularised by Jacobs, and the theory-of-the-firm approach suggested by Alonso, to explore the relative significance of aggregate urban rents, of quasi-rents, and of competition in moulding urban form.

Differential land fertility in cities

Ricardo, as a stocktrader, would have appreciated the ability of professional–commercial activity to create sharp land-rent differentials. The fertility of land in a contemporary city also arises from its usefulness for residential and industrial purposes. An ordering of these uses in accordance with a monocentric city would yield a land 'fertility' pattern similar to that represented in figure 1. Just as Ricardo argued that it was the margin of least fertile land as contrasted with that more interior which determined interior rents, so it can be argued that the urban rent surface is determined by the superiority of interior land as a location in avoiding transportation costs. Further, residential rents must compete with agricultural rents and reflect the urban transportation differentials; industrial rents must compete with the most central competitive residential rents but, in general, are more or less uniform over the industrial belt; the commercial rents must smoothly relate to the most central industrial rent, and rise with increased centrality in a manner determined by the 'transportation' costs involved in face-to-face communication. This being the case, little harm is done if employment in the commercial core is considered constant. It will be ignored in the following.

Based on this scenario, a simple Ricardian model of urban development can be developed. The analytical concepts employed are aggregate demand and supply curves for urban firms and population.

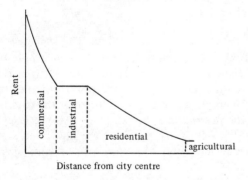

Figure 1. Rent pattern in a monocentric city.

A Ricardian model of aggregative city size

It is convenient to adopt the fiction that a city produces some amorphous aggregate good which is exported *in toto* at a fixed price, and then imports all the good required locally at the same price. This good (q) is produced by a number of profit-seeking firms which employ a labour force (h). The output per man (q/h) for each of these firms is dependent upon the number of firms (n) in the city as a whole (the evidence for this assumption has been collected by Alonso, 1970, pages 72–76) and upon the capital employed per man (k/h); so we have for the representative man [1]

$$\frac{q}{h} = F\left(n, \frac{k}{h}\right) .$$

As the firms are of uniform size, an aggregate production function (Q) exists (aggregate variables are identified by capital italic letters, variables attributable to firms or households by lower case) and is given by [2]

$$Q = nhF\left(n, \frac{k}{h}\right) .$$

This aggregation technique is similar to that used by Frankel (1962).

The effect of increases in city size (number of firms) on output per man may reflect agglomerative economies, diseconomies, or constant returns. For the remainder of this section it is assumed that firms maintain a fixed capital intensity ϕ, so $k = \phi h$.

If raw material is freely available locally, and Q is measured such that its price is unity (the price of the city's export good is assumed constant with regard to changes in the city's output and employment), then the firm's profit on industrial activity is given by

$$y = q - j - r - c ,$$

where y is the profit, j the wage bill, r the rent on industrial land, and c the cost of capital. j is given by

$$j - (s + ig)h + T(u, G)h ,$$

where $T(u, G)$ represents the transportation cost paid by an employee located at the margin of the city (located at u) as measured from the industrial belt's outer edge—it is a payment in addition to the net transfer wage s required to lure the employee from a small town or the countryside; and ig is the interest on the *per capita* public debt g; G is the level of infrastructure investment [3]. We assume the firms are of a fixed size, $\bar{h}$. If a positive profit is made, new firms are 'born' of the same size.

[1] The labour-force participation rate is assumed constant. Households and labourers are therefore interchangeable except for a factor of proportionality. 'Technology' is to be broadly construed in the present context, and includes the prevailing institutional arrangements of the city (that is work mores, governmental effectiveness and goals, size distribution of a firm), the prevailing state of social, human, and physical capital that does not belong to the firm (in the sense of the capital stock of the city), and engineering technology.

[2] Note that we assume all goods are traded interregionally for convenience. The effect of an alternative specification, say the addition of a service sector that does not export, would be to introduce a base service multiplier effect.

[3] The empirical implication, that wage rates rise with city size, is well-established. See the excellent discussion by Evans (1972, pages 53–56).

The employee is, *ceteris paribus*, willing to pay a premium over house construction costs of *up to* T(u, G) for a dwelling unit of standard quality at the city centre, that is it involves no transportation cost. The size of the unit thus occupied depends on a large number of factors, particularly upon the price per unit at various centralities. This unit price together with the transportation outlay involved in commuting from the given centrality may be taken as a constant, equal to T(u, G), and is determined by the level of infrastructure investment (G), the density of the city, and other factors. But the city's past history and existing building stock has the predominant role, so we will take the density and congestion gradient as given, and assume density on the city's margin as given by the conditions of a single-family-residence production. We can then view the changes in the size of the radius of the city as dependent on incremental changes in the city's size as measured in households and infrastructure investment, so

$$T(u, G) = T(H, G),$$

where H is the number of households in the city. Further, if x is some location interior to u, we may write the transportation cost perceived by the resident at x as T(H, G, x) which approaches T(H, G) as x approaches u. (For simplicity it is assumed that the cost of traveling to the city center from a given x does not change as the city grows.)

Returning to the industrial costs of production, we consider first industrial rent. If θ represents the number of households per acre at the point of greatest residential density, then θT(H, G) is the rent per acre at this location. Industrial users of land must meet this rent and, with the assumption that the industrial belt is of uniform industrial accessibility, this rent will prevail throughout the belt (we could repeat our argument about differentials in the residential belt, and assume different industrial densities and accessibilities, but this would needlessly increase the complication of the model). Assuming that z acres are required per worker, we have

$$r = z\theta T(H, G),$$

where r is the firm's cost of land per worker.

The cost of capital can be more simply presented. We have assumed that ϕ units of capital are required per man. If i is the user's cost of capital, the firm's capital cost is $c = i\phi$ per man. Thus the total cost of labour to the firm ('wage'), direct and indirect (w) is

$$w = [s + (g + \phi)i + (1 + z\theta)T(H, G)]\bar{h},$$

where firms are of fixed size $\bar{h}$. The total wage cost of the city is $W = nw$. So long as $Q/n > w$, new entrepreneurs will wish to enjoy supernormal profit and the number of firms will increase. In the process of city growth T(H, G) will rise, as will Q/n because of agglomeration effects.

If T(H, G) rises more quickly than Q/n as H increases, each new firm will enjoy smaller profit, until such point as profit is zero and the birth of new firms ceases. The city then attains an equilibrium size (rent, transportation outlay, and profits are assumed to accrue to absentee receivers).

Urban industrial organisation and growth policy

The framework just presented can be used to explore several cases of urban industrial growth. We will consider the competitive case, that is output set by a process of the birth of profit-seeking firms; and, with some modification, the managerial case, that is output set by exogenous demand managed nationally, regionally, or locally.

Let us begin by considering an entrepreneurially active environment— Jacobs' (1970) 'inefficient' city. It is easily seen from the above that the average firm product is equal to $\bar{h}F(n, \phi)$; this of course is the city's average social revenue product as well. (The marginal labour costs of the firm are not defined, as the firm does not alter its labour force size.) The city's marginal firm product is given by

$$\frac{\partial Q}{\partial n} = n\bar{h}\frac{\partial F}{\partial n} + \bar{h}F(n, \phi) .$$

These magnitudes are functions of n and are plotted in figure 2 for the agglomerative case. It is also clear from the above that the firm's total labour costs are w, and w is the city's *average* social cost of a firm.

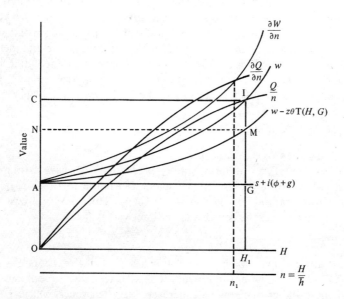

Figure 2.

The marginal cost of an additional urban firm is given by:

$$\frac{\partial W}{\partial n} = [s + i(\phi + g) + (1 + z\theta)\mathrm{T}(H, G)]\bar{h} + (1 + z\theta)\frac{\partial T}{\partial H}\frac{\partial H}{\partial n}\overline{hn} \; .$$

These cost magnitudes are also plotted in figure 2, as functions of H and n, where $H = \overline{hn}$.

The birth process of the city's firms will result in a city population for which the marginal (and average) gain accruing to an additional firm is just offset by marginal (and average) cost, that is n_1 on figure 2. At this point firms will earn no quasi-rent (although they did in the process of expansion to n_1) and proceeds of urban production above the cost of labour will accrue to transportation and land. Taking w as the boundary, the area AMIC represents aggregate urban rent (AMN is the residential rent, and NMIC the industrial rent), AMG represents the aggregate transportation outlay, and AGH_1O the wage outlay. The results of competition and profit-seeking among urban firms is the *maximisation of aggregate rent*.

Let us now consider the 'efficient' managerial case in which the city's output and employment are set by exogenous demand factors as interpreted by a dominant industry consisting of $\bar{n}$ firms, each with variable labour force size. Then $\bar{n}h = H$. In order to avoid restricting ourselves to a constant average-revenue product-of-labour case, we modify the production function to $Q = H\mathrm{F}(H, \phi)$. Q is assumed to be independent of the city's wage level but may be influenced by various measures under the control of a city's private and public policy makers, such as tax concessions, a 'friendly' atmosphere, willingness to make special concessions on zoning or pollution control, and so on. What level of urban product should the urban policy aim for?

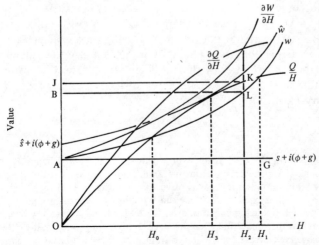

Figure 3.

One candidate is given by the intersection of marginal social product of the industry with marginal cost, which gives a city of size H_2 in figure 3. Note that the urban labour's real wage s remains unchanged (by assumption), but aggregate rent and transportation cost is reduced, while the dominant industry is favoured with a quasi-rent on its restrictive practice (profits are now JBLK). This is the familiar monopolistic outcome in a new guise. The interests of the established, dominant industry is in stabilising growth, providing it is not in a position to capture land rents. An exception to this logic is where the industry can influence a growth-oriented policy in which the city itself captures a substantial portion of the aggregate rent and applies it to infrastructure investment. This has the effect of lowering the congestion-cost gradient and increasing the aggregate rent-profit potential of the city. The dominant industry expands, but not so far as it might have in the case of a competitive industrial organisation.

Is maximum expansion necessary?

Is maximum expansion necessarily desirable, consistent with average *per capita* productivity, and *per capita* costs? The answer is that it is not, except where it is a national policy to employ labour most efficiently and obtain, thereby, the maximal return on its employment (we abstract, of course, from the obvious vested interest of city fathers in aggregate rent-oriented property taxes).

To see how this might work, note that the possibility of profit over the range of population H_0 to H_1 may lead to the organisation of more cities of this size class. (The problem of what forces assist, and what barriers obstruct, the organisation of new urban centres is neglected here.) Interregional competition for labour will lead to upward shifts of s and its associated curves, until such time as $\hat{w}$ becomes tangential to $F(H, \phi)$, that is at H_3. At H_3 the relevant marginal curves also would intersect and a comparative static equilibrium of urban development is achieved.

Note too that this 'long run' equilibrium yields a city of somewhat smaller size than at the peak of the city's growth—precisely because the firms operating in the city were able to earn short-run quasi-rents in the period of city expansion[4].

---

[4] An important difficulty of dynamic adjustment should be noted here. If an increase in public infrastructure investment (G), designed to reduce urban congestion, is financed by a tax on urban rent, as is often the procedure, the fiscal solvency of urban areas may be threatened by the 'long run' equilibrium adjustment indicated by H_3. For as cities invest in reducing congestion on the basis of the current tax revenues derived from rents, they may find their aggregate rents falling as a result of the competitive movement of the transfer wage from w to $\hat{w}$, which results in an erosion of their tax base.

These implications have been drawn on the assumption that $F(H, \phi)$ exhibits agglomeration economies, so that

$$\frac{\partial F(H, \phi)}{\partial H} > 0 .$$

The alternative specifications, $\partial F(H, \phi)/\partial H = 0$ or $\partial F(H, \phi)/\partial H < 0$, which correspond to constant returns or agglomerative diseconomies, are of some interest. The rule of thumb which emerged where there was agglomerative economy (maximise aggregate rent if you wish to maximise urban productivity and wages) may not hold in the cases of constant returns or agglomerative diseconomy. These two cases are portrayed in figure 4.

Consider the first. It can be clearly seen (in figure 4a) that the maximisation of rent (choice of city size H_1) implies the maximisation of employment for any given set of cities, but that the demand for labour, combined with the ability of small cities to avoid congestion costs, implies the organisation of more, and smaller, units of production until only minimum-sized cities remain.

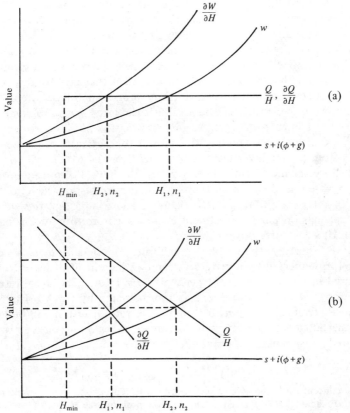

Figure 4.

The same result occurs where there is agglomerative diseconomy, only more so (figure 4b). Note that if the average product curve $F(H, \phi) = Q/H$ has an elasticity less than unity, the maximisation of rent does not maximise employment. Similar conclusions can be drawn for the competitive case.

Investment and growth

The discussion has thus far led to a rule for choosing a city size, measured in households, based on a policy of maximising land rent. The discussion was limited to the case of a static private-production relationship, $F(H, \phi)$ or $\bar{h}F(n, \phi)$, and an equally static congestion function, $T(H, G)$. A full treatment of the problem of growth policy when private and public investment is possible is beyond the scope of this paper, but it is important to note that the public authorities (as they well realise) have at their command levers of growth other than their ability to influence interregional industrial location via persuasion. These levers, to choose the two most universally recognised are: (a) investment in public, social, overhead capital; and (b) the influencing of the rate of private investment through measures to lower the cost of capital. Let us now inquire as to the social justification, if any, for each of these two policies.

As is commonly recognised, arguments for social investment and subsidisation arise out of benefits which cannot be privately captured. In the context of the present discussion, it is clear that private firms will make decisions regarding their investment programmes based upon their private return, whereas it is evident that their investment programmes will have a direct impact on aggregate rent (raising the $\partial W/\partial n$ curve and the w curve in figures 2 and 3). It is this impact (on aggregate rent), which results from private investment, which measures the *social value* of the private investment[5]. Note, however, that the impact of private investment on aggregate rent depends on the slope of the congestion curve, over the range of intersection (around H_1, figures 2 and 3) and that this slope, in turn, depends on public investment in infrastructure to reduce congestion (which tilts the curve downward).

Figure 5 portrays the problem graphically for the agglomerative case. The return expected by a private firm on an increment of investment, measured in increase in output per worker, is $I - A$. The social return, in the absence of public investment, is approximated by $C - A$. The result is too little private investment, for the private rate of return will be lower than the public. A subsidy provided out of taxes on urban rent is indicated if agglomerative economies prevail.

---

[5] The concept that economic surplus measured in rent is a measure of welfare gain is of long standing. For a recent critique of the position, see Margolis (1968) or, more recently, Goldberg (1972).

If constant returns prevail, no divergence between the private and social value of capital will occur. If we have diminishing returns, the anticipated private return will exceed the public, and we may have private over-investment.

The situation is further complicated if public officials are contemplating infrastructure investment, which would lower the *w* curve. The inter-dependency of private and public investment is complex, but it is obvious that coordination is required or too little investment will be undertaken on both sides of the urban economy.

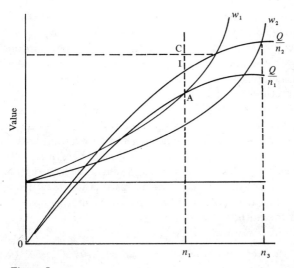

Figure 5.

Conclusion
The Ricardian logic employed here suggests that the question of the city as a generator of economic growth is more complicated than choice of a managerially 'efficient' as compared to a *laissez faire* 'inefficient' industrial organisation, as suggested by Jacobs (1970) in her popular book. The presence of a *laissez faire* industrial structure has the advantage of assuring that the growth of a city will not be stunted by a dominant, oligopolistic industry's efforts to maximise profits. But *laissez faire* is not enough, by itself, to ensure that the social profit of urban growth—aggregate rent—does not fall into infertile hands. The environmentally static, price-taking nature of *laissez faire* firms ensures that, in the absence of urban development planning, they will undertake too little investment in the agglomerative case. It is equally true that, without proper coordination with the investment plans of the private sector, the amount of public investment will be wrong.

The upshot of these considerations is that the historical concern of municipal officials for the promotion of urban growth was, and is, well-founded. Both in the managerial and the *laissez faire* case it would appear likely that the private sector will underestimate the benefits of urban growth. It should be emphasised, however, that this nearsightedness arises out of the inability of the private sector to capture urban rents. In the case of a company town where urban property is owned by the firm, the problem is not likely to arise, and no subsidy is called for. The implications of this argument for regional growth incentives schemes may be worthy of reflection.

Aggregate urban rent, then, is one measure of economic surplus appropriate for judging urban growth. But it should be recognised that this measure is only one of many measures of surplus. The appropriate measure depends on the relative stickiness of the factors of production. Our discussion has emphasised rent as a measure *if* a competitive industrial and residential structure prevails. If competition does not exist industrially, profit will not be converted to rent, and rent will not reflect urban surplus accurately. Alternatively, artificial, ghetto-like restrictions on the freedom of residents to locate will generate monopoly rents in certain areas, which again will distort rent as a welfare measure. Nonetheless, in a well-functioning competitive urban market, rent should serve as a reasonably accurate measure of the social value of an infrastructure investment; as well as an indicator of the relative desirability of promoting growth in one city as compared to another.

References
Alonso, W., 1971, "The economics of urban size", *Papers, Regional Science Association,* **XXVI**, 67-84.
Angel, S., Hyman, G. M., 1970, "Urban velocity fields", *Environment and Planning,* **2**, 211-224; see also Angel, S., Hyman, G. M., 1975, *Urban Fields* (Pion, London).
Beckman, M. J., 1969, "On the distribution of urban rent and residential density", *Journal of Economic Theory,* **1** (1), 60-67.
Beckman, M. J., 1972, "Von Thunen revisited: A neoclassical land use model", *The Swedish Journal of Economics,* **74** (1), 1-7.
von Böventer, E., 1970, "Optimal spatial structure and regional development", *Kyklos,* **23**, 903-926.
Evans, A. W., 1972, "The pure theory of city size in an industrial economy", *Urban Studies,* **9**, 49-77.
Frankel, M., 1962, "The production function in allocation and growth", *American Economic Review,* **52**, 998-999.
Goldberg, M. A., 1972, "An evaluation of the interaction between urban transportation and land use systems", *Land Economics,* **XLVIII** (4), 338-346.
Jacobs, Jane, 1970, *The Economy of Cities* (Random House Books, New York).
Leven, C. L., 1969, "Determinants of the size and structural form of urban areas", *Papers, Regional Science Association,* **XXII**, 7-28.
Leven, C. L., Legler, J. B., Shapiro, P., 1970, *An Analytical Framework for Regional Development Policy,* Regional Science Study 9 (MIT Press, Cambridge, Mass.).
Margolis, J., 1968, "The demand for urban services", in *Issues in Urban Economics,* Ed. H. Perloff (Johns Hopkins University Press, Baltimore).

Marshall, A., 1966, *Principles of Economics,* 8th edition (Macmillan, London).

Mills, E. S., 1967, "An aggregative model of resource allocation in a metropolitan area", *American Economic Review,* **57**, 197-210.

Mirrlees, J. A., 1972, "The optimal town", *The Swedish Journal of Economics,* **74**, 114-135.

Muth, R., 1969, *Cities and Housing* (University of Chicago Press, Chicago).

Neutze, G. M., 1971, *Economic Policy and the Size of Cities* (A. M. Kelly, New York).

Richardson, H. W., 1971, "Review of *Analytical Framework for Regional Development Policy* by C. L. Leven *et al.*", *Journal of Economic Literature,* **IX**, 1235-1237.

Richardson, H. W., 1972, "Optimality in city size, systems of cities and urban policy: A sceptics view", *Urban Studies,* **9**, 29-48.

Solow, R. M., Vickrey, W. L., 1971, "Land use in a long narrow city", *Journal of Economic Theory,* **3**, 430-447.

Stigler, G. T., 1969, "Alfred Marshall's lectures on progress and poverty", *Journal of Law and Economics,* **12**, 181-226.

Walters, A. A., 1968, *The Economics of Road User Charges,* World Bank Occasional Paper 5, International Bank for Reconstruction and Development (Johns Hopkins University Press, Baltimore).

Wingo, L., Jr., 1961, *Transportation and Urban Land* (Resources for the Future,

Retailers' Profits and Consumers' Welfare in a Spatial Interaction Shopping Model

A.G.WILSON
University of Leeds

1 The problems to be studied

1.1 Profits, welfare, and behaviour

Spatial interaction models of flows of goods to shops have been in common use since the work of Huff (1964) and Lakshmanan and Hansen (1965). A typical model can be expressed as

$$S_{ij} = A_i e_i P_i W_j^\alpha \exp(-\beta c_{ij}) \,, \tag{1}$$

where

$$A_i = \frac{1}{\sum_j W_j^\alpha \exp(-\beta c_{ij})} \,. \tag{2}$$

This ensures that

$$\sum_j S_{ij} = e_i P_i \,. \tag{3}$$

The variables are as follows:

S_{ij} is the flow of cash from residents of zone i to shops in zone j;
e_i is the expenditure *per capita* on shopping goods by residents of zone i;
P_i is the population of zone i;
W_j is the attractiveness of shops in zone j, usually measured by size, say of floorspace in square feet;
c_{ij} is the cost of travel from zone i to zone j;
α and β are parameters; and
A_i is a balancing factor, defined by equation (2).

The basis of this paper turns on a simple idea. In the model described above, we stop short of making hypotheses about the changes in shopping centres, measured say as sizes W_j, over time. Hotelling (1929), in a famous paper, offered some such behavioural assumptions for a very simple case. He showed that for inelastic demand evenly spread along a straight line served by two outlets, A and B, the stable competitive equilibrium for the shopkeepers, would be together at the centre, shown as A_1 and B_1 in figure 1, but that the consumers' optimum location for the outlets would be at the outer quartiles, shown as A_2 and B_2. The first position could be

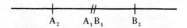

Figure 1

described as the profit-maximising optimum and the second as the welfare optimum. Hotelling's analysis has long been recognised as offering an explanation of the clustering of shops—even of the clustering of similar types of shops on particular streets—which is so frequently seen in cities. It seems interesting, therefore, to try to build his hypotheses into a more realistic model such as the spatial interaction model described at the beginning of this section. The investigation of this is carried out in section 2 later.

There appears to have been relatively little previous work of this kind. Huff (1966) presents an algorithm for determining optimum retail location using a spatial interaction model. However, he is not completely explicit in a mathematical sense, and it appears that his algorithm does not necessarily converge to an overall optimum. His viewpoint is very much that of the retailers. So also is that of Parry Lewis (1971) who explored the concept of 'probability in a shopping model'. He calculated sales per square foot predicted by a simple gravity model, but also goes on to discuss shopkeepers' decisions given a notion of profit. The approach is somewhat different to that used in this paper, but some of his results are echoed below.

1.2 Optimisation
But the idea becomes more complicated, because it also seems worthwhile to integrate the basic notion above with a number of other recent developments in shopping modelling or related fields. First, since we are examining optimisation problems associated with shop (or more generally, service facility) location, we can relate our investigation to optimisation methods more generally. Facility location problems have been much studied recently as so-called location–allocation problems (for example see Scott, 1971), usually with mathematical programming techniques. This provides the first avenue for extending our investigation. The second arises from the recent work of Evans (1973) and Senior and the present author (Senior and Wilson, 1974; Wilson and Senior, 1974) that connects entropy-maximising and mathematical programming models. Since we are exploring an optimisation problem within the framework of an entropy-maximising spatial interaction model, such connections become relevant. These two 'optimisation' avenues are explored in section 3.

1.3 Shopping-model disaggregation
The third step in the argument follows the recognition that more interesting problems can be analysed if more detail is added to the model of equations (1) and (2). First, we can allow for travel by different modes. Second, it is important to add trips from workplaces as well as from home. Third, we can distinguish different types of good, and particularly the availability of different types at different centres. This enables connections to be made with the model of Bacon (1971) and

Evans (1972), and with central-place theory. Such disaggregation is explored in section 4.

Some alternative behavioural assumptions are explored briefly in section 5, relating to the work of Alonso (1964), Gannon (1971; 1972), and Hartwick and Hartwick (1971).

1.4 Summary of the argument

Our main purpose, therefore, is to add more explicit behavioural assumptions to the supply side of the spatial interaction shopping model. This enables us to try to say something about 'competition' and 'dynamics' and to emulate Hotelling in a more complicated model. We can explore connections to a more microlevel of theory, and we can use the most recent results on optimisation.

2 Retailers' profits and consumers' welfare

2.1 Retailers' profits: preliminary discussion

How are profits to be measured? In a perfectly competitive world, competition ought to reduce profits to zero; but in that case, our intuitive notion of profit could be translated into one of rent, and if the definition of 'retailer' was expanded to include the owners of shopping floorspace or associated land, then rent maximisation could be analysed. However, while bearing such fundamental points in mind, we postpone further discussion to section 5, and proceed with some simpler notions of profit which are directly related to the spatial interaction model above.

Suppose retailers set the W_j's so that profits are maximised. Then, whatever the definition of 'profits', we can distinguish between local maximisation, where the W_j's are set so that profits in each zone are maximised, and global optimisation, where profits in the area as a whole are maximised. The first possibility is likely to be the more realistic for shopping, though there may be other services (banking, for example) where the second is better. We consider each in turn in sections 2.2 and 2.3 below, and some considerations of profit equalisation across space in section 2.4.

2.2 Local maximisation of retailers' profits

A crude index would be sales per square foot in zone j, defined as

$$\rho_j = \frac{\sum_i S_{ij}}{W_j} \, , \tag{4}$$

and this could be maximised. Alternatively, we might define profits occurring in zone j as

$$\Pi_j = \gamma_j \sum_i S_{ij} - W_j p_j \, , \tag{5}$$

where γ_j is the proportion of total sales which is an operating profit, while

p_j is the 'rent' per square foot of shopping space. This formula only really becomes interesting when p_j is specified as a function of other variables. The simplest assumption would be

$$p_j = \epsilon \rho_j \,,\tag{6}$$

where ϵ is some constant. But it is easy to see that, on substituting for p_j from equation (4),

$$\Pi_j = (\gamma_j - \epsilon) \sum_i S_{ij} \,,\tag{7}$$

and this leads to rather uninteresting results (unless γ_j was an interesting function of location variables). This arises because

$$\frac{\partial \left(\sum_i S_{ij} \right)}{\partial W_j} > 0 \,,\tag{8}$$

so that retailers, on this view, would continually increase their size.

Next we look at the rate of change of ρ_j with W_j. It can be shown that[1]

$$\frac{\partial \rho_j}{\partial W_j} = \frac{1}{W_j^2} \sum_i \langle S_{ij} \{ \alpha [1 - A_i W_j^\alpha \exp(-\beta c_{ij})] - 1 \} \rangle \,.\tag{9}$$

Note that if $\alpha \leqslant 1$,

$$\frac{\partial \rho_j}{\partial W_j} \leqslant 0 \;;\tag{10}$$

then sales per square foot could never be increased by addition to floorspace. If $\alpha > 1$, then

$$\frac{\partial \rho_j}{\partial W_j} > 0 \,,\tag{11}$$

if also

$$A_i W_j^\alpha \exp(-\beta c_{ij}) \leqslant \frac{\alpha - 1}{\alpha} \text{ for each } i;\tag{12}$$

or alternatively, by using equation (1)

$$\frac{S_{ij}}{e_i P_i} \leqslant \frac{\alpha - 1}{\alpha} \text{ for each } i.\tag{13}$$

A similar result was obtained by Parry Lewis (1971) with his simpler gravity model. It would be possible to adopt a rule of retailers' behaviour in this case that W_j was increased for the next time period if equations (11) and (12) were satisfied, and reduced if equation (10) held.

[1] These and other derivations used later are set out in the Appendix.

This could be expressed, in an obvious notation, by

$$W_j(t+T) = W_j(t) + \nu \frac{\partial \rho_j}{\partial W_j} , \tag{14}$$

where ν is a positive constant. Equation (9) indicates that $\partial \rho_j / \partial W_j$ is (for $\alpha > 1$) positive for low W_j and negative for large W_j, indicating a relationship of the form shown in figure 2.

The position of (ρ_j max, W_j max) will depend on a host of other variables, of course, which turn up in the A_i term in equation (9) as well as those which are shown explicitly.

The next step is to consider local profit maximisation using equation (5), but written here with p_j shown as a function of all the W_k and other unknown variables X_k; for convenience, we take γ_j as γ, independent of j.

$$\Pi_j = \gamma \sum_i S_{ij} - W_j p_j(W_1, W_2, ..., X_1, X_2, ...) . \tag{15}$$

We have

$$\frac{\partial \Pi_j}{\partial W_j} = \frac{\gamma \alpha}{W_j} \left[\sum_i S_{ij} \frac{(1-S_{ij})}{e_i P_i} \right] - p_j - W_j \frac{\partial p_j}{\partial W_j} . \tag{16}$$

This will be positive if

$$\frac{\gamma \alpha \sum_i S_{ij}}{W_j} > \frac{\gamma \alpha}{W_j} \sum_i \frac{S_{ij}^2}{e_i P_i} + p_j + W_j \frac{\partial p_j}{\partial W_j} . \tag{17}$$

Note that

$$\sum_i \frac{S_{ij}^2}{e_i P_i} = \sum_i S_{ij} A_i W_j^\alpha \exp(-\beta c_{ij}) , \tag{18}$$

and that

$$A_i W_j^\alpha \exp(-\beta c_{ij}) = \frac{W_j^\alpha \exp(-\beta c_{ij})}{\sum_k W_k^\alpha \exp(-\beta c_{ik})} \tag{19}$$

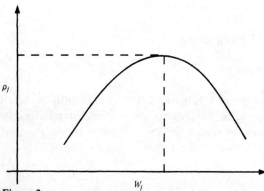

Figure 2

is likely to be $\ll 1$ unless j is the dominant centre. Thus, typically, the inequality (17) is saying that profits can be increased if the profits gained (γ) from an increase in sales per square foot, $(\sum_i S_{ij}/W_j)$, modified by α to allow for scale economies, is greater than the rent, p_j, plus its increase from the increase in size, $W_j \partial p_j/\partial W_j$. The first term on the right-hand side could often be neglected, but allows for the fact that as W_j increases, bigger increases are needed to attract trade away from other centres.

Once again we could have an operational rule that W_j are increased if $(\partial \Pi_j/\partial W_j) > 0$ and decreased otherwise, say

$$W_j(t+T) = W_j(t) + \nu \frac{\partial \Pi_j}{\partial W_j} , \qquad (20)$$

in the manner of equation (14). This formulation could be made more explicit if the functional form of p_j was known.

2.3 Global maximisation of retailers' profits
In the previous section, we have discussed the behaviour of a retailer in a particular zone and defined a process of adjustment over time for different kinds of local profit maximisation. Using the varieties and coefficients defined in that section, we can note that the global profit is

$$\Pi = \sum_j \Pi_j \qquad (21)$$

$$= \gamma \sum_j \sum_i S_{ij} - \sum_j p_j W_j . \qquad (22)$$

The global optimum occurs when

$$\frac{\partial \Pi}{\partial W_j} = \sum_k \frac{\partial \Pi_k}{\partial W_j} = 0 , \qquad (23)$$

for each j.

$$\frac{\partial \Pi_k}{\partial W_j} = -\alpha S_{ik} A_i W_j^{\alpha-1} \exp(-\beta c_{ij}) - W_k \frac{\partial p_k}{\partial W_j} \qquad (24)$$

for $k \neq j$, so the equations (23) become

$$\frac{\partial \Pi}{\partial W_j} = \sum_{k \neq j} \left[-\gamma\alpha \sum_i S_{ik} A_i - W_j^{\alpha-1} \exp(-\beta c_{ij}) - W_k \frac{\partial p_k}{\partial W_j} \right]$$

$$+ \frac{\gamma\alpha}{W_j} \sum_i S_{ij} [1 - A_i W_j^\alpha \exp(-\beta c_{ij})] - p_j - W_j \frac{\partial p_j}{\partial W_j}$$

$$= 0 \qquad (25)$$

$$= \frac{\gamma\alpha}{W_j} \sum_i S_{ij} - \gamma\alpha \sum_{ki} \left[S_{ik} A_i W_j^{\alpha-1} \exp(-\beta c_{ij}) - W_k \frac{\partial p_k}{\partial W_j} \right] - p_j$$

$$= 0 . \qquad (26)$$

By any standards, this is an extremely complicated set of simultaneous equations in the W_j's and the hope of finding the global optimum except by some heuristic, probably iterative, procedure must be slim. (Though it may be worthwhile to explore the $\alpha = 1$ case to see if any considerable simplification could be achieved.) However, this analysis does make it clear that the global optimum is different from the local optima.

2.4 A note on a problem

A marker should be set up at this point about a problem. It could be argued that under certain assumptions profits per square foot should be equal across the study area. The procedures outlined above would not guarantee this. It would be possible in principle to guarantee equality by the addition of constraints to the maximisation problems, but this is left for further investigation.

2.5 The maximisation of consumers' welfare

We are now considering another kind of $\{W_j\}$ adjustment process: control is assumed to be exercised by planners in order to maximise consumers' welfare. First we need a definition of consumers' welfare. We assume a tradeoff between the advantages of shopping centre size and the disutility of having to travel. If we write

$$W_j^\alpha = e^{\alpha \ln W_j} , \tag{27}$$

and rewrite equation (1) as

$$S_{ij} = A_i e_i P_i \exp\left[\beta\left(\frac{\alpha}{\beta}\ln W_j - c_{ij}\right)\right] \tag{28}$$

it can be argued that $(\alpha/\beta)\ln W_j$ represents the 'size' benefits of shopping at j and c_{ij} the disutility of travel. Thus, each consumer needs to maximise $(\alpha/\beta)\ln W_j - c_{ij}$. This could be represented within a mathematical programming formulation, but we postpone that to section 3. Further, only the global optimum seems to be of interest in this case. So the planners task is to choose $\{W_j\}$ to maximise total consumers' welfare, which is

$$Z = \sum_{ij} S_{ij}\left(\frac{\alpha}{\beta}\ln W_j - c_{ij}\right) , \tag{29}$$

where the S_{ij} are given by equation (28). Written in full this is

$$Z = \sum_i A_i e_i P_i \sum_j \exp\left[\beta\left(\frac{\alpha}{\beta}\ln W_j - c_{ij}\right)\right]\left(\frac{\alpha}{\beta}\ln W_j - c_{ij}\right) \tag{30}$$

$$= \sum_i \frac{e_i P_i}{\sum_l \exp\left[\beta\left(\frac{\alpha}{\beta}\ln W_l - c_{il}\right)\right]} \sum_j \exp\left[\beta\left(\frac{\alpha}{\beta}\ln W_j - c_{ij}\right)\right]\left(\frac{\alpha}{\beta}\ln W_j - c_{ij}\right) \tag{31}$$

This is obviously a very complicated nonlinear function of the W_j's. It can be shown that

$$\frac{\partial Z}{\partial W_k} = \sum_{ij}\left[-\alpha W_k^{\alpha-1}\exp(-\beta c_{ik})A_i S_{ij}\left(\frac{\alpha}{\beta}\ln W_j - c_{ij}\right)\right]$$

$$+ \sum_{i}\left[\alpha S_{ik}W_k^{-1}\left(\frac{\alpha}{\beta}\ln W_k - c_{ik}\right) + \frac{\alpha}{\beta}S_{ik}W_k^{-1}\right] \qquad (32)$$

and the task of solving the equations

$$\frac{\partial Z}{\partial W_k} = 0 , \qquad (33)$$

seems in general to be a very difficult one!

It may be possible to make some progress by taking approximate forms of Z—for example by assuming that the A_i's can be calculated using *current* W_j's and they are thereafter treated as constants. Alternatively, iterative solutions could be sought, and the $\alpha = 1$ situation explored as suggested for retailers' global profit maximisation.

2.6 First conclusions

We have now applied Hotelling's two alternative behavioural assumptions to the problem of predicting future W_j's in a world described by a spatial interaction shopping model. The results are not as obviously exciting as Hotelling's because the mathematics is so much more complicated. We have shown that the solutions are different, but the degree of clustering in the retailers' solution, and of dispersal in the consumers' solution, depend very much on the relative parameters of the model. The parameters α and β describe consumers' behaviour, and so α in particular must be taken as a measure of the *consumers'* scale economies. The retailers' scale economies are determined by the parameters of the functions γ_j, and p_j; and these functions will include parameters to describe other kinds of effects also.

The best way to proceed with this kind of study would be to develop simulation models of the two systems on the computer, since numerical solutions to the analytically intractable problems presented above would be possible. Alternative functional forms for γ_j and p_j could be tested (and indeed so could alternative forms for Π and Z). If the models then seemed in any way realistic, effort could be devoted to the empirical measurement of the parameters of these various functions.

Finally, we note that as yet, we are only half way to a representation of Hotelling's assumptions within a more realistic model. We have built in his *behavioural* assumptions for a spatial interaction model world. But an essential part of his model was the assumption of a small number of available outlets. This could be built into the formulation by setting a number of W_j to zero. But the problem then becomes a location-allocation problem which we will study in the next section.

3 Shopping models within optimisation problems
3.1 Typical location-allocation problems
A location–allocation problem for types of variables used already would
be as follows (cf Scott, 1971). Suppose there are n zones and m facilities
(say shopping centres) to be located in m of them. Let S_{ij} be the flow
variables and let $\lambda_i = 1$ if a facility is located in i, and 0 otherwise. Then
the problem is to find S_{ij} and λ_i such that some function

$$Z(S_{ij}, \lambda_i) \tag{34}$$

is a maximum, say. Many additional constraints could be imposed, for
example, setting minimum and/or maximum sizes for any or each facility.
Such problems are in general rather difficult to solve because of the
number of possible combinations to be investigated. The locational part
of the problem obviously involves ^nC_m possibilities and these multiply
into the even higher-dimensional allocation part. Usually there are some
simple cases, however, which can be solved using standard methods of
mathematical programming.

It is now clear that Hotelling's problem can be considered (and indeed
is so by Scott) as a location–allocation problem. Further, the methods of
analysis suggested in section 2 of this paper can be considered as an
alternative approach to some kinds of location–allocation problems:
instead of defining integer $(0, 1)$ location variables such as λ_i above, the
location of a facility can be represented by its size in any location, and
our W_j are such variables. This is most useful when $W_j > 0$ for all j, as
is likely to be the case for shopping. When some of the W_j are zero, say
$n - m$ of them, the usual ^nC_m combinatorial problem reappears. If this is
added to the models presented in section 2, we get a 'true' Hotelling problem
for a spatial interaction model world. Retailers would then be assumed to be
changing locations as well as deciding sizes in particular places.

3.2 Most probable suboptimal behaviour
As noted in the introduction, some recent work has established close
connections between mathematical programming models and entropy
maximising models. Evans (1973) showed in a specific case that a linear
programming model is the limit of an entropy-maximising model. In
general terms, the argument can be stated as follows. Suppose a set of
variables X is obtained by maximising an entropy function

$$S = S(X) , \tag{35}$$

subject to constraints

$$\left. \begin{array}{l} f_1(X) = C_1 \\ \quad\vdots \\ f_n(X) = C_n \\ f_{n+1}(X) = Z^{(1)} \end{array} \right\} . \tag{36}$$

Suppose then that X is estimated by maximising (or minimising, as appropriate)

$$Z = f_{n+1}(X) , \tag{37}$$

subject to

$$\left. \begin{array}{l} f_1(X) = C_1 \\ \quad \vdots \\ f_n(X) = C_n \end{array} \right\} . \tag{38}$$

Let β be the Lagrangian multiplier associated with the $(n+1)$th constraint in the entropy-maximising model, and let $X^{(1)}(\beta)$ be the solution expressed as a function of this (and it will also be a function of other multipliers). Let $X^{(2)}$ be the solution of the mathematical programming model given by equations (37) and (38). Then Evans showed that

$$X^{(2)} = \lim_{\beta \to \infty} X^{(1)}(\beta) , \tag{39}$$

and

$$Z = \lim_{\beta \to \infty} f_{n+1}(X^{(1)}) . \tag{40}$$

This result is also true for a range of functions other than S (Smith, 1974, private communication), but when S is an entropy function, $X^{(1)}$ can be considered, in the usual way, to be the *most probable* $X^{(1)}$ consistent with the suboptimal value, $Z^{(1)}$, of Z.

In the linear programming model given by equations (37) and (38), the dual variables associated with the constraints can often be interpreted as shadow prices, comparative advantages, or rents. Let these be $\lambda_1, ..., \lambda_n$ respectively. Let $\lambda_1^{(1)}, ..., \lambda_n^{(1)}$ be the Lagrangian multipliers associated with the first n constraints of the set (36), and we have already defined β as that associated with the last constraint. Then it has been conjectured, and shown to be true in particular cases (Senior and Wilson, 1974; Wilson and Senior, 1974), that

$$\lambda_i = \lim_{\beta \to \infty} \frac{\lambda_i^{(1)}}{\beta} , \tag{41}$$

for $i = 1, 2, ..., n$. Further, when β is finite, terms such as $\lambda_i^{(1)}/\beta$ can still be interpreted as rents for the suboptimal case. In one residential location example which was studied (Senior and Wilson, 1974) an increase in rent was identified which reflected the suboptimality of the situation and could be interpreted as such.

These results have very general implications. Any model stated as a mathematical programming optimising model can be transformed to a suboptimal, but often more realistic, entropy-maximising model, by adding the 'objective function' to the constraint set, to give equations (36) rather than (38). Conversely, many entropy-maximising models can be interpreted as suboptimal versions of mathematical programming models, and hence to represent imperfect 'market' but maximising (or minimising) behaviour. In that case, one of the constraints (or a linear combination of the constraints) has to be singled out as 'suboptimal objective function'.

These ideas can now be applied to the shopping model, taken in the form of equation (28), which is repeated here for convenience:

$$S_{ij} = A_i e_i P_i \exp\left[\beta\left(\frac{\alpha}{\beta} \ln W_j - c_{ij}\right)\right] . \tag{28}$$

If $\beta \to \infty$ and α remains finite, then $\alpha/\beta \to 0$ and all flows will be assigned to nearest centres and will be independent of $\{W_j\}$. Alternatively, we could let $\alpha \to \infty$ as $\beta \to \infty$ in such a way that $(\alpha/\beta) \to \nu$ where ν is finite. Then, for finite β, the model could be taken as

$$S_{ij} = A_i e_i P_i \exp[\beta(\nu \ln W_j - c_{ij})] , \tag{42}$$

where

$$A_i = \frac{\exp(-\lambda_i^{(1)})}{e_i P_i} = \left\{\sum_j \exp[\beta(\nu \ln W_j - c_{ij})]\right\}^{-1} , \tag{43}$$

with $\lambda_i^{(1)}$ the Lagrangian multiplier associated with

$$\sum_j S_{ij} = e_i P_i ; \tag{44}$$

and β that associated with

$$\sum_{ij} S_{ij}(\nu \ln W_j - c_{ij}) = Z , \tag{45}$$

where Z is a constant. ν gives the relative weighting of attractiveness, measured as $\ln W_j$, and travel disutility. The $\beta \to \infty$ limit would then give S_{ij} which maximised

$$Z = \sum_{ij} S_{ij}(\nu \ln W_j - c_{ij}) , \tag{46}$$

subject to equation (44), and the solution now would depend on W_j as well as c_{ij}. The term $\lambda_i^{(1)}/\beta$ could be interpreted as a measure of comparative advantage for shopping in the suboptimal situation.

3.3 Some uses of the programming–entropy-modelling relationship
We gave an example in the previous section of how an entropy-maximising shopping model could be interpreted as a suboptimal programming model, and that this gave us a measure of comparative advantage. Examples of the converse could also be given. But there are other uses: we saw in section 3.1 that a wide class of problems can be formulated as location-allocation models, almost always in mathematical programming terms. An implicit argument of this paper is that it is often right to attempt to optimise the *location* of facilities, but that the *allocation* is likely to be

suboptimal because of various imperfections. Thus the types of model outlined in section 2 can be considered as location–allocation models, with a mathematical-programming location part and an entropy-maximising allocation part. More generally, it will often be useful to transform the allocation parts of *any* location–allocation model to suboptimal entropy-maximising form. This has the added advantage that analytical expressions can be written down for the allocation variables. However, this will usually only be feasible if the objective function decomposes into separate location and allocation components.

A final comment: it may be possible to weaken the above optimising approaches further and have a suboptimal entropy-maximising calculation for the *location* variables also. This may be particularly appropriate for shopping when $\{W_j\}$ decisions are being made by a large number of retailers in an imperfect market.

4 The addition of more detail

4.1 Modal split; trips from workplaces; types of good

The basic shopping models discussed so far are inadequate in detail. Shopping patterns will clearly be influenced by the transport available by different modes, and will also differ by types of good. Further, trips to shops are also made from workplaces as well as homes. We will deal with the last point first, rather briefly. The $e_i P_i$ term has to be split between home-based and workplace-based shopping trips, and whatever model is being used can then be run separately for each category. The details are given elsewhere (Wilson, 1974, p.208). Lowry (1964) had these kinds of trips in his retail model, but few research workers since then have managed to do so. The difficulties are empirical, concerned with data availability rather than theoretical. We too will neglect it henceforth though the refinement can always be added easily.

In order to add modal split, it is necessary to distinguish person type. Let n indicate whether a person has a car available for shopping or not, and let k indicate mode. Then if S_{ij}^{kn} is the flow of cash from people of type n travelling by mode k, e_i^n is the *per capita* expenditure of type n people, p_i^n the number of type n people in zone i, W_j^k the attractiveness of j to users of mode k, and c_{ij}^k the cost of travel from i to j by mode k, a suitable model is (cf Wilson, 1974, chapter 9, and chapter 10, p.208)

$$S_{ij}^{kn} = A_i^n e_i^n P_i^n (W_j^k)^\alpha \exp(-\beta^n c_{ij}^k) \,, \tag{47}$$

where

$$A_i^n = \left[\sum_{jk} (W_j^k)^\alpha \exp(-\beta^n c_{ij}^k) \right]^{-1} . \tag{48}$$

Equation (47) can be written in the form

$$S_{ij}^{kn} = A_i^n e_i^n P_i^n \exp\left[\beta^n \left(\frac{\alpha}{\beta^n} \ln W_j^k - c_{ij}^k \right) \right] . \tag{49}$$

The overall consumers' welfare function, cf equation (29) or (46), is now

$$Z = \sum_{ijkn} S_{ij}^{kn} \left(\frac{\alpha}{\beta^n} \ln W_j^k - c_{ij}^k \right) . \tag{50}$$

However, we could now argue that

$$Z_i^n = \sum_{jk} S_{ij}^{kn} \left(\frac{\alpha}{\beta^n} \ln W_j^k - c_{ij}^k \right) \tag{51}$$

was the welfare achieved by type n people in zone i, and by calculating this, the more disaggregated model informs us about the *distribution* of welfare, both spatially and by person type. Thus the planner now has to think not only about the W_j^k which give the overall optimum, but whether the distribution is adequate also. The new overall function could be taken as

$$Z = \sum_{ijkn} \mu_i^n S_{ij}^{kn} \left(\frac{\alpha}{\beta^n} \ln W_j - c_{ij}^k \right) , \tag{52}$$

where μ_i^n are a set of value-laden weights to be determined!

Since many of the major new developments in shopping centres, such as hypermarkets, seem to favour particular types of person, this kind of disaggregation is important. However, there are usually considerable data problems. Further, if an index, say g, is added to represent different types of good, an array such as $\{S_{ij}^{kng}\}$ may have an uncomfortably large number of cells. Mackett (1973) and Smith (1973) have each tried to reduce this problem slightly by using a trip-end modal split, and by defining a P_i^k term rather than P_i^n. It would also be possible to use an alternative model representation (cf Wilson and Pownall, 1974). Mackett also runs the model separately for two types of good. This is obviously useful, but a more interesting question for the future is perhaps the development of a model in which centres are distinguished, perhaps in a hierarchy, by types of good available, and this possibility is pursued in the next section.

4.2 Types of good by centre

Let S_{ij}^g be the flow of cash from i to j for purchase of goods of type g, e_i^g the demand for good g *per capita* at i, P_i the population of i, W_j^g the attractiveness of the centre at j for g-type goods and c_{ij} the travel cost. This leads to the model

$$S_{ij}^g = A_i^g e_i^g P_i (W_j^g)^{\alpha^g} \exp(-\beta^g c_{ij}) \tag{53}$$

where α^g is assumed to vary with g, or alternatively

$$S_{ij}^g = A_i^g e_i^g P_i \exp\left[\beta^g \left(\frac{\alpha^g}{\beta^g} \ln W_j^g - c_{ij} \right) \right] , \tag{54}$$

where

$$A_i^g = \left[\sum_j (W_j^g)^{\alpha^g} \exp(-\beta^g c_{ij}) \right]^{-1} , \tag{55}$$

to ensure that

$$\sum_j S_{ij}^g = e_i^g P_i \; ; \tag{56}$$

and β^g is calculated to ensure that

$$\sum_{ij} S_{ij}^g c_{ij} = C^g \, , \tag{57}$$

where C^g is a constant giving the expenditure on travel for the purchase of g-type goods. This allows different types of good to have different ranges. It would also be possible to allow for a hierarchy of centres by setting W_j^g to be zero if goods of type g are not sold at j. For non-zero W_j^g the measurement question is an interesting one: should W_j^g, for example, be the size of the whole centre, or some function of the size which is deemed to be attributable to goods of type g? This question would bear a lot of further research.

The consumers' welfare function in this case would be

$$Z = \sum_{ijg} S_{ij}^g \left(\frac{\alpha^g}{\beta^g} \ln W_j^g - c_{ij} \right) \, . \tag{58}$$

Retailers profits could also be calculated for this model using the methods of section 2. Either of the major options of section 2 could then be used to set up hypotheses about the future development of the W_j^g, but with the additional interesting question of deciding when particular centres moved up the hierarchy. This may allow a connection to be made to central place theory.

The linear programming limit can be obtained in the usual way by letting $\beta \to \infty$, first setting $\alpha/\beta = \nu$, and keeping ν constant. If we took a special case by setting $W_j^g = 0$ if goods of type g were not available, but 1 otherwise, then the linear programming limit produces a solution which is close to that of Bacon (1971) and Evans (1972). However, it will be slightly inferior because it would not allow for the fact that a single trip for a higher order good could *also* be used to collect lower order goods.

5 Alternative behavioural assumptions

The spatial interaction model lends itself to analysis at a fairly coarse level of resolution both on the demand and on the supply sides. The behavioural hypotheses introduced in section 2 on the supply side could be refined by further analysis at a more micro scale. The best framework for this is probably the theory of the firm in a city adopted by Alonso (1964) (and described in Wilson, 1974, pp.191–199). This is likely, though, to leave the usual problems of aggregation. However, the fact that these have been solved in a residential location context using linear programming methods in the optimum case (Herbert and Stevens, 1960) and entropy-maximising methods in the most probable suboptimal case (Senior and Wilson, 1974) suggests hope for a shopping model of such a type. Since such a model

has an explicit market-clearing mechanism, there would also be a good
chance of dealing with the problems raised in section 2.4 and of finding a
mechanism for equalising rents across space, though ultimately this would
have to take place within the framework of a more general model which
included the actions of other land users. Such methods should also
sharpen the concepts of rent and profit to be used in analyses of this
type. Other approaches exist also. Gannon (1971; 1972) builds on the
work of Lösch (1940) in an analysis of spatial demand. Hartwick and
Hartwick (1971) build on Hotelling (1929) in their analysis of duopoly in
space. Thus, there are at least three major threads of theoretical work,
and to these should be added the work on central-place theory, which
could eventually be integrated with the approaches outlined in this paper.

6 Concluding comments
The detailed conclusions of section 2 were given in subsection 2.6. We
showed that Hotelling's behavioural hypotheses could be added to a spatial
interaction shopping model, but that the resulting optimisation problems,
while giving some insights, were analytically intractable and would only
yield to computer simulation or solution in an approximate form.

In section 3, we showed that the problems in section 2 were location–
allocation problems of a special type. They could be considered as part of
an expanded class of such problems generated by supplementing the usual
mathematical programming formulations with some entropy-maximising
calculations of at least the allocation variables.

More detail was added, with respect to modal split and types of good in
section 4. It would be a straightforward exercise in theory to combine
these two dimensions of disaggregation, though the resulting model would
typically prove difficult to handle in practice. A number of alternative
approaches to building shopping models were mentioned in section 5, and
it would be a major research task to integrate these with the models of
this paper. But the existence of such a variety of approaches indicates
that this field of modelling still has a long way to progress.

One final comment is in order: the approaches described in this paper
are all essentially static. There is a developing literature on dynamic
location–allocation problems (Scott, 1971; Sheppard, 1974), and a
further research task is to reformulate the models and analyses of this
paper in such terms.

References
Alonso, W., 1964, *Location and Land Use* (Harvard University Press, Cambridge, Mass.).
Bacon, R. W., 1971, "An approach to the theory of consumer shopping behaviour",
    Urban Studies, 8, 55-64.
Evans, A., 1972, "A linear programming solution to the shopping problem posed by
    R. W. Bacon", *Urban Studies*, 9, 221-222.

Evans, S. P., 1973, "A relationship between the gravity model for trip distribution and the transportation problem in linear programming", *Transportation Research*, **7**, 39-61.

Gannon, C. A., 1971, "Fundamental properties of Löschian spatial demand", *Environment and Planning*, **3**, 283-306.

Gannon, C. A., 1972, "Consumer demand, conjectural interdependence and location equilibria in simple spatial duopoly", *Papers, Regional Science Association*, **28**, 83-107.

Hartwick, J. M., Hartwick, P. G., 1971, "Duopoly in space", *Canadian Journal of Economics*, **4**, 485-505.

Herbert, J., Stevens, B. H., 1960, "A model for the distribution of residential activity in urban areas", *Journal of Regional Science*, **2**, 21-36.

Hotelling, H., 1929, "Stability in competition", *Economic Journal*, **39**, 41-57.

Huff, D. L., 1964, "Defining and estimating a trading area", *Journal of Marketing*, **28**, 37-48.

Huff, D. L., 1966, "Optimal retail location", *Land Economics*, **42**, 293-303.

Lakshmanan, T. R., Hansen, W. G., 1965, "A retail market potential model", *Journal of the American Institute of Planners*, **31**, 134-143.

Lösch, A., 1940, *Die Raumliche Ordnung der Wirtschaft* (Gustav Fischer Verlag, Jena); English translation by W. H. Woglom with the assistance of W. F. Stolper, 1954, *Economics of Location* (Yale University Press, New Haven, Conn.).

Lowry, I. S., 1964, "A model of metropolis", Rand memorandum 4035-RC, Rand Corporation, Santa Monica, USA.

Mackett, R. L., 1973, "Shopping in the city—the application of an intra-urban shopping model to Leeds", working paper 30, Department of Geography, University of Leeds, England.

Parry Lewis, J., 1971, "Profitability in a shopping model", *Urban Studies*, **8**, 285-288.

Scott, A. J., 1971, *Combinatorial Programming, Spatial Analysis and Planning* (Methuen, London).

Senior, M. L., Wilson, A. G., 1974, "Explorations and syntheses of linear programming and spatial interaction models of residential location", *Geographical Analysis*, **6**, 209-237.

Sheppard, E. S., 1974, "A conceptual framework for dynamic location-allocation analysis", *Environment and Planning A*, **6**, 547-564.

Smith, A. P., 1973, "Retail allocation models—an investigation into problems of application to the Rotherham sub-region", working paper 50, Department of Geography, University of Leeds, England.

Wilson, A. G., 1974, *Urban and Regional Models in Geography and Planning* (John Wiley, London).

Wilson, A. G., Pownall, C. E., 1974, "A new representation of the urban system for modelling and for the study of micro-level interdependence", working paper 64, Department of Geography, University of Leeds, England.

Wilson, A. G., Senior, M. L., 1974, "Some relationships between entropy maximising models, linear programming models and their duals", *Journal of Regional Science*, **14**, 207-215.

Appendix

Calculations of various derivatives
If

$$S_{ij} = A_i e_i P_i W_j^\alpha \exp(-\beta c_{ij}) , \tag{A1}$$

and

$$A_i = \left[\sum_k W_k^\alpha \exp(-\beta c_{ik}) \right]^{-1} , \tag{A2}$$

then

$$\frac{\partial S_{ij}}{\partial W_j} = \alpha A_i e_i P_i W_j^{\alpha-1} \exp(-\beta c_{ij}) - \frac{e_i P_i W_j^\alpha \exp(-\beta c_{ij})}{\left[\sum_k W_k^\alpha \exp(-\beta c_{ij}) \right]^2} \alpha W_j^{\alpha-1} \exp(-\beta c_{ij})$$

$$= \alpha \frac{S_{ij}}{W_j} [1 - A_i W_j^\alpha \exp(-\beta c_{ij})] . \tag{A3}$$

If

$$\rho_j = \frac{\sum_i S_{ij}}{W_j} , \tag{A4}$$

then

$$\frac{\partial \rho_j}{\partial W_j} = \frac{1}{W_j} \sum_i \frac{\partial S_{ij}}{\partial W_j} - \frac{1}{W_j^2} \sum_i S_{ij} . \tag{A5}$$

Substitution for $\partial S_{ij}/\partial W_j$ from equation (A3) then gives

$$\frac{\partial \rho_j}{\partial W_j} = \frac{1}{W_j^2} \sum_i \langle S_{ij}\{\alpha[1 - A_i W_j^\alpha \exp(-\beta c_{ij}) - 1]\} \rangle , \tag{A6}$$

which is the result used in equation (9). Since

$$A_i W_j^\alpha \exp(-\beta c_{ij}) = \frac{S_{ij}}{e_i P_i} , \tag{A7}$$

the right-hand side of this equation is sometimes used as an alternative for the left in various derivatives.
If

$$Z = \sum_{ij} S_{ij} \left(\frac{\alpha}{\beta} \ln W_j - c_{ij} \right) , \tag{A8}$$

as in equation (29) then

$$\frac{\partial Z}{\partial W_k} = \sum_{ij} \frac{\partial S_{ij}}{\partial W_k} \left(\frac{\alpha}{\beta} \ln W_j - c_{ij} \right) + \sum_{ij} \delta_{jk} S_{ij} \frac{\alpha}{\beta} \frac{1}{W_j} , \tag{A9}$$

where δ_{jk} is a Kronecker delta.

$$\frac{\partial S_{ij}}{\partial W_k} = \frac{-\alpha W_k^{\alpha-1} \exp(-\beta c_{ij}) e_i P_i W_j^\alpha \exp(-\beta c_{ij})}{\left[\sum_l W_l^\alpha \exp(-\beta c_{il}) \right]^2} + A_i e_i P_i \delta_{jk} \alpha W_k^{\alpha-1} \exp(-\beta c_{ik})$$

$$= -\alpha W_k^{\alpha-1} \exp(-\beta c_{ik}) A_i S_{ij} + \alpha \delta_{jk} \frac{S_{ik}}{W_k} . \tag{A10}$$

Substituting from equation (A10) into (A9), we obtain

$$\frac{\partial Z}{\partial W_k} = \sum_{ij} \left[-\alpha W_k^{\alpha-1} \exp(-\beta c_{ik}) A_i S_{ij} + \frac{\alpha \delta_{jk} S_{ik}}{W_k} \left(\frac{\alpha}{\beta} \ln W_j - c_{ij} \right) \right]$$

$$+ \sum_{ij} \delta_{jk} S_{ij} \frac{\alpha}{\beta} \frac{1}{W_j}$$

$$= \sum_{ij} \left[-\alpha W_k^{\alpha-1} \exp(-\beta c_{ik}) A_i S_{ij} \left(\frac{\alpha}{\beta} \ln W_j - c_{ij} \right) \right]$$

$$+ \sum_{i} \left[\alpha S_{ik} W_k^{-1} \left(\frac{\alpha}{\beta} \ln W_k - c_{ik} \right) + \frac{\alpha}{\beta} S_{ik} W_k^{-1} \right]$$

$$= \sum_{ij} \left[-\alpha W_k^{\alpha-1} \exp(-\beta c_{ik}) A_i S_{ij} \left(\frac{\alpha}{\beta} \ln W_j - c_{ij} \right) \right]$$

$$+ \sum_{i} \alpha S_{ik} W_k^{-1} \left(\frac{\alpha}{\beta} \ln W_k - c_{ik} + \frac{1}{\beta} \right) , \tag{A11}$$

which is the expression used in equation (32).

Analysing Multiple Connectivities

R.H.ATKIN
University of Essex

0 Introduction

This paper is an introduction to the mathematical techniques which have
been developed over the past few years and which, being referred to
generally as *Q*-analysis, have been applied to urban and community
structures. Specific illustrations are to be found in the four published
research reports of the Urban Structure Research Project (financed by the
Social Science Research Council) 1971–1974 at the University of Essex
(Atkin, 1972; 1973a; 1973b; 1974c), and also in more recent publications
(Atkin, 1974a; 1974d; 1975).

The analysis is based on a multidimensional representation of any binary
relation, viewed as a simplicial complex. This abstract structure possesses
both a global and a local geometry (which is naturally nonmetrical). In
this paper only the global geometry is studied, and this gives rise to an
examination of *q*-connectivity, eccentricity, patterns and *t*-forces, and the
ideas of a structure-vector/obstruction-vector in the associated *Q*-space.

The significance of the local geometry is illustrated in Atkin (1974b;
1974c; 1974d; 1975).

1 Mathematical relations

We are concerned with binary relations between finite sets. If λ is such a
relation between sets Y and X, where

$$Y = \{Y_i;\ i = 1, 2, ..., m\} \quad \text{and} \quad X = \{X_i;\ i = 1, 2, ..., n\}\ ,$$

then we write $Y_i \lambda X_i$ if Y_i is λ-related to X_i. Alternatively we can regard λ
as a subset of the Cartesian product $Y \times X$ and in that case we write
$\lambda \subset Y \times X$. Compatible with this idea is the notation

$$(Y_i, X_j) \in \lambda \quad \text{whenever} \quad Y_i \lambda X_j\ .$$

For a given relation $\lambda \subset Y \times X$ there is a naturally defined *inverse
relation* $\lambda^{-1} \subset X \times Y$. This is defined by setting

$$(X_j, Y_i) \in \lambda^{-1} \quad \text{whenever} \quad (Y_i, X_j) \in \lambda\ .$$

Each such relation λ may be represented by an *incidence matrix* Λ in
which

$$\Lambda = (\lambda_{ij})\ , \quad \text{and} \quad \begin{aligned}\lambda_{ij} &= 1 \quad \text{if } (Y_i, X_j) \in \lambda \\ &= 0 \quad \text{otherwise.}\end{aligned}$$

The incidence relation which corresponds to the inverse relation λ^{-1} is then the *transpose* Λ^T of Λ. Thus

$$\Lambda^T = (\mu_{ij})$$

with

$$\mu_{ij} = \lambda_{ji} \qquad \text{for} \quad i = 1, ..., m , \quad \text{and} \quad j = 1, ..., n.$$

It follows that Λ is an $m \times n$ matrix whereas Λ^T is an $n \times m$ matrix.

We also find it convenient, in applications, to consider matrices **M** which contain entries other than 0 or 1. We assume that the entries are integers $n \in J$, and we shall say that the matrix then corresponds to a *weighted relation* μ.

Associated with such a μ is a whole series of incidence matrices (binary relations) obtained by the process of *slicing* as follows. Take a set of parameters θ_i which are to characterise the matrix **M**. For example θ_i might refer to row i, for $i = 1, ..., m$; or θ_i might be θ_{ij}, where each value refers to the (ij) element of **M**. Call the $\{\theta_i\}$ the set of *slicing parameters* for **M**, and obtain a relation λ by defining its incidence matrix $\Lambda = (\lambda_{ij})$ in terms of elements $m_{ij} \in M$ as follows:

$$\lambda_{ij} = 1 \qquad \text{if} \quad m_{ij} \geqslant \theta_k(m_{ij})$$
$$= 0 \qquad \text{otherwise.}$$

Thus, if we 'slice by rows' we would select a numerical value for each θ_i, $i = 1, ..., m$, and take $\lambda_{ij} = 1$ if $m_{ij} \geqslant \theta_i$ $(j = 1, ..., n)$; $\lambda_{ij} = 0$ otherwise. Equally well we can take $m_{ij} \leqslant \theta_i$ as the condition.

This procedure gives a set of mathematical relations, dependent on the choices of the slicing parameters, and this latter choice is determined by consideration of the applications of the method.

2 Simplicial complexes
We use the idea of a simplicial complex (or complex of simplices) to represent a mathematical relation $\lambda \subset Y \times X$, in the following way.

If there exists at least one $Y_i \in Y$ such that a $(p+1)$-subset of X is related to it, we call that $(p+1)$-subset of X a *p-simplex*. If its members are $\{X_1, X_2, ..., X_{p+1}\}$ we write the simplex as

$$Y_i = \langle X_1, X_2, ..., X_{p+1} \rangle , \qquad \text{or as} \quad Y_i = \sigma_p ,$$

and call Y_i its name (possibly among many). Any subset of this $(p+1)$-subset of X is also λ-related to Y_i and is therefore another simplex, say a q-simplex. This q-simplex, σ_q, is said to be a *face* of the first σ_p, and this is written

$$\sigma_q \leqslant \sigma_p .$$

Each $Y_i \in \lambda$ therefore identifies a p-simplex (for some p) with all its faces, and this collection of simplices is called a *simplicial complex K*.

More precisely we shall denote the complex by $K_Y(X; \lambda)$. This notation is
to indicate that the members of the set Y are to be names of simplices,
whilst the set X is referred to as the *vertex set* for K.

It is clear that $K_Y(X; \lambda)$ is *closed* under the partial ordering denoted by
$\leqslant$ and, in our discussions, we shall usually assume that the set Y is the
domain of λ whilst X is its *range*. The *vertices* of K, or the $X_j \in X$, can
be identified with the 0-simplices σ_0^i $(i = 1, ..., n)$ and we naturally write

$$\sigma_0^i = \langle X_i \rangle \qquad \text{for} \quad i = 1, ..., n \; .$$

The largest value of p for which $\sigma_p \in K$ is called the *dimension* of K and
written $\dim K$. We shall try to reserve the letter N for this quantity,
$N = \dim K$. Otherwise we say that p is the dimension of σ_p (see next
section).

Associated with $K_Y(X; \lambda)$ will be that complex defined by λ^{-1}, and this
we write as $K_X(Y; \lambda^{-1})$ and say it is *conjugate* to the first. When λ is
understood we shall refer to these complexes by the symbols $K_Y(X)$ and
$K_X(Y)$.

The vertices of the simplex Y_i in $K_Y(X)$ can be identified by looking
along the ith row of the incidence matrix Λ, then X_j is such a vertex if
there is a 1 in that jth column. A vertex of the simplex X_j in $K_X(Y)$ is Y_i
if there is a 1 in the ith row of that jth column. This suggests that much
of the computing involved in this study centres around the incidence
matrices Λ, Λ^T.

A notation for reminding ourselves of the various roles is the following:

$$\begin{array}{c|c} \lambda & X \\ \hline Y & K_Y(X) \end{array} \qquad \text{and} \qquad \begin{array}{c|c} \lambda^{-1} & Y \\ \hline X & K_X(Y) \end{array}$$

Since the empty set is a subset of every set, it seems reasonable to include
it as a face of every simplex in $K_Y(X)$. When this is done we denote the
empty set by the (-1)-simplex, σ_{-1}, and say that the complex K is
thereby *augmented*; we write it as K^+ or as $K \cup \sigma_{-1}$.

Finally, there is a natural way in which a complex K may be given an
orientation, ω. Since the vertices, say X, are given the ordering of the
natural numbers, we say that the p-simplex,

$$\sigma_p = \langle X_{\alpha_1}, X_{\alpha_2}, ..., X_{\alpha_{p+1}} \rangle \; ,$$

possesses a *positive orientation* if the sequence $\{\alpha_1, \alpha_2, ..., \alpha_{p+1}\}$ is an *even
permutation* of the same numbers with their natural ordering, and that it
possesses a *negative* orientation when that permutation is *odd*. In the first
place we denote the simplex by σ_p, or $+\sigma_p$, and in the second case by
$-\sigma_p$. In this way every simplex σ_p, $p > 0$, possesses an orientation which
is *naturally induced* and when this is done we say that the complex K
possesses an orientation.

3 A geometrical representation

A complex $K_Y(X; \lambda)$ can be represented in a *Euclidean space* E^H in the following way for a suitable choice of H.

Each p-simplex, typically $\sigma_p = \langle X_1, X_2, ..., X_{p+1} \rangle$, is made to correspond to a *convex polyhedron* in E^H, with $(p+1)$ vertices which themselves correspond to $X_1, X_2, ..., X_{p+1}$. Thus, in an intuitive sense, in E^H the simplex σ_p is represented by the 'solid' polyhedron with $(p+1)$ vertices. The complex $K_Y(X)$ is then represented by a collection of polyhedra suitably connected to each other by sharing 'faces' (or sub-polyhedra).

This geometrical representation is always possible by suitably choosing H, it being remembered that each σ_p requires p dimensions for its accommodation. It might be somewhat surprising therefore that an economical theorem exists which demonstrates that the value of H need only be taken as

$$H = 2N + 1 , \qquad \text{where} \quad N = \dim K .$$

This is independent of how many N-simplices are contained in K, or of how they are mutually connected. But this means that, in the realm of social science, the *Euclidean spaces* which can accommodate the various mathematical relations will commonly be of much greater dimension than the 3-dimensional structure demanded by the physicist.

We illustrate the geometrical representation by a simple numerical example, allowing for the fact that perspective limits a plane representation to a value of $N = 3$.

Example. Given $\lambda \subset Y \times X$, $m = 6$, $n = 8$, and the incidence matrix as

$$\Lambda = \begin{bmatrix} 1 & 1 & 1 & 1 & 0 & 0 & 0 & 0 \\ 0 & 0 & 1 & 1 & 1 & 0 & 0 & 0 \\ 0 & 0 & 0 & 0 & 1 & 0 & 0 & 1 \\ 0 & 0 & 0 & 0 & 0 & 1 & 1 & 1 \\ 0 & 0 & 1 & 0 & 0 & 0 & 1 & 0 \\ 0 & 0 & 0 & 1 & 0 & 1 & 0 & 1 \end{bmatrix} .$$

Considering $K_Y(X; \lambda)$:

$\langle X_1 X_2 X_3 X_4 \rangle$	is a σ_3 whose name is Y_1	(row 1),
$\langle X_3 X_4 X_5 \rangle$	is a σ_2 whose name is Y_2	(row 2),
$\langle X_6 X_7 X_8 \rangle$	is a σ_2 whose name is Y_4	(row 4),

and similarly $\langle X_4 X_6 X_8 \rangle = Y_6$, $\langle X_5 X_8 \rangle = Y_3$, $\langle X_3 X_7 \rangle = Y_5$.

A geometrical representation is shown in figure 1. A representation of the conjugate, $K_X(Y; \lambda^{-1})$, is shown in figure 2.

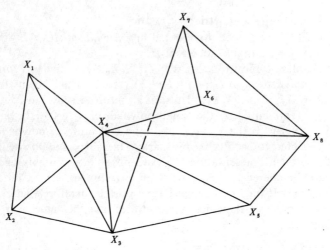

Figure 1. $K_Y(X; \lambda)$.

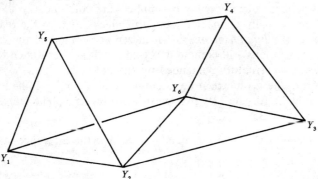

Figure 2. $K_X(Y; \lambda^{-1})$.

4 Chains of q-connection in K

Given two simplices σ_p, σ_r in K we shall say they are joined by a chain of connection if there exists a finite sequence of simplices

$$\sigma_{\alpha_1}, \sigma_{\alpha_2}, ..., \sigma_{\alpha_h}$$

such that

(1) $\sigma_{\alpha_1} \leqslant \sigma_p$,

(2) $\sigma_{\alpha_h} \leqslant \sigma_r$,

(3) σ_{α_i} and $\sigma_{\alpha_{i+1}}$ share a common face (say) σ_{β_i}, $i = 1, ..., (h-1)$.

We shall say that this sequence is a *chain of q-connection* (or that it is a *q-connectivity*) if q is the *least* of the integers

$$\alpha_1, \beta_1, \beta_2, ..., \beta_{h-1}, \alpha_h .$$

The *length* of the chain will be taken as $(h-1)$ and, when needed, the chain may be denoted by $[\sigma_p, \sigma_r]_q$.

As a special case we see that a p-simplex σ_p must be p-connected to itself by a chain of length 0, although it cannot be $(p+1)$-connected to any simplex.

It is easy to see that if σ_p and σ_r are q-connected then they are also $(q-1)$-, $(q-2)$-, ..., 1-, 0-connected in K.

If we refer to the numerical example of section 3, and figure 1, we can see that $Y_1 = \langle X_1 X_2 X_3 X_4 \rangle$ is 1-connected to $Y_2 = \langle X_3 X_4 X_5 \rangle$, since they share the 1-simplex $\langle X_3 X_4 \rangle$, whereas $Y_5 = \langle X_3 X_7 \rangle$ is (only) 0-connected to $Y_4 = \langle X_6 X_7 X_8 \rangle$. Similarly we can see that

$$Y_1 \xrightarrow{0} Y_5 \xrightarrow{0} Y_4 \xrightarrow{1} Y_6$$

is a 0-connectivity.

For a particular simplex, σ_r, in K it is consequently possible to identify two values of q. The first value is $\check{q}$ (the *bottom-q*), which is the least value of q for which σ_r is q-connected to any distinct simplex. The second value is $\hat{q}$ (the *top-q*), which is the dimension of that simplex (in this case $\hat{q} = r$). These two values have been referred to in Atkin (1972; 1973b; 1974a; 1975) where their relevance in applications has been explored. Closely associated with $(\check{q}, \hat{q})$ is a quantity called the *eccentricity* of σ. This is a rational number given by

$$\text{ecc}(\sigma) = \frac{\hat{q} - \check{q}}{\check{q} + 1} \cdot$$

This quantity is defined for all values except $\check{q} = -1$, and then we say $\text{ecc}(\sigma) = \infty$. This 'infinite' value for the eccentricity occurs when σ is totally disconnected from the rest of the complex. Possible significance in its use as a measure is discussed in Atkin (1972; 1973b; 1975).

5 Q-analysis

The process of identifying those pieces of K which are q-connected, for all values of q from 0 to N, constitutes a sequence of partitionings of the simplices of K. To see this we introduce, for a fixed q, a relation γ_q on the simplices of K, defined by

$$(\sigma_p, \sigma_r) \in \gamma_q , \qquad \text{if and only if} \quad \sigma_p \text{ is } q\text{-connected to } \sigma_r.$$

This γ_q is reflexive, symmetric, and transitive and is therefore an equivalence relation. The *equivalence classes*, under γ_q, are the members of the *quotient set* K/γ_q and constitute a partition of K (or more accurately of all simplices of K which are of order $\geqslant q$).

We denote the cardinality of K/γ_q by Q_q. This equals the number of distinct q-connected components in K. When we analyse K by finding all the values of

$$Q_0, Q_1, Q_2, ..., Q_N , \qquad \text{where} \quad N = \dim K ,$$

we say that we have performed a *Q-analysis* on K.

Referring to the numerical example of $K_Y(X; \lambda)$ and figure 1, we can obtain these Q_q-values by inspection. Since there is only one σ_3, $\langle X_1 X_2 X_3 X_4 \rangle$, we have $Q_3 = 1$. At the level of $q = 2$ the separate components are $\langle X_1 X_2 X_3 X_4 \rangle$, $\langle X_3 X_4 X_5 \rangle$, $\langle X_4 X_6 X_8 \rangle$, and $\langle X_6 X_7 X_8 \rangle$, no two of which are 2-connected. Thus $Q_2 = 4$. At $q = 1$ we obtain $Q_2 = 4$ since now Y_1 and Y_2 share a 1-face, as do Y_4 and Y_6, but Y_3 and Y_5 are new 1-simplices. At $q = 0$ we have $Q_0 = 1$ since the complex K is in 'one piece'.

The value of Q_0 is the same as the topologist's zero-order Betti number—it gives the number of (arc-wise) connected components of K. The higher-order Betti numbers equal the number of free generators of the homology groups. These are not the same as the higher Q-numbers. Our analysis therefore gives a generalisation of the zero-order Betti number different from that provided by homology theory. A discussion of the latter, showing for example, that the homology group of conjugate complexes are isomorphic, is given in Dowker, 1952.

6 An algorithm for Q-analysis

If the cardinalities of the sets Y and X are m and n respectively, the incidence matrix Λ is an $(m \times n)$ matrix with entries 0 or 1. In the product $\Lambda\Lambda^T$ the number in position (i, j) is the result of the inner product of row i with row j, taken from Λ. This number equals the number of 1's common to rows i and j in Λ. It is therefore equal to the value $(q+1)$, where q is the dimension of the shared face of the simplices σ_p, σ_r represented by rows i and j. The algorithm can therefore be summarised as follows:

To find the shared-face q-values between all pairs of the Y's in $K_Y(X; \lambda)$,
(1) form $\Lambda\Lambda^T$, an $(m \times m)$ matrix,
(2) evaluate $\Lambda\Lambda^T - \Omega$, where $\Omega = (w_{ij})$ and $w_{ij} = 1$ for $i, j = 1, 2, ..., m$.

The analysis for $K_X(Y; \lambda^{-1})$ follows by forming $\Lambda^T\Lambda - \Omega^1$ where Ω^1 is an $(n \times n)$ matrix of 1's.

The complex $K_Y(X; \lambda)$ of section 3 gives the following q-pattern for the shared faces. We reproduce only the upper triangular 'half' of the symmetric matrix $\Lambda\Lambda^T - \Omega$ for ease of analysis, and we write '−' for $q = -1$ (the case of disconnection).

Y_1	Y_2	Y_3	Y_4	Y_5	Y_6	
3	1	−	−	0	0	Y_1
	2	0	−	0	0	Y_2
		1	0	−	0	Y_3
			2	0	1	Y_4
				1	−	Y_5
					2	Y_6

The integers in the diagonal are the dimensions of the Y_i as simplices; the Q-analysis follows by inspection.

$N = 3 = \dim K$ since Y_1 is a 3-simplex

    at $q = 3$ we have $Q_3 = 1$, viz. $\{Y_1\}$;

    at $q = 2$ we have $Q_2 = 4$, $\{Y_1\}$, $\{Y_2\}$, $\{Y_4\}$, and $\{Y_6\}$;

    at $q = 1$ we have $Q_1 = 4$, $\{Y_1, Y_2\}$, $\{Y_3\}$, $\{Y_4, Y_6\}$, and $\{Y_5\}$;

    at $q = 0$ we have $Q_0 = 1$, $\{all\}$.

7 Q-space and the structure vector

We associate with the whole family of complexes a vector space over a field F which we shall call Q-*space*. (In fact in our studies so far we are only concerned with the ring of integers J in place of F. This makes the Q-space an algebraic module instead of a vector space.) This must be of sufficient dimension to accommodate any of the finite dimensional complexes which interest us. Then, given a complex K with $\dim K = N$, we introduce a (first) *structure vector* $Q(K)$,

$$Q = \{Q_N, Q_{N-1}, ..., Q_1, Q_0\} \ .$$

In the numerical example discussed in section 6 we obtain the structure vector

$$Q = \{ \overset{3}{1} \quad 4 \quad 4 \quad \overset{0}{1} \} \ ,$$

where the superscripts denote the q-values.

This Q-space is not necessarily equipped with an inner product, or a metric, but possesses only the structure of the vector space (or module).

If $Q_0 > 1$, the complex K is in Q_0 pieces and can therefore be regarded as the union of disjoint complexes; the resultant Q is then the vector sum of the separate Q_i associated with the K_i, where

$$K = \underset{i}{\cup} K_i$$

It later transpires that there is (applied) significance in a vector which is closely associated with Q and defined by it. This associated vector is given the name of *obstruction vector* and written $\hat{Q}(K)$, or simply $\hat{Q}$.

We restrict ourselves to a complex K for which $Q_0 = 1$ and introduce the vector U which gives the *unit point* (affinely), viz.,

$$U = \{1, 1, ..., 1\} \ ,$$

and we shall use the same letter to denote the projection of U on the N-dimensional subspace containing $Q(K)$. The obstruction vector is now defined as

$$\hat{Q} = Q - U$$

or

$$\hat{Q} = \{Q_N - 1, \ Q_{N-1} - 1, \ ..., \ Q_1 - 1, \ Q_0 - 1\} \ ,$$

where of course

$$Q_0 - 1 = 0 \ .$$

In later sections we shall see that this obstruction vector $\hat{Q}$ is a property of the complex K which acts as an obstruction (or obstacle) to the free flow of patterns on K.

In general we can see our structure vector $Q(K)$ as a first measure of some of the *global structure* to be found there by virtue of the property of q-connectivity. It overlooks, of course, the internal structure of any one component of K.

8 Patterns on a complex

By a pattern π, on a complex K, we shall mean a mapping

$$\pi : \{\sigma_p^i ; \ 0 \leqslant p \leqslant N, \ \text{all } i\} \to J \ ,$$

where J is (usually) the integers. Thus π is defined on every simplex of K and, because these are graded by their q-values, it is natural to grade the pattern itself. Thus we can write

$$\pi = \pi^0 \oplus \pi^1 \oplus ... \oplus \pi^t \oplus ... \oplus \pi^N \ ,$$

where

$$N = \dim K \ , \qquad \text{and where} \quad \pi^t = \pi | \{\sigma_t^i ; \ \text{fixed } t\} \ .$$

Each π^t is therefore a *set function*, defined on specified $(t+1)$-subsets of the vertex set X of K.

The mapping need not be (1–1) nor, at this stage, is there any question of its being an homomorphism.

The 'face' ordering, $\leqslant$, is to be manifest by the restriction map, so that

$$\sigma_q \leqslant \sigma_p \qquad \text{implies that} \quad \pi(\sigma_q) = \pi | \sigma_q \ .$$

9 An algebraic representation of K

Let X be totally ordered by the natural ordering of the integers and let the set

$$V = \{x_1, x_2, ..., x_n\}$$

be made to correspond (1–1) to the set $X = \{X_1, X_2, ..., X_n\}$. Construct the *exterior algebra* ΛV, over the n-dimensional module $\{V, +, J\}$, in which $\Lambda^0 V = J$.

Then there is an algebraic representation of K via the map

$$\rho : K \to \Lambda V \ ,$$

where

(1) $\rho = \{\rho_p\,;\ p = 0, 1, ..., N\}$,

(2) $\rho_0 : \langle X_i \rangle \to x_i \in \Lambda^1 V$,

(3) $\rho_p : \langle X_{\alpha_1}, X_{\alpha_2}, ..., X_{\alpha_{p+1}} \rangle \to x_{\alpha_1} x_{\alpha_2} ... x_{\alpha_{p+1}} \in \Lambda^{p+1} V$,

$p = 1, 2, ..., N$,   and $N \leqslant n-1$,

(4) when K is augmented, there exists a map ρ_{-1} such that
$\rho_{-1} : \sigma_{-1} \to 1 \in J$.

This representation means that K possesses an orientation (in ΛV)
expressed in the antisymmetry of the exterior product. Thus

$$\langle X_i X_j \rangle = -\langle X_j X_i \rangle \qquad \text{in } K$$

becomes

$$x_i x_j = -x_j x_i \qquad \text{in } \Lambda V .$$

The natural grading of the exterior algebra, viz.

$$\Lambda V = \Lambda^0 V \oplus \Lambda' V \oplus ... \oplus \Lambda^{p+1} V \oplus ... \oplus \Lambda^{N+1} V \oplus ... \oplus \Lambda^n V ,$$

corresponds to the grading of the augmented K, viz.

$$K = K^{-1} \oplus K^0 \oplus ... \oplus K^p \oplus ... \oplus K^N ,$$

in which

$$K^p = \{\sigma_p^i\,;\ \text{fixed } p\} ,$$

and

K^p corresponds to $\Lambda^{p+1} V$.

Now every p-simplex in K, σ_p, possesses a unique representation (via
products of distinct basis elements) in $\Lambda^{p+1} V$, and so the whole complex
K may be represented by a polynomial in ΛV, of the form

$$\pi_0 = 1 + x_1 + x_3 + x_1 x_2 x_4 + x_3 x_2 x_7 + \text{etc.} ,$$

representing, in this algebraic sense, the formal sum

$$\pi_0 = \sigma_{-1} + \sum_i \sigma_0^i + \sum_i \sigma_1^i + ... + \sum_i \sigma_p^i + ... + \sum_i \sigma_N^i .$$

10 The face operator f and coface operator Δ

The process of finding the faces of a simplex σ_p can be expressed in the
algebraic representation by a suitable operator, f, defined as follows: if

$$\sigma_p = \langle X_{\alpha_1}, X_{\alpha_2}, ..., X_{\alpha_{p+1}} \rangle \qquad \text{where } \alpha_1 < \alpha_2 < ... < \alpha_{p+1} \text{ and } p > 0 ,$$

then

$$\mathrm{f}\sigma_p = \mathrm{f}(x_{\alpha_1} x_{\alpha_2} ... x_{\alpha_{p+1}}) = \sum_{i=1}^{p+1} x_{\alpha_1} x_{\alpha_2} ... \hat{x}_{\alpha_i} ... x_{\alpha_{p+1}} , \qquad \in \Pi_p .$$

Thus, for example,

$$f(x_2x_4x_5) = x_4x_5 + x_2x_5 + x_2x_4 , \qquad \in \Pi^2 .$$

(Notice that this is not to be confused with the boundary operator ∂ of conventional homology theory.)

The face operator f now acts on a pattern polynomial π via linear extension to give a linear map f with the properties:

1. $f(\alpha, \sigma_p) = \alpha(f\sigma_p) , \qquad \alpha \in J ,$
2. $f(\sigma_p + \sigma_q) = (f\sigma_p) + (f\sigma_q) , \qquad$ taken together with
3. $f\sigma_0 = \sigma_{-1} = 1 \in \Lambda^0 V ,$
4. $f\sigma_{-1} = 0 \in \Lambda V .$

With the face operator f we can associate the dual coface operator, Δ, defined in the following.

Denote the image

$$\pi(\sigma_p) \in J \qquad \text{by the inner product notation} \quad (\sigma_p, \pi) ,$$

and let Δ be a map

$$\Delta : \Pi^t \to \Pi^{t+1}$$

such that

$$(f\sigma_p, \pi) = (\sigma_p, \Delta\pi) .$$

If we denote $f|K^p$ by f_p then it is appropriate to write

$$\Delta = \{\Delta_p\} ,$$

where

$$\Delta_p : \Pi^p \to \Pi^{p+1} \qquad \text{and} \qquad (f_p\sigma_p, \pi^{p-1}) = (\sigma_p, \Delta_{p-1}\pi^{p-1}) .$$

If $\pi = \pi^p$ is a graded pattern, associated exclusively with the p-dimensional simplices of K, then

$$\Delta\pi \equiv \Delta\pi^p \in \Pi^{p+1}$$

is a $(p+1)$-pattern, associated with those $(p+1)$-simplices whose p-faces are associated with π^p.

By requiring that linearity should be preserved under Δ, we can naturally extend it to a *homomorphism* (also denoted by Δ),

$$\Delta : \Pi \to \Pi ,$$

on the ring of pattern polynomials on K. In this context we need to notice that, in ΛV,

$$\Delta(\pi_1 \wedge \pi_2) = (\Delta\pi_1) \wedge \pi_2 + \pi_1 \wedge (\Delta\pi_2) ,$$

$$\Delta^2(\pi_1 \wedge \pi_2) = (\Delta^2\pi_1) \wedge \pi_2 + 2(\Delta\pi_1) \wedge (\Delta\pi_2) + \pi_1 \wedge (\Delta^2\pi_2) ,$$

which suggests that if we write

$$\Delta = \Delta_1 + \Delta_2 ,$$

then

$$\Delta^k = (\Delta_1 + \Delta_2)^k ,$$

in which we suppose

$$\Delta_1 = \Delta|\pi_1 \qquad \text{and} \qquad \Delta_2 = \Delta|\pi_2 .$$

It also follows that we can interpret Δ^r, $r > 1$, by way of the definition of f^r. Thus

$$(f^r \sigma_{p+r}, \pi^p) = (f^{r-1}\sigma_{p+r}, \Delta\pi^p) = \text{etc.}$$
$$= (f^{r-s}\sigma_{p+r}, \Delta^s\pi^p)$$
$$= (f_{p+r}, \Delta^r\pi^p) .$$

Thus $\Delta^r\pi^p$ is a map defined on $(p+r)$-dimensional simplices. The mutual actions of f and Δ on the graded ring Π, are illustrated by the scheme:

$$\Pi^0 \oplus \Pi^1 \overset{f}{\underset{\Delta}{\rightleftarrows}} \Pi^2 \oplus ... \oplus \Pi^p \overset{f}{\underset{}{\rightleftarrows}} \Pi^{p+1} \oplus ... .$$

If we move to the exponential face operator $\hat{f}$, we obtain a dual operator $\hat{\Delta}$, via $(\hat{f}\sigma_p, \pi) = (\sigma_p, \hat{\Delta}\pi)$. Since

$$(\hat{f}^t\sigma_p, \pi) = \frac{1}{t!}(f^t\sigma_p, \pi) = \frac{1}{t!}(\sigma_p, \Delta^t\pi)$$

it follows that

$$\hat{\Delta}^t = \frac{1}{t!}\Delta^t , \qquad t \geq 0 .$$

11 The role of the obstruction vector $\hat{Q}$

A Q-analysis of the complex K gives us a first structure vector

$$Q = \{Q_N, Q_{N-1}, ..., Q_1, Q_0\} ,$$

where Q_r is the number of components at the r-level of connectedness.

Suppose σ_r is an r-simplex in one of the Q_r components but that it is not a face of any σ_{r+1} simplex; thus there is no $(r+1)$-simplex, σ_{r+1}, such that

$$\sigma_r \leq \sigma_{r+1} .$$

It is precisely this circumstance that results in Q_r taking a value greater than unity.

It follows that if $(\sigma_r, \pi^r) \in J$, then $\Delta\pi^r$ is not defined with respect to this σ_r. Thus the value of π_r on σ_r cannot be redistributed over those

σ^i_{r+1} for which $\sigma_r \leqslant \sigma^i_{r+1}$ since they do not exist. Hence this kind of σ_r acts as an obstruction to allowed changes $\Delta\pi^r$. The obstruction is inherent in the geometry of K.

If $Q_0 = 1$ and $Q_N = 1$, K is an N-simplex, σ_N, and the only obstruction occurs at $r+N$. There is zero obstruction at all levels r such that

$$0 \leqslant r < N ,$$

that is to say, the geometry of K freely allows $\Delta\pi^r$, given π^r.

If $Q_0 = 1$, but K is not a single N-simplex, then there exists a nontrivial *filtration* of K such that

$$K = \underset{p}{\cup} K^p , \qquad p = 0, 1, ..., N$$

and

$$K^N \subset K^{N-1} \subset ... \subset K^p \subset K^{p-1} \subset ... \subset K^1 \subset K^0 = K .$$

We can now form a *graded complex K* by

$$K = \underset{p}{\oplus} K_p \qquad \text{and} \qquad K_p = K^p/K^{p+1} ,$$

consisting of classes—each one of which has a representative p-simplex that is not a face of any $(p+1)$-simplex. It follows that

$$Q_r = \text{card} K_r$$

meaning that

$$Q_r = \text{card}\{\text{equivalence classes in } K_r\} .$$

It follows that if $Q_r > 1$, $0 < r < N$, there are exactly $(Q_r - 1)$ r-simplices which act as obstructions to Δ.

Thus we see that the obstruction vector

$$\hat{Q} = \{Q_N, Q_{N-1} - 1, Q_{N-2} - 1, ..., Q_1 - 1, 0\}$$

is a measure of the obstruction to Δ at any level r such that $0 < r < N$. In a previous paper (Atkin, 1972) the obstruction vector was written so as to include the component $(Q_N - 1)$ but whereas this is harmless for $r < N$, we can see that in general such a component disguises the existence of obstruction at the N-level.

Finally we can see that when $Q_0 > 1$ then K consists of Q_0 disjoint complexes $K^{(i)}$, $i = 1, ..., Q_0$, and the above argument applies to each $K^{(i)}$ separately.

12 Incremental changes $\delta\pi$ in a pattern π
Each pattern π on a complex K, regarded as a polynomial in the exterior algebra $\Lambda(X_n)$, may be associated with a pattern $\Delta\mu$ where Δ is the coface operator. If $\sigma_p \in K$, then we need only write

$$(\sigma_p, \pi) = \sum_i (f_{-1}\sigma_p, \Delta\mu) ,$$

where

$$f_{-1}\sigma_p = \{\sigma^i_{p+1}\,;\ \sigma_p \leqslant \sigma^i_{p+1}\}\ .$$

This means that $\Delta\mu$ is the pattern, associated to the $f_{-1}\sigma_p$, at the $(p+1)$-level, which corresponds to the (given) pattern π at the p-level.

Now an increment $\delta\pi$, in a pattern π, may thereby be associated to such a $\Delta\mu$ via

$$(\sigma_p, \delta\pi) = (f_{-1}\sigma_p, \Delta\mu)\ , \qquad \text{for all } p.$$

In the applications of the idea of patterns (Atkin, 1972), we interpret an incremental change $\delta\pi$ as a *force* in the structure; if $\delta\pi \equiv (\delta\pi)^t$ then we speak of a *t-force* in the complex K. This t-force is therefore associated to a pattern $(\Delta\mu)$ defined at the $(t+1)$-level, and it is in this sense that we interpret the incremental $\delta\pi$ in the abstract geometry of K.

A motivation for this association arises via a consideration of the notion of δv, where v is a velocity (a 1-pattern) defined on a σ_1 (say) $\langle P_1, P_2 \rangle$. Then δv is a measure of a 'force' throughout an interval of time δt, and this δv is associated to a triangle (a σ_2) of which $\langle P_1, P_2 \rangle$ is a face. Thus we are saying that the physicist's 'force' δv is naturally tied to a 2-pattern defined on (say) $\langle P_1 P_2 P_3 \rangle$ via

$$(\langle P_2 P_3 \rangle, \delta v) = (\langle P_1 P_2 P_3 \rangle, \Delta\mu) = (\langle P_1 P_2 P_3 \rangle, \text{force})\ ,$$

and this is illustrated in figure 3.

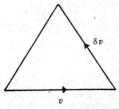

Figure 3. Δ associated with δ.

The *intensity* of a t-force, on a particular σ_t, is defined as:

$$\text{intensity} = \frac{[\sigma_t, (\delta\pi)^t]}{(\sigma_t, \pi^t)}\ ,$$

when that exists; and this is associated to the ratio

$$\sum_i (f_{-1}\sigma_t, \Delta\mu) \Big/ (\sigma_t, \pi^t)\ .$$

References

Atkin, R. H., 1972, Urban Structure Research Project Report I, University of Essex, Colchester, Essex, England.

Atkin, R. H., 1973a, "A survey of mathematical theory", Urban Structure Research Project Report II, University of Essex, Colchester, Essex, England.

Atkin, R. H., 1973b, "A study area in Southend-on-Sea", Urban Structure Research Project Report III, University of Essex, Colchester, Essex, England.

Atkin, R. H., 1974a, "An approach to structure in architectural and urban design. 1 Introduction and mathematical theory", *Environment and Planning B*, **1**, 51-67.

Atkin, R. H., 1974b, "An approach to structure in architectural and urban design. 2 Algebraic representation and local structure", *Environment and Planning B*, **2**, 173-191.

Atkin, R. H., 1974c, "A community study: the University of Essex", Urban Structure Research Project Report IV, University of Essex, Colchester, Essex, England.

Atkin, R. H., 1974d, *Mathematical Structure in Human Affairs* (Heinemann Educational Books, London).

Atkin, R. H., 1975, "An approach to structure in architectural and urban design. 3 Illustrative examples", *Environment and Planning B*, **2**, 21-57.

Dowker, C. H., 1952, "Homology groups of relations", *Annals of Mathematics*, **56**, 84.

Heuristic Methods for Solving Combinatorial Problems

T.B.BOFFEY
University of Liverpool

1 Introduction

Many mathematical models in regional science yield problems which are combinatorial in nature. For some combinatorial problems, such as the assignment or minimal spanning tree problems, there are special-purpose algorithms which are reasonably efficient, but this is not very often the case. It then becomes necessary to use some method of complete (implicit) enumeration, such as branch-and-bound or dynamic programming, or to resort to the use of heuristic methods. This paper is concerned with the area for which special-purpose algorithms are not known, and with the improvement of enumerative and heuristic techniques.

To illustrate the discussion, two path-minimisation problems will be used. The shortest route problem deals with the minimal length route through a network between two specified points, S and F. The travelling salesman problem provides a mathematical model for various scheduling problems, and also occurs as a subproblem in methods for solving realistic problems concerning vehicle scheduling.

2 Branch-and-bound techniques

Consider the shortest-route problem which requires that a shortest route from S to F should be found by using the map of figure 1. It may be assumed that the towns $S, a, ..., F$ are accurately placed on the map, but the roads are shown conceptually by straight lines, and so the map distance between two towns is not always a true reflection of the actual road distance (for example the road Sb).

A first simplification that will be made is that roads will be used only in a left to right direction on the map (thus ruling out the route $S\ a\ c\ b\ e\ F$ for example). For the particular network under consideration this simplification does not in fact rule out any optimal solution.

From S one has the choice of travelling to a or to b and so the set of all solutions (feasible routes from S to F) can be split into two subsets $\{Sa\}$ and $\{Sb\}$ where $\{Sxy ... t\}$ denotes the set of solutions starting with the 'partial route' $Sxy ... t$. $\{Sa\}$ can be split into subsets $\{Sac\}$ and $\{Sad\}$ and so on. This splitting process is termed *branching* and if carried on for as long as possible results in the *complete enumeration tree* shown in figure 2a. The value alongside each node $\{Sxy ... ut\}$ is the 'distance travelled so far' given by

$$g\{Sxy ... ut\} = d_{Sx} + d_{xy} + ... + d_{ut} .$$

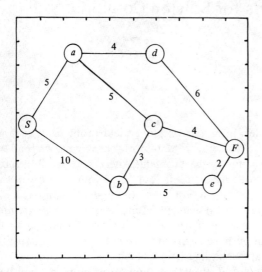

Figure 1. Find the shortest route from S to F with the use of the above map.

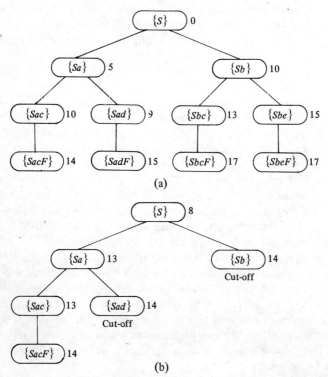

(a)

(b)

Figure 2. (a) The complete enumeration tree for the problem of figure 1. (b) The branch-and-bound tree obtained by using the tighter set of bounds described in the text.

By comparing the values of g at the four terminal nodes it is seen that
SacF is the sole optimal route from *S* to *F*.

Since all distances involved are positive it follows that g{*Sxy ... t*} is a
lower bound for the lengths of all the routes in {*Sxy ... t*}. Hence once
{*SacF*} has been bounded it is no longer necessary to *develop* {*Sbe*} with
value 15, by creating *SbeF*. That is there is a *cut-off* at {*Sbe*}.

Branching and bounding are the two main constituents of branch-and-
bound methods and the associated enumeration tree with cut-offs will
be termed a *branch-and-bound tree*.

A second improvement can be made by noting that, by the principle
of optimality, any optimal route from *S* to *F* via *x* must be such that the
partial route from *S* to *x* is itself an optimal route (from *S* to *x*). This
leads to a cut-off at {*Sbc*} since g({*Sac*}) < g({*Sbc*}).

A third improvement can be obtained by tightening the bounding rule
as follows. Considering the set {*Sa*} for example, it is seen that there is
some minimal distance, $h^*(\{Sa\})$ say, which still has to be travelled. Now
the distance from *a* to *F* is at least as great as the map distance, which in
turn is slightly greater than 8, and so g({*Sa*})+8 provides a tighter lower
bound for the set {*Sa*}. Extending this we have a new lower bounding
function f, where

$$f(\{Sxy \dots t\}) = g(\{Sxy \dots t\}) + h(\{Sxy \dots t\}),$$

and h({*Sxy ... t*}) ≡ h(*t*) is a lower bound on the distance from *t* to *F*.
By using map distance and taking h(*S*) = 8, h(*a*) = 8, h(*b*) = 4, h(*c*) = 3,
h(*d*) = 5, h(*e*) = 1, and h(*F*) = 0 leads to the branch-and-bound tree of
figure 2b. Clearly, improved bounds lead to more cut-offs and in general:

*The tighter the bounding rule the smaller the branch-and-bound tree tends
to be.*

However, tighter bounds almost always require more effort to compute.
Despite this it is usually the case that:

Tighter bounding rules tend to lead to less overall effort.

In order to illustrate the possibility of various bounding rules we now
look at some possible branch-and-bound approaches to the travelling
salesmen problem. For branching rule we use an *inclusion–exclusion*
strategy in which a set of solutions *X* is split into two disjoint subsets
$X_{\overline{ij}}$ and X_{ij} (see Little *et al.*, 1963) where

$X_{\overline{ij}}$ is that subset of towns which do not contain link *ij*, and
X_{ij} is that subset of towns which do contain link *ij*.

Exclusion of link *ij* is effected quite simply by replacing the
corresponding cost, C_{ij}, of travel between *i* and *j* by some very large
number. Inclusion of link *ij* can be effected by deleting row *i* and column
j of the cost matrix (C_{rs}) and replacing C_{kl} by some very large number

where kl is that link which together with ij and links already assigned would give rise to a closed 'tour' *not* containing all nodes (see Little *et al.*, 1963).

The problem of choosing a bounding function remains. $g(X)$ is just the sum of the costs of links committed to the tour by X, but what of $h(X)$? Some possibilities are given below, but for simplicity the bounds are given in the form $f(X)$, rather than $g(X)$ and $h(X)$ being given separately. Also it is convenient at this point to present the following result.

Theorem 1: If the cost matrix is modified by replacing C_{ij} by $C_{ij} - p_i - q_j$ (for all i, j) then the relative values of the various tours remain unchanged.

This is true since there is a link to each node and a link from each node and so the value of each tour is reduced by the same amount R,

$$R = \sum_{\alpha} (p_\alpha + q_\alpha).$$

Rule R_0: $f(X) = g(X)$,
that is, $h(X) = 0$ for all X.

Rule R_1: At each node of the branch-and-bound tree the associated matrix is reduced as explained above by subtracting the minimum element of each row from every element in that row and then reducing the columns in the same way. At any node X we can set

$f_1(X) =$ aggregate of reductions in reaching X .

Rule R_2: The reductions can frequently be increased by, for example, adding a constant to one row and subtracting the same constant from two columns.

$f_2(X) =$ aggregate of improved reductions .

Rule R_3: The maximum reduction can be obtained by solving the corresponding assignment problems (see for example Christofides, 1972),

$f_3(X) =$ aggregate of maximum reductions .

Rule R_4: To go from an assignment solution to a solution for a travelling salesman problem the subtours must be 'joined'. This can be shown to imply an extra cost of at least $\delta f(X)$ (see Christofides, 1972):

$f_4(X) = f_3(X) + \delta f(X)$.

Other schemes exist, for example those based on minimal spanning trees (Held and Karp, 1971).

In the above discussion it was implicitly assumed that the branch-and-bound tree was 'grown', at any stage, by developing a node with a minimal lower bound. Whilst this leads to a minimal-sized tree being developed, it is often not the best strategy to adopt since it is very expensive on storage requirements, and sometimes expensive on computation because of the overheads involved in dodging back and forth across the tree. Moreover, as pointed out in the next section, it is a bad strategy to adopt if the method is to be used heuristically, since the first feasible solution to be found may be generated only at the very end! There is some discussion of development strategies in Little *et al.* (1963).

3 Heuristic methods

The growth rate in effort required to solve combinatorial problems tends to be high and frequently the required effort grows approximately exponentially in the 'size' of the problem. Thus, whilst it may be moderately easy to solve a problem of size 10, it may be quite infeasible to solve exactly one of size 30. When a problem is too large to solve exactly, or when the effort required is not justified, then it is necessary to resort to heuristic methods. Some general classes of heuristic methods are outlined below together with illustrations.

3.1 Improvement methods

A set of permissible transitions $x \to y$, between pairs of solutions (x, y), must be prescribed by the problem solver. This leads to a graph structure on the set X of feasible solutions which may be pictured as follows. The links correspond to sections of road in a hilly region, the nodes (feasible solutions) correspond to points at which road sections join, and the value $\phi(x)$ of solution x corresponds to the height of the corresponding road intersection.

If we change in this subsection only, to maximisation problems, the *hill climb* can now be described. It consists of selecting (perhaps at random) a point x_0, then moving via a permissible transformation to a neighbouring point x_1 which is higher, $\phi(x_1) > \phi(x_0)$, then moving again to a higher point x_2 and so on until a point x^* is reached at which no further improvement is possible. That is, x^* is a *local* optimum though not necessarily a *global* optimum. x^* can now be taken as a solution to the problem. If the above procedure is related back to the analogy of a road network in a hilly region, the term 'hill climb' is readily appreciated.

As an example of this approach consider the travelling salesman problem, and two tours x and y. Take $x \to y$ (and $y \to x$) to be an allowable transformation if and only if y results from x by interchanging two nodes, x_r and x_s say. That is if

$$x = u_1 u_2 \dots u_{r-1} u_r u_{r+1} \dots u_{s-1} u_s u_{s+1} \dots u_n u_1 \, ,$$

then y must be given by

$$y = u_1 u_2 \dots u_{r-1} u_s u_{r+1} \dots u_{s-1} u_r u_{s+1} \dots u_n u_1 \, .$$

A solution to the travelling salesman problem is then found by hill climbing as described above. Other systems of allowable transitions are described by Shen Lin (1965).

The approach can be improved by taking several starting points $x_0^{(1)}, ..., x_0^{(s)}$ and by performing separate hill climbs to the local optima $x^{(1)*}, ..., x^{(s)*}$. The best of these local optima is then selected as the solution. The number s of starting points may be predetermined or determined dynamically in order to try to minimise the effort required to achieve a 'desired quality of solution' (see Reiter and Sherman, 1965).

Backtracking may also be incorporated if desired, by retracing some way along the path to x^* and then branching off in a different direction. This has been done for the travelling salesman problem (Doran, 1968) by using permissible transitions as defined by Shen Lin.

3.2 Constructive methods

These are much the same as improvement methods, but now X also contains elements which correspond to nonfeasible solutions. An infeasible solution is taken as starting point, and transitions, which must result in moves 'toward feasibility' to be permissible, are performed until a feasible solution x^* is *constructed*. If there is a fixed starting point then x^* is taken as the solution, otherwise several starting points could be taken and the best of the resulting local optima selected as solution.

If we take the travelling salesman problem as an example, the start could be with a partial tour consisting of just one node, u_1 say. The partial tour is then built up by adding the shortest link $u_1 u_2$, then the shortest link $u_2 u_3$ not resulting in a circuit, and so on until the partial tour $u_1 u_2 u_3 ... u_n$ is obtained. The tour is completed by adding the link $u_n u_1$.

The design of constructive methods is very often such that the transitions are selected by reference to g(x) (see for example Ward, 1963; and section 2). However, from the earlier discussion on branch-and-bound methods it is easily seen that the transitions could be selected with reference to f(x) = g(x) + h(x) instead, and it may be expected that this would lead to better results. The evidence from branch-and-bound methods tends to confirm this, though in this case the branching strategy complicates the situation somewhat.

Backtracking can be incorporated, with the result that the method becomes rather like branch-and-bound. Indeed branch-and-bound is often used 'heuristically' but in this case it should be so arranged that a good feasible solution is found early on and so that further search is directed at possible improvements. This means that a 'branch from lowest bounded node' strategy is not the one to be employed (see section 2).

3.3 Decomposition

A third approach is to decompose the problem into smaller subproblems (see also problem reduction in section 4). For example consider the case of the shortest route problem in a network with an articulation point t (that is the removal of node t disconnects the network). Then the problem of finding a shortest route from S to F is clearly equivalent to solving the two simpler problems of finding shortest routes from S to t and from t to F.

The faster the amount of computation required to solve a particular problem with the use of a particular method grows, the more desirable decomposition becomes. In fact if overheads involved in decomposing are ignored, then decomposition results in computational saving provided the computational requirement grows faster than linearly with the size of the problem.

3.4 Approximation of the problem
Instead of using an approximation method for solving a problem, the problem itself can be approximated by another problem which is then solved, exactly or approximately, to obtain a solution x^*_{approx}. x^*_{approx} is then related by some mapping to a solution x^* of the original problem which may or may not be optimal. An example of this is afforded by the case of a pure integer programming problem. The integrality constraints are relaxed and the resulting linear programming problem solved to obtain a solution x^*_{approx} in which some components may be fractional. The solution to the integer problem is then taken to be the nearest feasible solution x^* all of whose components are integers.

Problem approximation will not be laboured since this is a familiar exercise which is performed when going from real-world problems to mathematical-model problems.

4 Some ideas from artificial intelligence
The field of artificial intelligence, which is little more than 15 years old, though its origins go somewhat further back, is concerned with 'intelligence' and the implementation of mechanical problem solvers for solving problems which may be regarded as 'requiring intelligence for their solution'. Such problems are frequently combinatorial in nature, but because of their size and complexity (as is the case for the game of chess for example) they are often not amenable to anything approaching complete enumeration either explicit or implicit.

In the early days of artificial intelligence considerable emphasis was laid on tree searching methods which bore close affinity to tree searching methods in other fields. However, as the subject progressed it was realised that in order to significantly improve the performance of 'problem solving' systems different techniques would have to be employed, and a start has already been made on the investigation and implementation of some such techniques. The following subsections contain short accounts of some of the more conventional tree searching methods from artificial intelligence and also some indication of present trends in the field. For a general introduction to artificial intelligence see Michie (1974).

4.1 Improving branch-and-bound methods
If a variety $R_1, R_2, ..., R_s$ of bounding rules is available (as was shown to be the case for the travelling salesman problem in section 2) then it may

be better to use a derived rule $\tilde{R}$, where $\tilde{R}$ is one of $R_1, ..., R_s$, which particular one depending on the value of some heuristic guiding function γ. γ should be a relatively easily evaluatable function with $\gamma(x)$ depending on, for example, the bound of the parent node of x, the particular value of the best solution obtained so far, the depth down the tree, the particular nature of x, etc.

Providing the overheads [incurred through having to evaluate $\gamma(x)$] are small then it seems that $\tilde{R}$ will probably lead to improved results, since it allows one to direct more effort to where it is needed and less effort to where only a small amount is required.

Again, branch-and-bound methods can be made more flexible by passing knowledge gained in one region of the tree across to other regions of the tree. Thus, for example, if on one line of development for the travelling salesman problem it is found that joining nodes i and j leads to trouble then this could be taken account of in other lines of development where the joining of i and j is being contemplated.

The knowledge referred to above may be termed acquired knowledge, as opposed to initial knowledge, which is provided at the outset. The proper use of knowledge is currently receiving much attention from artificial-intelligence researchers and, on the whole, they have found that sole reliance on tree searching methods is often inadequate.

The proper utilization of knowledge is important.

4.2 Approximate branch-and-bound methods

It has been noted above (section 2) that the tighter the bounds, the better a branch-and-bound method works. Hart *et al*. (1968) went further in suggesting the use of the function f where

$$f(x) = g(x) + \bar{h}(x)^{(1)}, \qquad \text{for all } x,$$

and where $\bar{h}(x)$ is an *estimate* of $h^*(x)$ (see section 2). Whilst this approach should lead to less effort being expended, it is heuristic in nature because there is in general no guarantee that the final solution obtained will be optimal. However, provided the estimates are reasonably accurate, the final solution should not be too far from optimal. Indeed if $\bar{h}(x)$ is known to be a lower bound to $h^*(x)$ for each x, then (in the finite case) the method of Hart *et al*. (1968) becomes a branch-and-bound method with a branch from lowest-bound strategy.

Pohl (1969) investigated the error that can be introduced through the use of the estimates $\bar{h}(x)$ by employing a function f_w where

$$f_w(x) = (1-w)g(x) + w\bar{h}(x), \qquad \text{for all } x, \qquad 0 \leqslant w \leqslant 1.$$

He put forward some theoretical results relating to the possible error

---

(1) Strictly, Hart *et al*. use an estimate $\tilde{g}(x)$ of $g(x)$. However, provided $\bar{h}$ is consistent (Nilsson, 1971) $\tilde{g}(x)$ will always equal $g(x)$.

incurred through the use of f_w and performed some limited simulation experiments.

However, in using the above approach it is possible for a *catastrophe* to occur because a computational procedure (a) terminates (because of time and spare constraints) without finding a feasible solution, or (b) terminates with an insufficiently good solution being obtained. To overcome this Pohl (1973) uses the function

$$f_\alpha(x) = g(x) + w(x)\bar{h}(x) , \qquad \text{for all } x , \qquad 1 < w(x) \leqslant \infty ,$$

in which the weight varies dynamically with node x, and is such that $w(x)$ decreases with the depth of x in the search tree. Pohl applied his methods to the travelling salesman problem of Croes (1958) with encouraging results.

4.3 Bidirectional search

An idea that seems attractive is to work 'simultaneously from both ends of a problem'. It will be recalled that this is often advantageous when proving theorems in mathematics, and its use in combinatorial problems is well illustrated by the shortest route problem in which one can explore the network from S and from F. Two smaller trees will be grown instead of one larger one and, since the number of nodes in a tree usually grows faster than linearly with its maximum depth (in terms of number of links) from the root to a terminal node, this may be expected to lead to computational savings. Figure 3 shows two trees that could be grown for the problem of figure 1 by alternately developing a node from the first tree and a node from the second tree. From these it is seen that *SacF* is an optimal route from S to F.

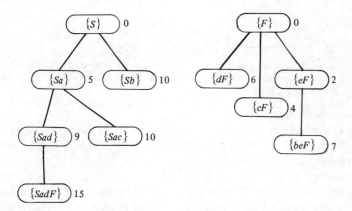

Figure 3. The two trees grown during a bidirectional search of the network of figure 1 as described in the text. $\{u \dots F\}$ denotes the set of all solutions ending with the partial path $u \dots F$.

It will be appreciated after a glance at figure 3 that various overheads will be involved in checking that a pair of nodes, one from each tree, yield a path from S to F (for example $\{Sac\}$ and $\{cF\}$, and $\{Sad\}$ and $\{dF\}$). Also there is a danger of the two trees 'missing each other' as illustrated in figure 4, where one tree will correspond to the part of the network marked A and the other will correspond to the part of the network marked B. For such reasons the idea of *bidirectional* search is not as attractive as it appears at first sight, and Dreyfus (1969) states that when using an exact method based on g(x) (see section 2) a *unidirectional* search leads to less computational effort in general. However, Pohl has demonstrated that computational savings can be achieved using bi-directional search for the shortest route problem in the heuristic case based on the use of f(x) = g(x) + h̄(x) (see section 4.2), provided bookkeeping aspects are treated carefully. A theory has been developed by Kowalski (1972) which contains the bidirectional search of Pohl and other search methods as special cases.

In the exact case bidirectional search may be termed 'double branch-and-bound', since two trees are grown. Hall (1971) generalises this to multiple branch-and-bound but, as far as the author is aware, no applications have been made to date where more than two trees are involved.

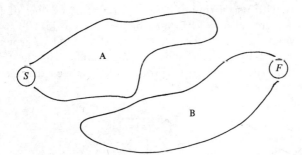

Figure 4. An illustration of how the two trees developed during a bidirectional search can tend to 'miss each other'—tree one has 'grown over the region A' and tree two has 'grown over the region B'.

4.4 Adaptive methods

Increased flexibility has been introduced into the methods discussed in sections 4.1 and 4.2 by the use of the guidance function γ and the weighting function w. However, these methods are *not* adaptive since they would always produce the same solution to a given problem. On the other hand, a human being would tend to improve his performance at solving problems, within a given domain, as time passes. That is, the human learns from experience. In section 4.1 it was shown that experience could be used within a problem by the acquisition and use of knowledge, but the element of learning was absent as this experience was not utilised by the problem solver when tackling later problems.

A simple form of learning can be achieved by *parameter optimisation*. Thus, for example, the estimate $\bar{h}(x)$ may be chosen to be of the form

$$\bar{h}(x) = a_1 q_1(x) + a_2 q_2(x) + \ldots + a_t q_t(x) = aq ,$$

where $q_i(x)$ is the value of some feature i of the 'state' x, and the a_i are parameters. One way of finding 'good' values for the a_i is as follows. First, initial values are chosen for the a_i and a few selected problems solved. a is now varied to $a + \delta a$ and more problems are solved. If superior performance is achieved then a is replaced by $a + \delta a$ otherwise the system reverts to using just a. In this way variations in a are continually tried out and when improved performance results a is updated thus leading to an a which varies with time. It should be noted that this approach leads to a being adapted in response to changes in the type (within the given domain) of problem presented. (For example travelling salesman problems could vary because the nodes become more clustered.)

An example of parameter optimisation with one parameter is afforded by allowing just w to vary in the formula

$$f(x) = (1 - w)g(x) + w\bar{h}(x) .$$

4.5 Representation of problems

Suppose a *representation* $\mathcal{R}$ of a problem (for example as a symmetric directed graph for the travelling salesman problem) has been chosen, then it may be possible to choose another representation $\mathcal{R}'$ which is simpler (for example as an undirected graph) but which retains the essential features of the problem under consideration. Before starting to solve a

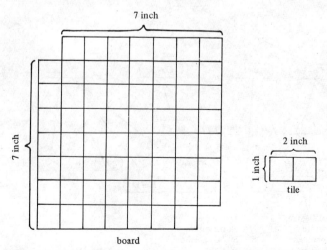

7 inch

7 inch

2 inch

1 inch

tile

board

Figure 5. Is it possible to cover the board using 1 inch × 2 inch tiles in such a way that no two tiles overlap?

problem, the sensible problem solver will try to find simplifications

$$\mathcal{R} \to \mathcal{R}' \to \mathcal{R}'' \dots ,$$

in representation.

Although it is obvious that it is preferable to have a good representation, this is a difficult area in which little has been discovered to date. However, in order to illustrate the importance of a good representation consider the following problem (Michie, 1973): can the board of figure 5 be completely covered by 1 inch x 2 inch tiles such that no two overlap? It may take the reader some time to prove that this is impossible. However, the result is immediate if one thinks of the board as being a chess board with the two white corner squares missing, since each tile must cover one white square and one black square!

4.6 Problem reduction

Frequently a problem can be split into two smaller problems both of which must be solved. To illustrate this consider the problem of planning a route from Colchester to Liverpool. This is solved if one can solve the two subproblems of finding routes from Colchester to Leicester, and Leicester to Liverpool; or the two subproblems of finding routes from Colchester to Northampton, and Northampton to Liverpool.

Subproblems can themselves be further split into 'subsubproblems' and an AND–OR tree is generated. An example of such a tree is given in figure 6. It often happens that the same subproblem may be generated

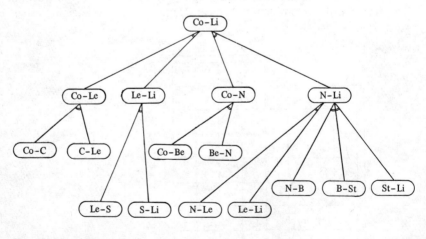

Key   B   Birmingham   Li   Liverpool
      Be   Bedford   N   Northampton
      C   Cambridge   S   Stoke-on-Trent
      Co   Colchester   St   Stafford
      Le   Leicester

Figure 6. Part of a possible AND–OR tree (see text).

more than once (for example the subproblem Le–Li in figure 6) in which
case these common subproblems can be identified leading to the generation
of an AND–OR graph. (It may be noted that the decision trees considered
earlier may be described as OR trees.)

   A treatment of AND–OR graphs is given in Nilsson (1971). Daniel
(1973) applies AND–OR graph techniques to decision critical path analysis,
which is an extension of the more familiar critical path analysis but allows
alternative ways of performing some of the constituent tasks.

   Probably of more interest to regional scientists is the work of de Feu
(1971) in which heuristic programming techniques are applied to the
problem of locating new residential development by using threshold
analysis. Such a problem is very complex, and the number of possible
solutions is likely to be impossibly large. To overcome this de Feu made
various simplifications; in particular he 'discretised' the area in question
into grid squares, and used a heuristic method based on the familiar idea
of first simplifying a problem in general terms, followed by a closer look
at the aspects of especial interest. This was done by first aggregating the
grid squares into groups (of about 10 squares say), solving the problem at
this level of detail, and then refining those groups that proved to be
interesting. The implementation of this approach involved the use of
AND–OR graphs which, when redundancies were eliminated, specialised
to AND graphs.

5 The man–machine system
It has been suggested above that artificial intelligence is leading towards
the production of programs which display some form of intelligence and
use suitable knowledge bases. However, despite the progress being made,
as yet and perhaps for some time to come, the human being is significantly
ahead in this area. On the other hand, the computer excels when it comes
to computation. Now it frequently happens that large and complex
problems go beyond the computing abilities of the human and beyond the
'intelligence' of the computer. The sensible way out of this would seem
to be to try to optimise the overall man–machine system by assigning to
each partner those aspects of the problem for which 'he' is best suited.
This would entail an interactive system in which, as the program is run,
it performs routine calculations, and periodically 'asks for advice', thus
allowing the human to exercise his judgement; and/or is suspended by the
human when he wishes to give advice or directions.

   Whilst the human may be better with questions that involve judgement,
this is no argument against providing the program with such elements of
deduction and judgement as may be feasible, or against providing the
program with as much knowledge as may reasonably be incorporated.
Such matters should be decided after consideration of the nature of the
problem to be solved. Indeed Michie et al. (1968) suggest, from their
experience with the travelling salesman problem, that if methods for a

particular problem are still relatively unsophisticated, an interactive approach may be better, but as the available methods become more powerful, reliance on the computer alone becomes more attractive. Of course in the latter phase the human has already provided knowledge and judgement from the outset in the form of an advanced method.

Krolak and Nelson (1972) describe the man–machine approach to urban problems. They discuss the following distribution problems: the travelling salesman problem; the truck dispatching problem; school busing; and school busing for racial balance.

For the solution of the travelling salesman problem described in Felts (1970) and Krolak *et al.* (1971), the human who can view the scene as a whole devises the best tour that he can. With his global view he is able to avoid the pitfalls of a 'nearest neighbour approach'. The computer program can now perform small tour-to-tour improvements along the lines suggested in section 3.1. This is a simplification of the work of Felts (1970) and Krolak *et al.* (1971), but illustrates their interactive approach. Their results were quite promising and the solutions obtained were generally of a high quality.

References

Christofides, N., 1972, "Bounds for the travelling salesman problem", *Operational Research,* **20**, 1044–1055.

Croes, G. A., 1958, "A method for solving travelling salesman problems", *Operational Research,* **6**, 791–812.

Daniel, L., 1973, "AND–OR graphs and critical path", memo number 71, internal report, Department of Computational Logic, University of Edinburgh, Scotland.

Doran, J. E., 1968, "New developments of the graph traverser", in *Machine Intelligence,* volume 2, Eds E. Dale, D. Michie (Oliver and Boyd, Edinburgh), pp.119–135.

Dreyfus, D., 1969, "An appraisal of some shortest path algorithms", *Operational Research,* **17**, 395–412.

Felts, W. J., 1970, "Solution techniques for stationary and time varying travelling salesman problems", Ph.D. dissertation, Vanderbilt University, Nashville, Tennessee.

de Feu, D., 1971, "An application of heuristic programming to the planning of new residential development", memo number 49, internal report, Department of Machine Intelligence and Perception, University of Edinburgh, Scotland.

Hall, P. A. V., 1971, "Branch-and-bound and beyond", in *Second International Joint Conference on Artificial Intelligence—Advance Papers* (British Computer Society, London), pp.641–650.

Harris, B., 1971, "Planning as a branch and bound process", *Papers of the Regional Science Association,* **26**, 53–63.

Hart, P., Nilsson, N., Raphael, B., 1968, "A formal basis for the heuristic determination of minimum cost paths", *IEEE Transactions on Systems, Man and Cybernetics,* **4** (2), 100–107.

Held, M., Karp, R. M., 1971, "The travelling salesman problem and minimum spanning trees: Part II", *Mathematical Programming,* **1**, 6–25.

Kowalski, R., 1972, "And-or graphs, theorem-providing graphs and bidirectional search", in *Machine Intelligence,* volume 7, Eds. B. Meltzer, D. Michie (Edinburgh University Press, Edinburgh), pp.167–194.

Krolak, P. D., Felts, W., Marble, G., 1971, "A man-machine approach toward solving the travelling salesman problem", *Communications of the ACM,* **14** (5), 327-334.

Krolak, P. D., Nelson, J. H., 1972, "A man-machine approach for creative solutions to urban problems", in *Machine Intelligence,* volume 7, Eds B. Beltzer, D. Michie (Edinburgh University Press, Edinburgh), pp.241-266.

Little, J. D. C., Murty, K. G., Sweeny, D. W., Karel, C., 1963, "An algorithm for solving the travelling salesman problem", *Operational Research,* **11**, 979-989.

Michie, D., 1973, "Machines and the theory of intelligence", *Nature,* **241**, 5391, 507-512.

Michie, D., 1974, *Donald Michie on Machine Intelligence* (Edinburgh University Press, Edinburgh).

Michie, D., Fleming, T. G., Oldfield, J. V., 1968, "A comparison of heuristic, interactive, and unaided methods of solving a shortest route problem", in *Machine Intelligence,* volume 3, Ed. D. Michie (Edinburgh University Press, Edinburgh), pp.245-255.

Nilsson, N. J., 1971, *Problem-solving Methods in Artificial Intelligence* (McGraw-Hill, New York).

Pohl, I., 1969, "First results on the effect of error in heuristic search", in *Machine Intelligence,* volume 5, Eds B. Meltzer, D. Michie (Edinburgh University Press, Edinburgh), pp.219-236.

Pohl, I., 1971, "Bidirectional search", in *Machine Intelligence,* volume 6, Eds B. Meltzer, D. Michie (Edinburgh University Press, Edinburgh), pp.127-140.

Pohl, I., 1973, "New results in the theory of heuristic search", memo H-5, University of California Heuristic Theory Project, University of California, Santa Cruz, USA.

Reiter, S., Sherman, G., 1965, "Discrete optimizing", *Journal of the Society for Industrial and Applied Mathematics,* **13**, 864-889.

Shen Lin, 1965, "Computer studies of the travelling salesman problem", *Bell System Technical Journal,* **44**, 2245-2269.

Ward, J. H., 1963, "Hierarchical grouping to optimize an objective function", *Journal of the American Statistical Society,* **58**, 236-244.

A Maximum Likelihood Model for Econometric Estimation with Spatial Series

L.W.HEPPLE
University of Bristol

1 The problem of dependence

The standard linear regression model is

$$y = X\beta + u ,\tag{1}$$

where

y is the $n \times 1$ vector of observations on the dependent variable;
X is the $n \times k$ matrix of observations on the k independent variables;
β is the $k \times 1$ vector of regression coefficients; and
u is the $n \times 1$ vector of errors.

We assume that the error terms, u, are independent of one another, so that the variance–covariance matrix of errors is diagonal (and is also assumed to be homoscedastic):

$$E(uu') = \sigma^2 I ,\tag{2}$$

where I is the unit matrix. If the errors are in fact dependent on each other in some way, so that

$$E(uu') = \sigma^2 V ,\tag{3}$$

where V is nondiagonal, then the least-squares estimates of β may be shown to be inefficient and the standard errors and significance tests biased, except in certain very specialised instances. In estimation and model building with time-series data, econometricians generally recognise that the formulation in equation (3) is more plausible than that in equation (2), and this is frequently confirmed by tests for serial correlation in the errors. It is also increasingly common for econometricians not simply to test for serial correlation, but to incorporate the dependence within u into the estimation procedure. If V is known *a priori* then the generalised least-squares estimator:

$$\hat{\beta} = (X'V^{-1}X)^{-1}X'V^{-1}y ,\tag{4}$$

provides efficient estimates and facilitates valid hypothesis-testing (Theil, 1971). Only rarely is V completely known. If, however, V depends on only a few unknown parameters, these may be estimated from the sample data, together with $\hat{\beta}$. A commonly hypothesised generating process for the dependence in u is the first-order temporal autoregressive model:

$$u_t = \rho u_{t-1} + e_t , \qquad t = 1, 2, ..., n ,\tag{5}$$

where e is a random sample from an independent normal distribution with mean zero and variance σ^2, which we denote by $e \sim N(0, \sigma^2 I)$. For quarterly economic data, a fourth-order process is perhaps more plausible (Wallis, 1971). An alternative specification is a moving-average process, and complex mixed moving-average autoregressive processes may also be considered (Box and Jenkins, 1970; Dhrymes, 1971). The first-order autoregressive model is, however, still the formulation most frequently used in applied econometric work.

Equation (5) may be rewritten in matrix terms as

$$u = \rho M u + e \tag{6}$$

where M is the lag-operator matrix, that is it contains zeros apart from ones on the first subdiagonal. Denoting $P = I - \rho M$ in equation (6), except for the very first element p_{11}, which is $(1 - \rho^2)^{1/2}$, and is introduced to incorporate the variance of the first observation (see Dhrymes, 1971; or Hildreth, 1969), we may show that $P'P = V^{-1}$. For the temporal autoregressive model, it may then be shown that minimising $e'e$, which may also be written $u'V^{-1}u$, produces consistent and hence asymptotically unbiased and efficient estimates (Hildreth and Lu, 1960). This minimising may be achieved by direct nonlinear least-squares estimation of $\hat{\beta}$ and $\hat{\rho}$ simultaneously.

Alternatively a number of multistage linear least-squares estimation methods have been derived. Two well-known procedures of this type, due to Durbin (1960), and Cochrane and Orcutt (1949) are described in Johnston (1972) and most econometrics texts. This group of estimators that minimise $u'V^{-1}u$ are sometimes known as minimum chi-square estimators (Dhrymes, 1971). Similar methods have also been devised for incorporating temporal dependence into simultaneous equation systems (Goldfeld and Quandt, 1972).

The importance of incorporating autocorrelated errors into the estimation procedure has been neatly demonstrated in econometric studies of United Kingdom inflationary problems by Wallis (1971) and Godfrey (1971), where the inclusion of autocorrelation in both single-equation and simultaneous-equation models overturns the ordinary least-squares inferences on the effectiveness of incomes policy.

2 Estimation with spatial series

In regional science, urban economics, economic geography, and econometrics generally, large numbers of regression models of the form of equation (1) are estimated on the basis of a spatial cross-section of n regions, states, or counties. Increasingly, simultaneous-equation techniques are also being employed with spatial series (for example Lee, 1970; Steinnes and Fisher, 1974). The presence of *spatial* autocorrelation or dependence in both variables and regression residuals is increasingly recognised and statistically demonstrated (Cliff and Ord, 1973; Hepple, 1974a; 1974b), and it is no more plausible for spatial series than for time series that the error variance–covariance matrix of a regression model will be diagonal. Until recently, however, the problem was almost totally neglected [see Hepple (1974b) for a history of this neglect and recent research]. Tests for spatial autocorrelation amongst regression residuals are now available (Cliff and Ord, 1973; Hepple, 1974a), and the severe effects of neglecting autocorrelated errors in spatial regression have been studied (Hepple, 1974a); it is important to develop estimation procedures that incorporate *spatial* dependence into econometric estimation of both single-equation and simultaneous-equation models.

As in the temporal case, it is necessary to decompose V so that it depends on only a few parameters. The commonest form of spatial autocorrelation is positive dependence between adjacent regions, so that a generating process incorporating dependence on immediate neighbours should give a valid and parsimonious representation of V. One such representation is a first-order spatial autoregressive model of the form of equation (6), where M is now some form of spatial lag-operator. Let W be the $n \times n$ matrix of contiguities between regions, with entry $w_{ij} = 1$ if regions i and j are contiguous, and $w_{ij} = 0$ otherwise, and let M be matrix W with the rows each scaled to sum to unity. This gives a generating process in which each region is a linear function of the average contiguous value. M can also, of course, incorporate prior weightings based on other information about interregional linkages and flows. Other specifications of the generating process, such as spatial moving averages and Box–Jenkins models, are also possible, but as in the time-series literature, the autoregressive model is a useful starting point.

Estimation of the regression model with autocorrelated errors is more difficult in the spatial case than with temporal data. The least-squares or minimum chi-square procedures for time series do not have valid analogues in the spatial-series case. The validity of least-squares or minimum chi-square estimators in time-series models springs from the asymptotic equivalence of these procedures with maximum-likelihood estimators. In spatial models this equivalence does not exist, and minimum chi-square estimators are not consistent. The reasons for this will be examined in subsequent sections.

Since least-squares procedures are invalid, the more general context of maximum-likelihood estimators has to be investigated. Coefficient estimates that maximise the likelihood function have desirable properties of consistency (and hence asymptotic unbiasedness and efficiency) and asymptotic multivariate normality. These properties are set out in Cramer (1945) and Goldfeld and Quandt (1972). Under suitable regularity conditions, such as the existence of the relevant derivatives, the estimates may be obtained by finding values of the coefficients that fulfil the second-order conditions for a maximum when first derivatives are set to zero. The set of values giving rise to the largest maximum constitutes the maximum-likelihood estimates. The variance–covariance matrix of the coefficients, $\mathbf{R}$, may then be estimated by the negative inverse of the probability limit of the Hessian matrix (the matrix of second-order partial derivatives). $\mathbf{R}$ may then be used, together with the property of asymptotic multivariate normality, to provide asymptotic significance tests of the coefficients. In the following two sections the likelihood function, derivatives, and asymptotic distribution theory are developed for the regression model with spatially autocorrelated errors.

3 The likelihood function
The density function of a standard normal independent variable, e, is:

$$(2\pi)^{-n/2}\exp(-\tfrac{1}{2}e'e) , \qquad e \sim N(0, \mathbf{I}_n) . \tag{7}$$

Transforming to another variable, u, where $u = B + Ce$, gives:

$$(2\pi)^{-n/2}|\mathbf{C}^{-1}|\exp\{-\tfrac{1}{2}(u - B)'(\mathbf{C}^{-1})'\mathbf{C}^{-1}(u - B)\} . \tag{8}$$

The term $|\mathbf{C}^{-1}|$, the Jacobian of the transformation, is the determinant of the matrix of partial derivatives of the transformation, with typical element $\partial e_j/\partial u_i$. In a transformation such as $y = \mathbf{X}\beta + e$, $\mathbf{C}^{-1}$ is simply an identity matrix, so the term disappears. For $y = oe$, where o is scalar, then $\mathbf{C}^{-1}$ is diagonal. Where o_u^2 is not unity, so that o is the standard deviation, the density becomes:

$$(2\pi o^2)^{-n/2}\exp\left(-\frac{1}{2o^2}u'u\right) . \tag{9}$$

For an observed series, this gives the likelihood function. In most models $|\mathbf{C}^{-1}|$ is either unity or a simple diagonal form, as with the variance transformation. Only if u_j is related to elements of e other than e_j does the Jacobian become a problem.

It is usual for convenience to maximise the log-likelihood function. For formulation (9) the log-likelihood function is

$$L = -\frac{n}{2}\ln 2\pi - \frac{n}{2}\ln o^2 - \frac{1}{2o^2}u'u , \tag{10}$$

and for the normal multiple-regression model with independent errors:

$$L = -\frac{n}{2}\ln 2\pi - \frac{n}{2}\ln o^2 - \frac{1}{2o^2}(y - \mathbf{X}\beta)'(y - \mathbf{X}\beta) . \tag{11}$$

Minimisation of the quadratic component will maximise the log-likelihood. This minimisation is the equivalent of least-squares minimisation.

Now consider the likelihood function for models with autocorrelated errors, where the Jacobian element may be important. For both the

spatial and temporal autoregressive formulations, it follows from equation
(6) that $u = P^{-1}e$. Hence in both these models $C^{-1} = P$, and if we recall
that $P'P = V^{-1}$, the log-likelihood function is then:

$$L = -\frac{n}{2}\ln 2\pi - \frac{n}{2}\ln \sigma^2 + \ln|P| - \frac{1}{2\sigma^2}[(y - X\beta)'V^{-1}(y - X\beta)] \ . \tag{12}$$

In the time-series case, P is a matrix with diagonal entries of unity
[except for p_{11} which is $(1-\rho^2)^{1/2}$], and $-\rho$ on the first subdiagonal, with
all the other elements zero. P is therefore a triangular matrix. The
determinant of a triangular matrix is the product of its diagonal elements.
Hence, if we ignore p_{11}, $|C^{-1}|$ is unity, if we assume that σ^2 has already
been separated out, so that least-squares estimation (minimisation of the
quadratic component) is equivalent to maximum-likelihood estimation. If
we recognise that the first element of matrix P is not unity but $(1-\rho^2)^{1/2}$,
then the determinant $|C^{-1}|$ is $(1-\rho^2)^{1/2}$. However, as sample size n
increases, this term does not alter, its magnitude becoming swamped by
the quadratic component of the likelihood function, so that asymptotically
it is negligible (this is further clarified in section 6).

In the spatial series case the same results do not apply. In the spatial
model C^{-1} will not be a triangular matrix: region j influences region i,
which in turn influences region j. Both m_{ij} and m_{ji}, elements of M, will
be nonzero if regions i and j are adjacent, but they will probably not be
equal. The Jacobian is neither negligible nor invariant with sample size,
and does not collapse to a simple quantity. Whittle (1954), writing in a
spectral-methods context, was the first to note the problem of the
non-vanishing Jacobian. It was also noted in a biometric context by Mead
(1967). Independently of the present work, Cliff and Ord (1973) have
presented the likelihood in a regression context and provided an empirical
illustration. There has, however, been no study of the structure and
properties of the maximum-likelihood estimation, the role of the Jacobian,
distribution theory, or computational techniques. These are developed
here.

4 Derivatives and asymptotic distribution
The first partial derivatives of the log-likelihood function in equation (12)
for the spatial model are:

$$\frac{\partial L}{\partial \sigma^2} = -\frac{n}{2\sigma^2} + \frac{1}{2\sigma^4}u'V^{-1}u \ , \tag{13}$$

$$\frac{\partial L}{\partial \beta} = \frac{1}{\sigma^2}X'V^{-1}u \ , \tag{14}$$

$$\frac{\partial L}{\partial \rho} = -\text{tr}\,P^{-1}M + \frac{1}{2\sigma^2}(P'M + M'P) \ . \tag{15}$$

The probability limits of these derivatives may be shown to be zero (Hepple, 1974a; in preparation). The second partial derivatives are:

$$\frac{\partial^2 L}{\partial \sigma^2 \partial \sigma^2} = \frac{n}{2\sigma^4} - \frac{1}{\sigma^6} u' V^{-1} u \ , \tag{16}$$

$$\frac{\partial^2 L}{\partial \beta \partial \beta} = -\frac{1}{\sigma^2} X' V^{-1} X \ , \tag{17}$$

$$\frac{\partial^2 L}{\partial \rho \partial \rho} = -\operatorname{tr}(P^{-1}M)^2 - \frac{1}{\sigma^2} u' M' M u \ , \tag{18}$$

$$\frac{\partial^2 L}{\partial \sigma^2 \partial \beta} = -\frac{1}{\sigma^4} X' V^{-1} u \ , \tag{19}$$

$$\frac{\partial^2 L}{\partial \sigma^2 \partial \rho} = -\frac{1}{2\sigma^4} u' (P'M + M'P) u \ , \tag{20}$$

$$\frac{\partial^2 L}{\partial \beta \partial \rho} = -\frac{1}{\sigma^2} X' (P'M + M'P) u \ . \tag{21}$$

The probability limits (plim) of these derivatives are:

$$\operatorname*{plim}_{n \to \infty} \frac{1}{n} \frac{\partial^2 L}{\partial \sigma^2 \partial \sigma^2} = -\frac{1}{2\sigma^4} \ , \tag{22}$$

$$\operatorname*{plim}_{n \to \infty} \frac{1}{n} \frac{\partial^2 L}{\partial \beta \partial \beta} = -\frac{1}{n\sigma^2} X' V^{-1} X \ , \tag{23}$$

$$\operatorname*{plim}_{n \to \infty} \frac{1}{n} \frac{\partial^2 L}{\partial \rho \partial \rho} = -\frac{1}{n} \operatorname{tr} A^2 - \frac{1}{n} \operatorname{tr} A' A \ , \tag{24}$$

where $A = MP^{-1}$, with

$$\operatorname*{plim}_{n \to \infty} \frac{1}{n} \frac{\partial^2 L}{\partial \sigma^2 \partial \rho} = -\frac{\operatorname{tr} A}{n\sigma^2} \ , \tag{25}$$

and the probability limits of the cross-partials between β and σ^2, and between β and ρ, are zero. Let us denote the matrix of these probability limits by Ω.

$$\operatorname*{plim}_{n \to \infty} \frac{1}{n} \frac{\partial^2 L}{\partial \theta' \partial \theta} = \Omega \tag{26}$$

where $\theta = (\sigma^2, \beta, \rho)$.

The negative inverse of this matrix Ω is the asymptotic variance–covariance matrix of the maximum likelihood estimates. Ω may be partitioned so that $\hat{\beta}$ may be tested separately from $\hat{\rho}$ and σ^2. These results may be compared with those for temporal models (see for example Dhrymes, 1971; Hildreth, 1969). It is the elements containing ρ that differ from temporal models. The second partial for ρ in equation (24) naturally differs, and the probability limit for the cross-partial, equation (25), is zero in the temporal model.

5 Computation of maximum-likelihood estimates

The likelihood function is highly nonlinear, and numerical optimisation techniques are needed to determine the maximum. A wide variety of such techniques are now available (Fletcher, 1970; Himmelblau, 1972), some of which, such as Newton-type methods, require repeated evaluation of both first and second partial derivatives, others only the first partial derivatives (for example steepest ascent and Davidon's method), and some require neither set of derivatives, as in Powell's conjugate gradient algorithm (Powell, 1965). Where explicit expressions for the derivatives are available it is normally most efficient to employ them in the maximisation. However, if computation of these derivatives, even if available, is complex and time consuming—as in the present case where inversion of $n \times n$ matrices would be involved—methods such as Powell's may be faster and less subject to round-off error.

Powell's conjugate gradient algorithm is based on solving a sequence of one-dimensional maximisation problems. If there are k unknown coefficients to be estimated, each iteration basically consists of maximising the function sequentially in k conjugate directions. After each iteration either the k directions are retained, or one is abandoned and a new conjugate direction calculated. So for a quadratic function a maximum of k iterations are needed to find the maximum. The algorithm also has good convergence properties for more general functions and has found extensive use in econometric research (for example Hendry, 1971; Hendry and Trevedi, 1970). It is the method used in the empirical illustration below.

The major difficulty in numerical maximisation of the likelihood function is the necessity of evaluating the $n \times n$ determinant $|\mathbf{P}|$ at each step. Ostensibly this severely limits the general availability of the method. However, a simplification is possible for the model with first-order spatial autoregressive errors. (Simplifications are also possible for a number of other generating processes.) Recalling that $\mathbf{P} = \mathbf{I} - \rho\mathbf{M}$, we denote the eigenvalues of $\mathbf{P}$ by λ_i, $i = 1, ..., n$, and the eigenvalues of $\mathbf{M}$ by μ_i, $i = 1, ..., n$. It may be proved (see Hepple, 1974a; in preparation) that for each nonzero eigenvalue of $\mathbf{M}$, μ_i, there is a corresponding eigenvalue of $\mathbf{P}$, λ_i, equal to $1 - \rho\mu_i$. Since the determinant of a matrix is the product of its eigenvalues:

$$|\mathbf{P}| = \prod_{i=1}^{n} \lambda_i = \prod_{i=1}^{n} (1 - \rho\mu_i) \,. \tag{27}$$

The advantage of this formulation is that the eigenvalues of $\mathbf{M}$ may be determined once and for all at the beginning of the estimation. Unless the contiguity matrix $\mathbf{W}$ is 'regular', with each region in the lattice having the same number of adjacencies, $\mathbf{M}$ will not be a symmetric matrix. Hence the eigenvalues of a general real matrix must be extracted. This may be done by reducing the matrix to an upper-Hessenberg form and then using Francis' QR algorithm to extract the eigenvalues (Wilkinson, 1965). This procedure is quite practicable even for large matrices: for the American illustration below, the eigenvalues of a 49 × 49 nonsymmetric matrix were extracted. Given these eigenvalues of $\mathbf{M}$, $|\mathbf{P}|$ is easily obtained at each function evaluation.

6 The role of the Jacobian

It is useful to explore further the role of the Jacobian term, $|\mathbf{P}|$, in the estimation. Concentrating the log-likelihood function presented in equation (12) by eliminating σ^2 gives

$$L^* = -\frac{n}{2}(\ln 2\pi + 1) + \ln|\mathbf{P}| - \frac{n}{2}\ln u'\mathbf{V}^{-1}u \ , \tag{28}$$

$$= -\frac{n}{2}(\ln 2\pi + 1) - \frac{n}{2}\ln\frac{u'\mathbf{V}^{-1}u}{|\mathbf{P}|^{2/n}} \ . \tag{29}$$

Maximising the log-likelihood function is thus equivalent to globally minimising $u'\mathbf{V}^{-1}u/(|\mathbf{P}|^{2/n})$. This formulation is directly equivalent to expression (39) in Whittle's paper on a spectral approach to spatial estimation, where in his notation KU is the expression to be minimised (Whittle, 1954, p.44). K is $|\mathbf{P}|^{-2/n}$ and U is $u'\mathbf{V}^{-1}u$. Using this notation, K acts essentially as a penalty or weighting function on the sum of squares component $u'\mathbf{V}^{-1}u$. Least-squares estimates simply set $K = 1$ for all values of ρ.

Equation (29) also allows further clarification of the equivalence of maximum-likelihood and minimum chi-square estimators in the time-series model. In the time-series case the term to be minimised in maximum-likelihood estimation is

$$KU = \frac{u'\mathbf{V}^{-1}u}{(1-\rho^2)^{1/n}} \ . \tag{30}$$

As n tends to infinity it is clearly seen that

$$\lim_{n \to \infty} (1-\rho^2)^{1/n} = 1 \ , \tag{31}$$

so that the maximum-likelihood estimator is asymptotically equivalent to minimising $u'\mathbf{V}^{-1}u$. In any finite sample the minimum chi-square and maximum-likelihood estimates will differ numerically because of $(1-\rho^2)^{1/n}$; however, their asymptotic properties are the same.

It is possible that in the spatial maximum-likelihood model K is such a weak penalty function that omission of it makes very little difference to the estimates, so that the simpler nonlinear least-squares method might be used in place of the maximum-likelihood method. This is not the case, as may be shown by the following illustration.

The eigenvalues of $\mathbf{M}$ were extracted for spatial autoregression on the lattice of 49 states of the USA (48 continental states plus the District of

Columbia). **M** was scaled to have row sums equal to unity so that each state value was a linear function of the average contiguous value. This gives real eigenvalues of modulus $\leqslant 1\cdot 0$, with ρ in the range $-1\cdot 0 < \rho < +1\cdot 0$ permitted. K and $|\mathbf{P}|$ were then evaluated for $\rho = -1\cdot 0$ to $+1\cdot 0$ in steps of $0\cdot 01$, to trace out the form and magnitude of the penalty function. These are charted in figure 1. The form of K, growing greater than $1\cdot 0$ as ρ moves to either $+1\cdot 0$ or $-1\cdot 0$ penalises least-squares solutions that give large absolute $\hat{\rho}$ values. The very high penalty values as ρ approaches $\pm 1\cdot 0$ (there is a singularity at $+1\cdot 0$) restrict the maximum-likelihood estimates to within the feasible range; there is no such constraint in the least-squares estimator, with K set to unity, and values of ρ greater than

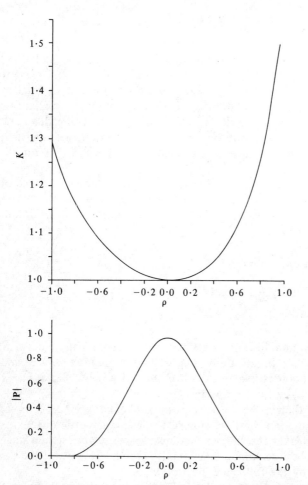

Figure 1. The Jacobian penalty term K and the Jacobian $|\mathbf{P}|$ for various ρ values in the lattice for the United States.

$1 \cdot 0$ are frequently generated as least-squares estimates. This structure of KU suggests that in general the least-squares estimator will be biased towards overestimating the absolute value of ρ.

The spatial maximum-likelihood model is in many ways similar to the simultaneous equation model of econometrics. As in the simultaneous-equation model, least-squares procedures are invalid because of the presence of a nonvanishing Jacobian element (though in the simultaneous-systems case there are adaptations of least-squares procedures, such as two- and three-stage least-squares, that take account of the Jacobian). The Jacobian in the spatial-series model also plays a role directly analogous to the Jacobian term containing the matrix of endogenous coefficients in simultaneous-equation systems. Thus in Haavelmo's (1947) consumption model for example, the Jacobian term $|1 - \alpha|^n$, where α is the endogenous coefficient, may be shown to be a penalty function, that compensates for the tendency of the minimum-sum-of-squares estimator to overestimate the absolute value of α (Zellner, 1971), as noted above for ρ in the spatial model.

7 Empirical application
In this section the maximum-likelihood model is illustrated by application to a regression equation in a paper by Hanna (1966). Hanna's paper is an econometric study of the effects of regional differences in sales taxes and transport charges across the United States on the pattern of car ownership or 'automobile consumption'. The models were set up in the form of the effects that taxes, etc. on new cars would have on the value of second-hand cars, and hence on the relative frequency of older cars from state to state.

The particular equation investigated was

$$y = \alpha + \beta x + u , \tag{32}$$

where y is the vector of 49 observations on the average value of 1955–1959 model cars in January 1960 for each state, and x is the vector of observations on new-car price differentials attributable to transport charges and sales taxes. Both variables are expressed in dollars. β is clearly expected to be >0 but probably <1. The least-squares estimates are given in table 1. These double-precision estimates differ slightly, but

Table 1. Ordinary least-squares estimates.

	α	β	
standard errors	$27 \cdot 20$	$0 \cdot 1947$	$\hat{\sigma}_u^2 = 3181 \cdot 97$
t values	$52 \cdot 76$	$3 \cdot 5245$	$r^2 = 0 \cdot 250$
	$y = 1435 \cdot 97 + 0 \cdot 6864 x + u$		

not significantly, from those given by Hanna (1966). The slope coefficient, $\hat{\beta}$, is $0 \cdot 686$, positive and <1, but significantly different from zero.

The least-squares regression residuals, $\hat{u}$, were then tested for spatial autocorrelation between adjacent states by the statistic

$$s = \frac{\hat{u}'W\hat{u}}{\hat{u}'\hat{u}} , \tag{33}$$

where W is the $n \times n$ matrix of contiguities, where entry $w_{ij} = 1$ if regions i and j are contiguous, and zero otherwise. Since $\hat{u} = G'u$ where G is the idempotent matrix $I - X(X'X)^{-1}X'$ (Johnston, 1972), the statistic s is distributed as

$$s = \frac{u'G'WGu}{u'Gu} . \tag{34}$$

Under independence of the errors u this may be shown (Hepple, 1974a) to be asymptotically normally distributed with mean value

$$E(s) = \frac{\text{tr}\,G'W}{n-k} , \tag{35}$$

and variance

$$\text{var}(s) = 2\left[\frac{(n-k)\,\text{tr}(G'W)^2 - (\text{tr}\,G'W)^2}{(n-k)^2(n-k+2)}\right] . \tag{36}$$

For Hanna's model, $s = 2 \cdot 763$. Under independence the expected value is $-0 \cdot 129$, with variance $0 \cdot 148$, thus giving a standard normal deviate of $7 \cdot 506$, which is highly significantly different from zero. This inference was also confirmed by the application of exact, small-sample tests. Since the tests indicate highly significant spatial dependence in the errors, the regression model with spatially autoregressive errors was estimated:

$$y = \alpha + \beta x + u , \tag{37}$$
$$u = \rho M u + e ,$$

with $e \sim N(0, \sigma^2)$. The eigenvalues of the 49×49 nonsymmetric matrix M were first computed, with M scaled so that row sums were unity, as in section 6, and the coefficients of equation (37) were then estimated by Powell's conjugate gradient algorithm. The algorithm converged to a maximum after eight iterations and 129 function evaluations. The estimates are given in table 2, together with asymptotic standard errors and significance tests. Incorporation of the dramatically large $\hat{\rho}$ value of $0 \cdot 816$ has significantly reduced the slope-coefficient estimate. It is now close to, and not significantly different from, zero. It is possible, though unlikely, that the high autoregressive coefficient is the result of a local rather than a global maximum in the likelihood function. To check this separate maximisations were started from initial ρ values of $0 \cdot 0$, $0 \cdot 4$, and $0 \cdot 8$, and each converged to the same estimates as in table 2, so that the estimates represent a global maximum.

In order to assess whether inclusion of the Jacobian term in the maximum-likelihood estimation makes a real difference in an empirical situation, the model was also estimated leaving out this term, that is by minimum chi-square, by minimising $u'V^{-1}u$ and assuming the Jacobian term to be one. Simultaneous estimation of α, β, and ρ by nonlinear least squares, again using Powell's algorithm, produced the following minimum chi-square estimates:

$$y = 1579 \cdot 11 + 0 \cdot 0534x + u,$$

$$u = 0 \cdot 9785Mu + e, \qquad \hat{\sigma}_e^2 = 966 \cdot 97,$$

with convergence after 62 function evaluations. The estimated $\hat{\rho}$ value is considerably larger than in table 2, $0 \cdot 979$, thus indicating that inclusion of the Jacobian penalty term works in the way suggested in section 6. The $\hat{\beta}$ estimate is still lower than in the maximum-likelihood estimation, at $0 \cdot 053$. Spatial versions of the Durbin procedure and the Cochrane–Orcutt method, both asymptotically equivalent to minimising $u'V^{-1}u$, produced very similar results in this application.

The maximum-likelihood results show the importance of incorporating spatial dependence into the estimation of econometric relationships. In this particular case, incorporation of spatial dependence results in rejection of the inference that new-car price differentials attributable to sales taxes and transport charges significantly affect the value of used cars. Comparison of the maximum-likelihood and minimum chi-square estimates also indicates that the simpler but inconsistent minimum chi-square procedures lead to substantially different numerical results to those by consistent maximum-likelihood estimation. Inclusion of the Jacobian term is therefore important.

Table 2. Maximum-likelihood estimates.

	Asymptotic standard error	Asymptotic t value
$\hat{\alpha}$	31·791	48·073
$\hat{\beta}$	0·121	0·820
$\hat{\rho}$	0·074	11·035

$$y = 1528 \cdot 17 + 0 \cdot 0992x + u,$$

$$u = 0 \cdot 8164Mu + e, \qquad \hat{\sigma}_e^2 = 1044 \cdot 74.$$

8 Concluding remarks

The maximum-likelihood spatial estimator in this paper suffers from the general drawback shared by the maximum-likelihood and minimum chi-square time-series estimators: the desirable statistical properties are all asymptotic. A further, highly theoretical qualification is discussed in the appendix. In small, finite samples maximum-likelihood estimates need not be unbiased and normally distributed. Hildreth has shown, for the time-series model, that it is likely that the distribution of $\hat{\beta}$ in autoregressive models rapidly approaches normality as the sample size increases, but that larger samples will be needed for normality of $\hat{\rho}$ and $\hat{\sigma}^2$ (Hildreth, 1969). Several Monte Carlo simulation studies of small-sample properties have been made for the time-series estimators (for example Griliches and Rao, 1969; Hendry and Trevedi, 1970). Some very preliminary small-sample Monte Carlo studies of the maximum-likelihood spatial model (Hepple, 1974a) suggest that there is some downward bias of $\hat{\rho}$, but that on both average bias and mean-square-error criteria, the maximum-likelihood estimates are superior to direct minimisation of the sum of squares, i.e. when the Jacobian term is ignored.

It may prove possible to construct more accurate approximations to the sampling distributions than by assuming normality. In the time-series case Hildreth has suggested the possibility of a beta-distribution for $\hat{\rho}$. An alternative approach is to stop focussing purely on the maximum of the likelihood, and study the whole likelihood function, or recast the estimation in Bayesian terms (Zellner, 1971). Suitable diffuse prior distributions still allow the likelihood to dominate the posterior distribution, and the method allows exact finite-sample inference, though not of course in the same terms as the classical inference of maximum likelihood. A Bayesian formulation and application of the present model will be presented in another paper.

The maximum-likelihood estimator does however extend readily to simultaneous-equation systems with spatially autocorrelated errors (Hepple, 1974a), whereas it is difficult, on purely computational grounds, to envisage a full Bayesian analysis of such models or of large multiple regressions, though marginal distributions may be obtained.

The maximum-likelihood model that has been outlined in this paper is only one of a family of possible models that build spatial dependence into econometric estimation. It is important to also explore moving average, Box–Jenkins, and other specifications of the error structure. Alternatively, the spatial autocorrelation in the residuals may be the result of misspecification of the actual regression structure, this requiring the introduction of spatially lagged X variables or lagged dependent variables, rather than directly modelling dependence in the errors. However the maximum-likelihood model presented here shows the main features and problems that arise in econometric estimation with spatial data, together with the empirical importance of incorporating spatial dependence into the estimation.

Acknowledgement. The author is indebted to Professor Peter Whittle for his helpful comments on this model.

References
Box, G. E. P., Jenkins, G. M., 1970, *Time Series Analysis, Forecasting and Control* (Holden-Day, San Francisco).
Cliff, A. D., Ord, J. K., 1973, *Spatial Autocorrelation* (Pion, London).
Cochrane, D., Orcutt, G. H., 1949, "Application of least-squares regressions to relationships containing autocorrelated error-terms", *Journal of the American Statistical Association*, **44**, 32-61.
Cooper, J. P., 1972, "Asymptotic covariance matrix of procedures for linear regression in the presence of first-order serially correlated disturbances", *Econometrica*, **40**, 305-310.
Cramer, H., 1945, *Mathematical Methods of Statistics* (Princeton University Press, Princeton).
Dhrymes, P. J., 1971, *Distributed Lags: Problems of Estimation and Formulation* (Oliver and Boyd, Edinburgh).
Durbin, J., 1960, "Estimation of parameters in time-series regression models", *Journal of the Royal Statistical Society*, 22B, 139-153.
Fletcher, R., 1970, *Optimization* (Academic Press, London).
Godfrey, L., 1971, "The Phillips curve: incomes policy and trade union effects", in *The Current Inflation*, Ed. H. G. Johnson and A. R. Nobay (Macmillan, London), pages 99-124.
Goldfeld, S. M., Quandt, R. E., 1972, *Nonlinear Methods in Econometrics* (North-Holland, Amsterdam).
Griliches, Z., Rao, P., 1969, "Small-sample properties of several two-stage regression methods in the context of autocorrelated errors", *Journal of the American Statistical Association*, **64**, 253-272.
Haavelmo, T., 1947, "Methods of measuring the marginal propensity to consume", *Journal of the American Statistical Association*, **42**, 105-122.
Hanna, F. A., 1966, "Effects of regional differences in taxes and transportation charges on automobile consumption", in *Papers on Regional Statistical Studies*, Ed. S. Ostry and T. K. Rhymes (Toronto University Press, Toronto), pp.199-223.
Hendry, D. F., 1971, "Maximum likelihood estimation of systems of simultaneous regression equations with errors generated by a vector autoregressive process", *International Economic Review*, **12**, 257-272.
Hendry, D. F., Trevedi, P. K., 1970, "Maximum likelihood estimation of difference equations with moving average errors: a simulation study", Discussion Paper No. 7, London School of Economics and Political Science, Department of Economics.
Hepple, L. W., 1974a, *Econometric Estimation and Model-Building with Spatial Series*, Ph. D. Thesis, University of Cambridge.
Hepple, L. W., 1974b, "The impact of stochastic process theory upon spatial analysis in human geography", in *Progress in Geography 6*, Eds C. Board, R. J. Chorley, P. Haggett and D. R. Stoddart (Arnold, London), pp.89-142.
Hepple, L. W., in preparation, *Econometric Estimation with Spatial Series* (Pion, London).
Hildreth, C., 1969, "Asymptotic distribution of maximum likelihood estimators in a linear model with autoregressive disturbances", *Annals of Mathematical Statistics*, **40**, 583-594.
Hildreth, C., Lu, J. Y., 1960, "Demand relations with autocorrelated disturbances", Research Bulletin 276, Agricultural Experiment Station, Michigan State University, East Lansing, Michigan, USA.

Himmelblau, D. M., 1972, *Applied Nonlinear Programming* (McGraw-Hill, New York).
Hoeffding, W., Robbins, H., 1948, "The central limit theorem for dependent variables", *Duke Mathematical Journal*, **15**, 773-780.
Johnston, J., 1972, *Econometric Methods*, 2nd edition (McGraw-Hill, New York).
Lee, M. L., 1970, "A model of the distribution of federal expenditures among States", *Journal of the American Statistical Association*, **65**, 136-149.
Mead, W. R., 1967, "A mathematical model for the estimation of interplant competition", *Biometrics*, **23**, 189-205.
Powell, M. J. D., 1965, "An efficient method for finding the minimum of a function of several variables without calculating derivatives", *Computer Journal*, **7**, 155-162.
Steinnes, D. N., Fisher, W. D., 1974, "An econometric model of intraurban location", *Journal of Regional Science*, **14**, 65-80.
Theil, H., 1971, *Principles of Econometrics* (Wiley, New York).
Wallis, K. F., 1971, "Wages, prices and incomes policies: some comments", *Economica*, **38**, 304-310.
Whittle, P., 1954, "On stationary processes in the plane", *Biometrika*, **41**, 434-449.
Wilkinson, J. H., 1965, *The Algebraic Eigenvalue Problem* (Clarendon Press, Oxford).
Zellner, A., 1971, *An Introduction to Bayesian Inference in Econometrics* (Wiley, New York).

Appendix

Properties of maximum-likelihood estimators

The classical proofs of the properties of maximum-likelihood estimators, the properties of consistency and asymptotic multivariate normality, were derived on the basis of independently distributed observations (Cramer, 1945, pages 500-504). Intuitively, these properties will also hold for temporal and spatial models where the observations are no longer independent, provided that the structure of the generating process is not peculiar (for example if matrix **M** were broken into disjoint 'islands'). To be completely rigorous, however, the properties of maximum-likelihood estimators need to be proved again for the temporal and spatial models. This theoretical problem has been largely ignored by econometricians and others studying time-series regression models (for example Cochrane and Orcutt, 1949; Cooper, 1972; Hendry and Trevedi, 1970), but in recent years a few papers have proved the maximum-likelihood properties for the regression model with temporally autoregressive errors (Dhrymes, 1971; Hildreth, 1969). Their proofs, based on the theory of m-dependent variables (Hoeffding and Robbins, 1948), are not easily extended to the spatial maximum-likelihood models discussed here. Nor have proofs yet been constructed for simultaneous equation models with temporally autocorrelated errors (Hendry, 1971). As in the time-series literature, it would be pedantic to delay exploration and application of the spatial maximum-likelihood models for want of this detailed proof. Equally, it would be valuable to have such a proof.

Constrained Random Simulation: The North Sea Oil Province†

K.E.ROSING, P.R.ODELL
Economisch Geografisch Instituut, Erasmus Universiteit, Rotterdam

Simulation modelling has been used by geographers in many contexts (for example land-use patterns, urbanization, and locational problems of economic activities) over the past ten or so years. These procedures are generally resorted to when there exists a complex net of relationships, particularly over a time dimension, which is not amenable to a probabalistic analytical solution. An alternative approach might be the derivation and solution of joint probability matrices culminating in a probability model capable of being tested inferentially (given the availability of real-world data for comparison); however, with the increasing order and increasing rank the solution of such matrices becomes increasingly cumbersome. When the phenomenon being investigated occurs along a time axis, a simulation model, with dynamic attributes, may also replicate more faithfully the real-world experience and give a more synthetic view, and hence a more enhanced understanding, than is possible through a static model.

For the above reasons it was felt that the development of a simulation model offered the best potential for the prediction of the future of discovery and production from the North Sea oil basin from 1968 into the 21st century. Any such model must eventually be judged in terms of its correspondence with reality. Such testing will not be possible in the case of the present model for many years. However, it is hoped, by basing it on a series of assumptions drawn from the development of other major oil provinces and by calibrating these assumptions in light of the early North Sea basin development, that such a correspondence will eventually be found.

The development of the North Sea province up to the end of March 1975 is shown in figure 1. With proven economically recoverable reserves already amounting to over 20 thousand million barrels (more than 3 thousand million tons) it is obviously a major province by any standards (see an earlier appreciation of its significance in Odell, 1973). In addition, the North Sea is a unique occurrence in that its development coincides in time with an increasing demand in Western Europe for an indigenous energy source and, perhaps even more important, in that it lies within a region of already high and intensive energy use.

---

† This paper is based on a study by Professor Odell and Dr. K.E.Rosing, *The North Sea Oil Province: An Attempt to Simulate its Development and Exploitation 1969-2029.* This is published by Kogan Page Ltd, 116a Pentonville Road, London N.1.

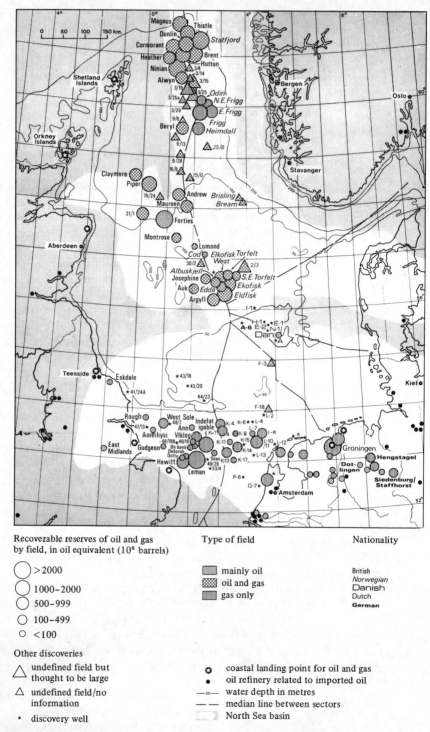

Figure 1. The North Sea basin: oil and gas discoveries up to the end of 1974. (© E.G.I.)

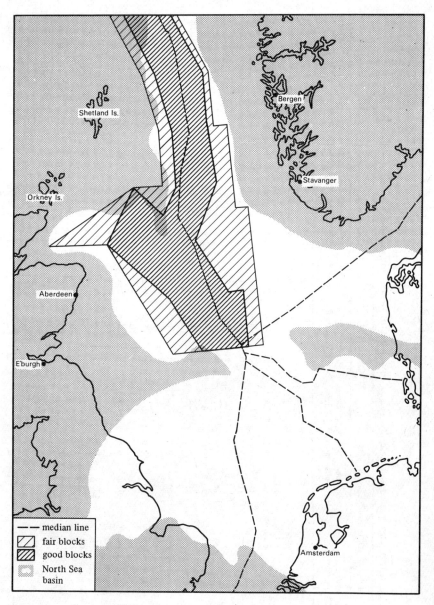

Figure 2. The North Sea basin: designated good and fair blocks in the oil province considered in this study. (© E.G.I.)

Table 1. The development of exploration and field discoveries—by classes of fields 1969–1988.

Year	Annual total number of wells	Annual total success rate (%)	Objective[a]	Class 1 fields number of wells	Class 1 fields success rate (%)	Class 1 fields number of fields	Class 2 fields number of wells	Class 2 fields success rate (%)	Class 2 fields number of fields	Class 3 fields number of wells	Class 3 fields success rate (%)	Class 3 fields number of fields	Class 4 fields number of wells	Class 4 fields success rate (%)	Class 4 fields number of fields
1 1969	8	6	cw	8	5·0	0·4	8	1·0	0·8	8	0·0	0·0	8	0·0	0·0
			ow												
2 1970	14	8	cw	10	7·0	0·7	4	7·0	0·28	14	0·0	0·0	14	0·0	0·0
			ow	4	1·0	0·04	10	1·0	0·1						
3 1971	20	10	cw	10	8·0	0·8	10	8·0	0·8	20	1·0	0·2	20	0·0	0·0
			ow	10	1·0	0·1	10	1·0	0·1						
4 1972	26	12	cw	8	9·0	0·72	18	9·0	1·62	26	1·0	0·26	26	0·5	0·13
			ow	18	1·5	0·27	8	1·5	0·12						
5 1973	34	12	cw	6	10·0	0·6	20	10·0	2·0	8	10·0	0·8	34	0·5	0·18
			ow	28	1·0	0·28	14	1·0	0·14	26	0·5	0·13			
6 1974	45	14	cw	3	11·0	0·33	22	11·0	2·42	20	11·0	2·2	45	1·2	0·54
			ow	42	0·8	0·34	23	1·0	0·23	25	1·0	0·25			
7 1975	60	14	cw	60	1·0	0·6	24	11·0	2·64	36	11·0	3·96	60	1·0	0·6
			ow				36	1·0	0·36	24	1·0	0·24			
8 1976	95	12	cw	95	0·67	0·62	17	10·0	1·7	53	10·0	5·3	25	10·0	2·5
			ow				78	0·67	0·52	42	0·67	0·28	70	0·67	0·49
9 1977	135	12	cw	135	0·5	0·68	5	10·0	0·5	75	10·0	7·5	55	10·0	5·5
			ow				130	0·75	0·94	60	0·75	0·45	85	0·75	0·64
10 1978	200	10	cw	200	0·4	0·8	2	8·0	0·16	93	8·0	7·44	105	8·0	8·4
			ow				198	0·53	1·04	108	0·53	0·57	95	0·53	0·5
11 1979	220	10	cw	220	0·3	0·66	220	0·5	1·1	44	8·0	3·52	176	8·0	14·08
			ow							176	1·2	2·12	44	1·2	0·53
12 1980	200	8	cw	200	0·3	0·6	200	0·3	0·6	24	7·0	1·68	176	7·0	12·32
			ow							176	0·4	0·7	24	0·4	0·1
13 1981	160	8	cw	160	0·3	0·48	160	0·3	0·48	14	7·0	0·98	146	7·0	10·22
			ow							146	0·4	0·58	14	0·4	0·06
14 1982	120	7	cw	120	0·1	0·12	120	0·3	0·36	8	6·0	0·48	112	6·0	6·72
			ow							112	0·6	0·67	8	0·6	0·05

Table 1 (continued).

Year		Annual total		Objective[a]	Class 1 fields			Class 2 fields			Class 3 fields			Class 4 fields		
		number of wells	success rate (%)		number of wells	success rate (%)	number of fields	number of wells	success rate (%)	number of fields	number of wells	success rate (%)	number of fields	number of wells	success rate (%)	number of fields
15	1983	90	7	cw	90	0·0	0·0	90	0·3	0·27	3	6·0	0·18	87	6·0	5·2
				ow		0·0	0·0				87	0·7	0·61	3	0·7	0·02
16	1984	75	6	cw	75	0·0	0·0	75	0·5	0·38	75	1·0	0·75	75	4·5	3·38
				ow												
17	1985	60	6	cw	60	0·0	0·0	60	0·5	0·3	60	1·0	0·6	60	4·5	2·6
				ow												
18	1986	50	5	cw	50	0·0	0·0	50	0·5	0·25	50	1·0	0·5	50	3·5	1·65
				ow												
19	1987	40	5	cw	40	0·0	0·0	40	0·0	0·0	40	1·5	0·6	40	3·5	1·4
				ow												
20	1988	25	5	cw	25	0·0	0·0	25	0·0	0·0	25	1·5	0·38	25	3·5	0·87
				ow												

[a] Class wells (cw): wells into structures expected to produce a discovery of the class shown; other wells (ow): wells producing a field outside the class expected.

In consequence in the model we have been able to assume that all oil discovered and technically producible will be produced and marketed as rapidly as possible at a normal or supernormal profit. Therefore the province will be developed as rapidly as the constraints of offshore technology, manpower, and hardware allow. Given this assumption the production potential becomes partly a function of the rates of discovery and appreciation and partly a function of the timing and speed of their depletion.

In order to simulate the development, and thereby arrive at a prediction of the development, a computer program was written to control the order and timing of the simulated discovery and appreciation, and to define the constraints for random variables. The various assumptions were quantified and written into this program. We shall now turn our attention to these assumptions and how they were made operational.

The average annual rate of discovery of initially declared reserves, a primary input, was defined as a function of the probable total number of wildcat wells, the variable success rate, and the various sizes of fields. There are 365 'prime blocks' in the North Sea, which we shall assume each require 3·3 wells for full exploration, and 261 'fair blocks' each requiring 1·8 wells per block (when all blocks are adjusted to the British size) (see Kitcat and Aitken, 1974), so giving a total of 1675 wildcat wells required for full exploration. All but 7 of these adjusted blocks lie within British or Norwegian waters (see figure 2). Legislation in these two countries requires that a licencee submit a work program of exploration prior to the granting of the licence. If the full exploration work is not carried out the company must relinquish the area, and the nation then may reallocate the area to another company. Therefore we may assume that these wildcats will be drilled (unless the country decides not to allocate blocks for drilling). Since the national laws also require the relinquishment of a substantial percentage of the area after a given time period with subsequent possible reallocation, and since there has also been a sequential allocation of blocks for exploration, then the total exploration effort will take place over a long period of time, during which the actual effort will be a function of the development of offshore drilling technology, manpower, and the availability of hardware.

These three constraints will dictate a buildup in the number of wildcat wells drilled, year by year, to a maximum of 220 in 1979 as shown in the second column of table 1. As shown in the third column of table 1 the assumed success rate varies from year to year and we assume, conservatively, that the highest rate (1:7 in 1974) has already been reached and will decline until it is uneconomic to continue exploration after the full 20-year period.

The remainder of table 1 is a joint probability matrix stratified by class of field size. (Since the total number of involved variables was relatively small the joint probability approach was possible.) There were, by

December 1974, over 173 different companies and consortia holding
exclusive licences on one or more blocks in the North Sea. Each of these
decision-making.groups orders its allocated blocks by rank and then it
plans to drill its largest and most promising structures first. Each wildcat
has some probability of finding a field of the size expected from the
inferential evidence (a 'class well', in table 1) but at the same time each
well has a lower probability of finding a field of a different size than
expected (an 'other well', in table 1). Thus the number of wells being
drilled in any year must be allocated between the four size-classes as class
wells with a probability, as shown, of finding a field in the class size, but
all wells aimed at a particular class of field also have a lower probability
of finding a field in one of the other classes, as shown in table 1. For
example, of the total number of 45 wells in 1974, 3 are exploring for
class 1 fields, 22 for class 2, 20 for class 3, and none for class 4. The 42
wells looking for class 2 and 3 also have a probability (0.8%) of finding a
class 1 field; the 25 looking for class 1 and 2 have a probability (1.0%)
of finding a class 3 field; the 25 looking for class 1 and 3 have a
probability (0.1%) of finding a class 2 field; and all 45 have a probability
(1.2%) of finding a class 4 field. Multiplying the probability times the
number of wells yields the average expected number of fields per class,
per year, and per type of objective.

The average number of fields per year and class is now transferred to
table 2 for each class. The number of class 4 fields is reduced by 25% on
the assumption that only 75% of the fields in this class will be of a size
that can be economically produced. The average number of fields (or in
the case of class 4, the average number of effective fields) is then multiplied
with an assumed average volume (see note 1 of table 2) for each class, so
giving a reserves figure for each class in each year (as given in table 2).
Summing across we arrive at the total addition to reserves for each year.

The calculated total reserves were then used as the expected mean
annual rate of the discovery of initially declared reserves. Figure 3 shows
the curve which was derived from these figures. Values were then read
off the curve to provide values in an array—the normal rate of discovery
of initially declared reserves—for the program.

Since the estimates and assumptions regarding each well and each
discovered field were confined to the joint probability matrix, and the results
are in the form of total yearly discoveries, the simulation itself deals only
with yearly discovered totals irrespective of the number of fields discovered
per year.

A similar series of values were developed for the coefficient of variation
of the average annual rate of discovery. This curve represents moderate
certainty about the volume of finds in the early years, increasing certainty
as the stratigraphic history becomes better understood, followed by
decreasing certainty for the second half of the period when less likely

Table 2. Derivation of mean curve of annually discovered reserves (initially declared).

Year	Class 1 fields		Class 2 fields		Class 3 fields		Class 4 fields		Annual total	
	number	reserves (10^6 ton)	number	reserves (10^6 ton)	number	reserves (10^6 ton)	number (and effective number)	reserves (10^6 ton)	fields	reserves (10^6 ton)
1 1969	0·4	80	0·08	8					0·48	88
2 1970	0·74	148	0·38	38					1·12	186
3 1971	0·9	180	0·9	90	0·2	10			2·0	280
4 1972	0·99	198	1·74	174	0·26	13	0·13 (0·09)	2	3·12	387
5 1973	0·88	176	2·14	214	0·93	47	0·18 (0·14)	3	4·13	440
6 1974	0·67	134	2·65	265	2·45	123	0·54 (0·41)	8	6·31	530
7 1975	0·6	120	3·0	300	4·2	210	0·6 (0·45)	9	8·4	639
8 1976	0·62	124	2·22	222	5·58	279	2·99 (2·24)	45	11·41	670
9 1977	0·68	136	1·44	144	7·95	398	6·14 (4·61)	92	16·21	760
10 1978	0·8	160	1·2	120	8·01	401	8·9 (6·7)	134	18·91	815
11 1979	0·66	132	1·1	110	5·64	282	14·61 (10·96)	219	22·01	743
12 1980	0·6	120	0·6	60	2·38	119	12·42 (9·32)	186	16·0	485
13 1981	0·48	96	0·48	48	1·56	78	10·28 (7·71)	154	12·8	376
14 1982	0·12	24	0·36	36	1·15	58	6·77 (5·08)	102	8·4	220
15 1983			0·27	27	0·79	40	5·22 (3·92)	79	6·28	146
16 1984			0·38	38	0·75	38	3·4 (2·55)	51	4·53	127
17 1985			0·3	30	0·6	30	2·6 (1·95)	39	3·5	99
18 1986			0·25	25	0·5	25	1·65 (1·24)	25	2·4	75
19 1987					0·6	30	1·4 (1·05)	21	2·0	51
20 1988					0·38	19	0·87 (0·65)	13	1·25	32
Total	9·14	1828	19·49	1949	43·93	2200	78·70	1182	151·26	7149

Notes:

(1) The number of fields in each class in each year is derived from table 1. The following average sizes have been assumed for fields in the different classes. Class 1—200 million tons; class 2—100 million tons; class 3—50 million tons; class 4—20 million tons. Only 75% of class 4 fields (the numbers given in brackets in the table) discovered are considered to be effective, on the assumption that the other 25% will be too small to be profitable to develop.

(2) Although further work remains to be done to validate the results of this analysis in respect of number of fields, field size, and total reserves *vis-à-vis* the accepted lognormal distribution of oil fields within a province, it may be noted that a largest field with >150 million tons of oil reserves (as declared on initial discovery), a smallest commercial field with 15 million tons, and a total of 151 fields appears to be compatible with a lognormal distribution of fields in a province with total reserves of the size indicated in the final column of the table.

structures are being drilled. These values are shown in figure 4 and were also incorporated in the program. The standard deviation for each year was then calculated from the coefficient of variation and the mean.

Subroutine GAUSS (IBM, 1970), a random-number generator, was provided with the set of mean values and standard deviations and returned a value for each year from a normal probability distribution. This value was taken to be the volume of oil initially declared as recoverable reserves from *all fields* discovered in 1 of the 20 years of exploration. Since a normal random-number generator was used, negative volumes were possible.

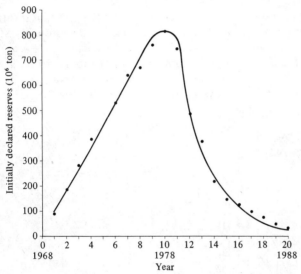

Figure 3. Mean curve of initially declared recoverable reserves derived from tables 1 and 2. (© E.G.I.)

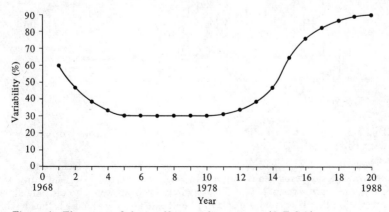

Figure 4. The curve of the coefficient of variation. (© E.G.I.)

However, since negative oil volumes cannot be found, these volumes were set equal to zero. Additionally, if any year's total volume of oil was less than 10 million tons, it was assumed to come from fields which were too small to produce[1] and the volume was set equal to zero. The annual volumes of oil initially discovered and the variability are displayed in figure 5 which is based on 100 iterations of the model.

When reserves are initially announced they are actually a probability statement based on test data. Over the years, with more drilling experience on an oil field and with production experience from the field, the variability of the probability field decreases and, generally, the estimate appreciates. The companies concerned also appear to be rather conservative in their public announcements of such commercially important information.

The phenomenon of reserves appreciation has been thoroughly studied in Alberta where a normal appreciation factor, relating 20th-year knowledge to the discovery-year estimate, has been found to be 8·89. On a world-wide basis such accurate information is not available but 4–5-fold appreciation seems to have occurred worldwide over the period

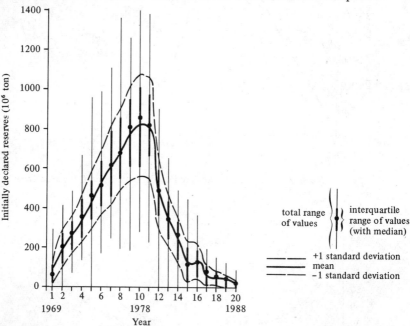

Figure 5. Results from 100 iterations of annual rates of discovery of initially declared reserves. (© E.G.I.)

[1]Note that this safeguard against 'using' reserves from fields which are too small to be economically developed is additional to the overall earlier safeguard introduced in the normal curves when 25% of discovered class 4 fields were also discounted on the assumption that they were too small to be of interest. The model is thus doubly conservative with respect to field sizes.

1950–1970 (for a detailed analysis of the appreciation of reserves see
Odell, 1974). The phenomenon is, indeed, already recognisable in the
case of the North Sea for the Ekofisk field has already appreciated by
over 50% to 1800 million barrels in 4 years; Brent by 125% to 2250
million barrels in 2 years, and Thistle by over 60% to 1300 million barrels
in less than one year.

Thus we must include the dynamic process of the appreciation of
reserves in any model such as this, but since new technology, which enables
initial declarations of reserves to come closer to the figure for ultimate
recovery, implies a decreasing importance for the appreciation factor (and
since this is in any case a conservative model) a mean appreciation factor
of only 2 (doubling) has been used. As simulated in this model, the
appreciations can occur in three stages; the first, randomly, from 1 to 3
years after discovery; the second, randomly, 2 to 6 years after the first
appreciation; and the third, also randomly, between 5 and 11 years after
the second appreciation (see table 3). The volumes of the appreciations
were related to the volume of the initial discovery, with the first appreciation
being the largest and the third being the smallest, so representing reality in
having successively smaller appreciations over time as the final producible
limits of a field are approached. The constraints on the volumes of the
appreciations are shown in table 3, which shows in addition their time
scale.

Subroutine RANDU (IBM, 1970) was used to generate a rectangular
probability field with cutoff points as specified in table 3 to determine
the volumes (and timing). Discoveries which had zero volumes or which
were set to zero because the field size was assumed to be too small could
not, of course, be appreciated. This is also conservative in the light of
world experience where uneconomically sized initial reserves can, and do
on reappraisal, become producible; but this is in line with the generally
conservative nature of the model. The year-by-year volume and variability
in the appreciation of reserves from 100 iterations of the model are shown
in figure 6.

Table 3.

Appreciation number	Volume of appreciation		Time of appreciation	
	minimum (%)	maximum (%)	minimum (no. of years)	maximum (no. of years)
1	25	85	1	3
2	15	45	2	6
3	0	30	5	11
Sum	40	160	8	20
Average	100		14	

The yearly total of discovered and appreciated reserves is, of course, a combination of the two phenomena—shown separately in the paper so far. They are now combined and, as figure 7 indicates, the degree of variability in the simulation for any year is quite high. The mean and standard deviation, and the median and inner quartile range, show a rapid increase to 1979, largely composed of discoveries, followed by a slow decline increasingly composed of appreciations. Although the last discovery occurs in 1988, new reserves are being added as late as 2008.

To simulate the production of each discovery or appreciation a set of eight depletion curves (see figure 8), each covering a period of 20 years, were drawn and their volumes set equal to unity. Although depletion curves are nearly infinitely variable, the eight used here represent a range

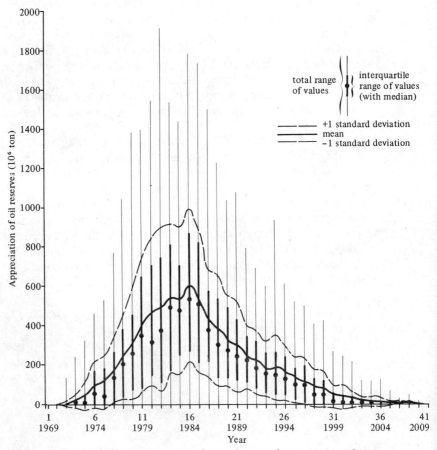

Figure 6. Results from 100 iterations of annual rates of appreciation of reserves 1969–2009. (© E.G.I.)

of occurrences within certain observed constraints. These constraints are:
(1) Full depletion of any set of reserves to take place over 20 years;
(2) 66–75% of the reserves to be depleted in production years 1–10 and
    the remaining 34–25% in years 11–20;
(3) The buildup period to peak production rate to be between 4 and 7
    years;
(4) The peak production rate itself to lie within the range of 6–10% of
    the original total of reserves to be depleted.

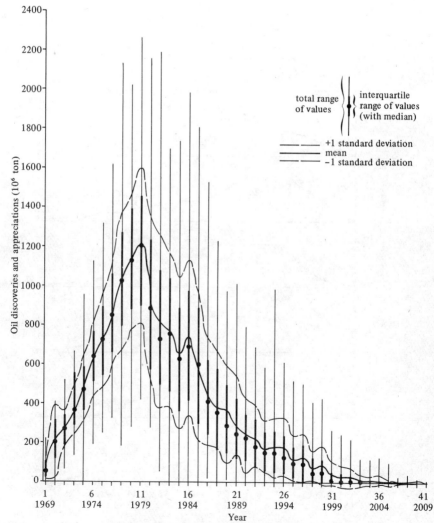

Figure 7. Results from 100 iterations of annual rates of discovery and appreciation
of reserves 1969–2009. (© E.G.I.)

These curves constituted additional data for the program. For each set
of reserves one of these curves was randomly selected (RANDU) and the
volume of the discovery or appreciation was multiplied by the height of
the curve for each year. For simplicity the assumption was made that all
fields discovered in one year would begin production at the same time as
each other; the lag between discovery and production was randomly

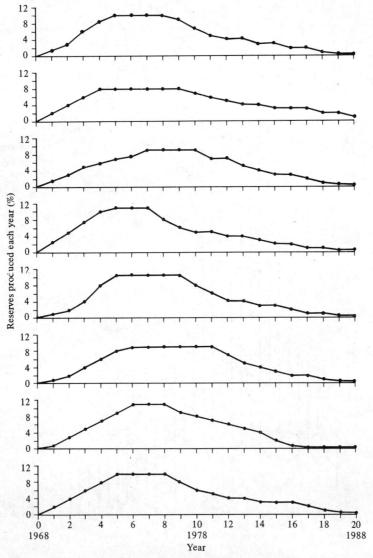

Figure 8. A range of eight curves within the given constraints for the depletion of
any set of reserves. (© E.G.I.)

Simulation of the North Sea oil province   119

chosen to be 2–5 years. A similar procedure was used for the sets of reserves emerging from the three appreciations. The resulting 80 scaled depletion curves were not plotted in a temporal sequence. Instead, the initial discovery of year 1 (1969) was plotted first, followed by the scaled depletion curve for the 1st appreciation of the 1969-discovered reserves, then the 2nd appreciation, and then the 3rd appreciation of the 1969 discoveries. The process was then repeated for the initially discovered

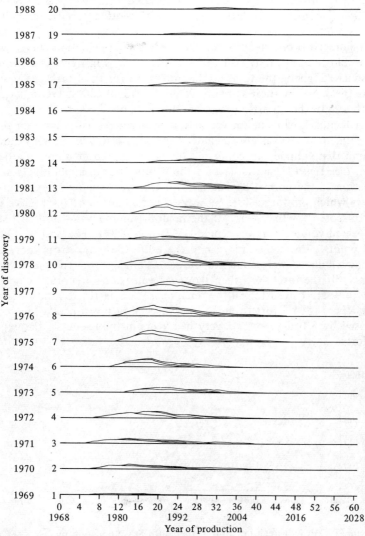

Figure 9. Year-by-year noncumulative production curves for each year calculated from the initially declared reserves and the three appreciations of the reserves. The volumes contained under the curves are all proportional. (© E.G.I.)

reserves of the 2nd, 3rd, ..., 20th year. Figure 9 shows the production
curves of each of the discovery years, together with the appreciations of
each, for one iteration.

A full iteration contains a maximum of 80 curves. However, an 0·02
probability of there being a disaster (for example a collapse of a rig; a
blowout; pollution leading to a shutdown, etc.) in any year was allowed.
In such a case the discovered reserves were eliminated from the model
together with all the appreciations associated with that year's discovery.
In figure 9 there is no discovery-year 1983 plotted because of such a
'disaster'.

Figure 10 is one iteration of the model. The depletion curves which
were plotted separately (for each discovery year) in figure 8 are now all
cumulated, giving the total production curve for the North Sea basin. As
it is the same iteration as figure 9, the four depletion curves associated
with 1983—the 'disaster year'—are not present.

A feedback element for the loss of management confidence in their
investment plans was also included. As each discovery year's volume was
found that volume was compared to the mean expected volume for that
year (see figure 3 and table 2) if the volume was disappointingly small in
relation to the normal expectation for that year (implying exploration
costs which produced little by way of potential rewards), negative points
were scored for that year. If the random volume was <30% of the mean
expected volume, −1 was scored. If it was <20%, −2; and for <10%,
−3 points. From the 3rd year to the 20th, the scores from the year
being simulated were added to the scores arising from the preceding 2
years. If the total ≤−5 then the mean values on the normal curve,
figure 3, are halved for all the remaining years in the iteration. In this
way there is an effort to model the cutback in investment which could be
caused by 3 bad years or 2 very bad years in the results of the exploration
efforts.

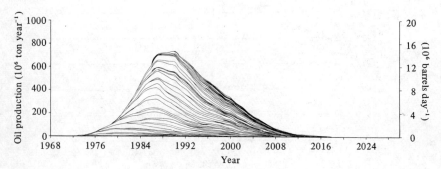

Figure 10. An individual iteration of the North Sea production model. (© E.G.I.)

If the above condition was fulfilled and the values were halved, then randomly chosen volumes for good years were checked as well; if the volume randomly discovered was >125% of the mean expected, +1 was scored; for >150%, +2; and >175%, +3. At the same time, checking continued for small discoveries which were negatively scored. A 3-year total of +5 resulted in a doubling, or a 3-year total of −5 resulted in a further halving. Additionally, if there was a disaster (see above) −1 was scored for the year in which it *should have* begun production.

This feedback had the most effect near the end of the period of exploration [when the coefficient of variation (figure 4) was large and the mean small]. The feedback often acted to cause exploration to tail off before the end of the 20 years. However, in one iteration an early failure—from which there was no recovery—resulted in a very low development both of reserves and of production (see figure 11).

The superimposed top lines from 100 iterations are shown in figure 11. Each of these represents an estimate of the likely minimum level of production over the period. The bottom 10 were eliminated to arrive at the 90% confidence limit (so following the practice of oil companies) and the mean of the remaining 90 curves was calculated. In figure 12 this mean curve is shown superimposed on the curve of 75% of the expected demand for oil in Western Europe over the rest of the present century (Odell, 1975). 75% of the expected demand for oil has been used because: (a) certain areas of Europe, for example southern France and Italy, will be more economically supplied with North African oil than North Sea oil; (b) some countries have or are entering into long-term commitments to purchase oil from existing suppliers; and (c) a certain amount of exogenous oil will always be required for refinery blending purposes with the light North Sea crudes in order to meet European product-demand patterns. This last will become less important, however, as northwestern

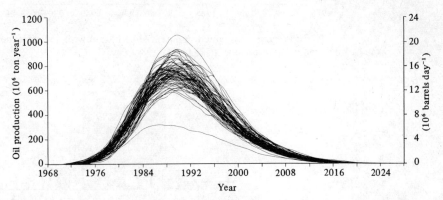

Figure 11. Results from 100 iterations of the production model. Note the 'failed' curve. This represents the 1% probability of a curve of minimum production as low as this. (© E.G.I.)

Europe increases its use of natural gas which, as it is being found associated with oil, will become more plentiful.

The mean result from the simulation model on the long-term oil potential from the North Sea basin indicates that it can indeed supply 75% of the total demand for oil for the 15-year period from 1982 to 1996, and so opens up the possibility that some constraints on the rate of the development of the basin might be appropriate so as to keep the production potential much more closely related to the developing Western European demand position, and so enable oil to be 'saved' for use in the first quarter of the 21st century.   Beyond that time it is conceivable that the Western European economy will become orientated to the use of other cheaper and/or preferred energy sources which, by then, will have been made available by technological developments.   In brief, the North Sea oil production potential may well be great enough—given full and appropriately timed development, as well as the efficient use of oil implied in the demand curve in figure 12—to see the whole of Western Europe through into the post-oil age without any further undue dependence on supplies of foreign oil.

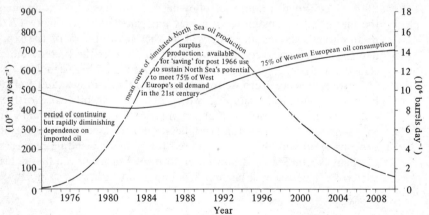

Figure 12. The mean curve of production potential compared with 75% of expected western European demand for oil. (© E.G.I.)

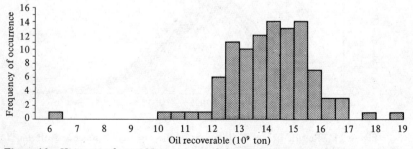

Figure 13. Histogram from 100 iterations of the total quantities of oil recoverable. (© E.G.I.)

The model has predicted the potential of the basin to be between two and nearly four times the volumes indicated by the oil companies (see figure 13). The oil companies figures are now being commonly quoted but the results of this investigation indicate the need to examine a broader range of policy options for the future of Western Europe's energy supply than those so far envisaged. The first requirement in looking at the broader range of options is an adequate international monitoring and evaluation system at a northwestern European level for the North Sea basin's development. Such monitoring of the basin's development would provide the essential device needed to give the information on which the shorter (5 to 10 year) policy options can be determined. Evaluation, based on adequate information, would then indicate options for the next two generations. In this respect, the simulation model as presented in this paper can, hopefully, be used as the prototype from which to develop a more sophisticated and a more elegant approach to the longer-term potential from the province—not only for oil, but also for natural gas, the availability of which will, of course, be increasing at the same time. The simulations of future possibilities can provide a control against which actual developments can be examined for their significance, and so provide a tool for determining policies such as those, for example, which seek to vary the rate of development of the oil and gas resources of this major oil and gas province for political and economic reasons.

References

IBM, 1970, *IBM System 360 Scientific Subroutine Package Version 3, Program Manual GH20-0202-4,* program 360a-CM-03X (IBM, New York), p.77.

Kitcat and Aitken, 1974, "The outlook for large mobile drilling rigs on the European continental shelf", Investment Research Division, Kitcat and Aitken, 9 Bishopsgate, London EC2.

Odell, P. R., 1973, "Indigenous oil and gas and Western Europe's energy policy options", *Energy Policy,* 1 (1), 47-63.

Odell, P. R., 1974, *Energy Needs and Resources* (Macmillan, London).

Odell, P. R., 1975, "European alternatives to oil imports from OPEC countries; oil and gas as an indigenous resource", *Energy Policy Planning in the European Community,* Ed. J. A. M. Alting van Genson (Sijthoff, Leiden).

Urban Commodity Flows and the Environmental Balance

S.M.MACGILL
University of Leeds

1 Introduction

We may consider that the ultimate aim of industrial activity in a given region is (a) to provide the stream of goods demanded by final consumers within that region or (b) to satisfy export demands. The activities themselves are interdependent, they require each others' inputs for the manufacture of their own outputs, and thus give rise to a movement of goods between the spatially separated industries in the region. The activities are also dependent on the environment, both as supplier of natural resources and as receptor of residual wastes.

The work below is an approach to modelling, at the urban level, those flows of materials generated by industrial activity. A model will be developed which can trace the flows of materials between the various sectors in the different zones of the city and which can at the same time predict the environmental impact of this process. There are therefore several aspects to consider—a spatial movement of goods, an intersectoral movement of goods, and what might be called the 'environmental repercussions' of the industrial system—and it is appropriate to consider briefly the existing work in these areas which might influence the development of the model in hand.

The modelling of the spatial movement of goods is not particularly well-developed (see for example Carroll, 1971; French and Watson, 1971) especially when compared with the state of the art of person–trips modelling. The reason for this lies in the nature rather than the importance of the flows—the movement of goods is a multifirm activity with no central organisation, and with enormous diversity in products; measurement and study of these flows is therefore difficult. Some work has, however, been done in this field; for example Maltby (1973) has used regression analysis to estimate the generation of goods movements from manufacturing establishments, and Chisholm and O'Sullivan (1973) have studied interregional freight flows for the British economy, but on a much larger scale than that envisaged for the present approach.

Despite its limitations (the strict linearity assumptions are probably the most obvious), the elegance, convenience, and comprehensiveness of input–output analysis has led to its widespread use for dealing with intersectoral flows in an economy. Its most familiar use is at the national level, but a significant number of urban and regional level input–output studies have also been made, such as Artle (1965) for the Stockholm economy, and Morrison (1973) for Peterborough, to name but two.

Urban or regional input–output accounts are compiled either by direct survey of local industries or, more usually, through some adjustment of the national input–output coefficients. There are several more theoretical problems which approaches of the type given here need to overcome. These concern (a) the representation of flows between the sectors of the urban area and the world outside, and (b) the flows between the spatially-separated industries within the city. Some sort of interregional input–output method is needed, and the approach of Leontief and Strout (1963) adopted by Wilson (1970a, chapter 3) is likely to be more appropriate for present purposes than the type given for example in Isard (1960). This point is discussed further below.

There is an increasing body of literature concerned with the environmental repercussions of industrial activity and its potentially dangerous effects, see for example Meadows *et al.* (1972), Dales (1968), and various attempts at modelling these aspects. Leontief (1970), for instance, extends the usual input–output table to incorporate residuals flows, and this has subsequently been taken up by other writers (including the present one); Wilen (1973) adopts what is possibly a more comprehensive approach, which introduces a full set of coefficients to depict the complete economic system–ecosystem interaction, but which requires a lot of data.

Victor (1972) reviews a number of such approaches, including those of Leontief (1970), Kneese *et al.* (1970), Isard (1969), and others, before introducing his own economic–ecological model.

2 Framework for the present model

The approach taken in developing the present model is to view the industrial activities and their associated materials flows as a materials balance problem (Kneese *et al.*, 1970). The weight of all materials used as inputs to the manufacture of goods must be fully accounted for at each stage in production; industrial processes are thus seen as a transformation of a set of inputs, including resources, into outputs (including wastes) and, stock increases aside, the total weight of inputs and of outputs must be the same. The model outlined below represents a translation of this materials-balance concept to the urban economy, and therefore involves the development of a system capable of quantifying the exchange of all types of materials between the various spatially separated sectors (industrial, household, and environmental) in such an economy.

The relevant flows are probably most easily explained with the help of a diagram (figure 1). Sector m in zone i represents a typical industry in the urban area. Its inputs take the form of imported goods from the rest of the world beyond the city boundary, manufactured products from other sectors within the city, or resources from the environment. Outputs produced by this sector are destined for final consumers in the region, other sectors in the region, or are exported.

In addition to these flows of what might be called 'useful goods', waste by-products are also produced and freely emitted into the ambient environment.

Final consumers are considered here as an exogenous component. Although we might recognise that they too require resources and emit wastes, and thus interact with the environment, the modelling of these flows is considered outside the scope of the present analysis. Hence no such flows are depicted in figure 1.

The basic variable chosen for the present model is X_{ij}^{mnk} which defines the flow of commodity k from industry m in zone i to industry n in zone j. In a model of this kind, it was thought desirable to distinguish between commodities and industries even though this increases the number of dimensions involved. Not all commodities are representative of any given industry, most industries produce more than one commodity, and the same commodity may be produced by a number of industries. Thus the usual but rather inappropriate assumption of a one-to-one correspondence between industries and commodities (often necessitated by the need to invert input–output relationships) is not considered here, and this is likely to prove particularly useful in further developments of the current model.

Commodity is a general term used to signify any material used or produced by industries; thus it may be a natural resource—water, air, sand, coal (but notice the distinction made below between coal as a resource and coal as a manufactured product); a manufactured (or intermediate) product—steel, cloth, and so on: a residual by-product—solid, liquid and gaseous of any kind.

Resources are taken from the environment and used by industries where they are found. Intermediate or manufactured products are supplied and used by industries[1] (or used by final consumers). Wastes are emitted by industries directly into the environment.

It is theoretically possible to use any level of classification for commodities in the model, but a very fine one would obviously lead to enormous dimensions, with associated data and computing problems.

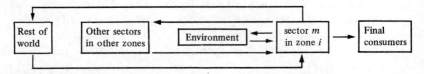

Figure 1. Materials flows for sector m in zone i.

---

[1] Unmined coal is considered a resource, but mined coal as an intermediate product. Once mined, the coal may be considered as an output from the mining industry rather than as an output from the environment.

The three kinds of commodities given above will be represented by k, distinguishing between $k \in R$, Q, or W depending on whether k is a resource, a manufactured product, or waste respectively.

As already implied, the sectors (labelled m or n) correspond largely to the industries of the region, following perhaps the industry groupings given under the Standard Industrial Classification. In terms of the given variable X_{ij}^{mnk}, the first superscript (m in this case) denotes the producing sector, and the second (n) the consuming sector. As with commodities, industries may be taken at various levels of classification. The environment may also be considered as a sector, but in recognition of its obvious differences from the urban industries, it will be given a distinctive label e. [It would probably be more useful to subdivide the environmental sector into three, namely land, air and water; it would be a straightforward matter to incorporate such an extension into the given model.]

The subscripts i and j represent the zones in the area under study (for example as given by administrative boundaries), the first subscript gives the origin of the flow and the second the destination. The spatial system is closed by representing the rest of the world by subscript o. Thus X_{io}^{mnk} denotes the export of k from industry m in zone i to industry n in the rest of the world; similarly X_{oj}^{mnk} is an import term for zone j. Both these terms will be treated as separate variables to be determined endogenously by the model.

The exogenous final-demand sector, labelled Y (with sub- and superscripts to be attached later), includes domestic consumers, public authorities, and net investment in stocks and capital equipment. Each of these ideally deserves separate consideration. They have been lumped together in one term for convenience.

Steady-state equilibrium is assumed, so that in addition to X_{ij}^{mnk} giving the flow of k defined above, we may sum over any of the indices. For example X_{*j}^{*nk},

where $X_{*j}^{*nk} = \sum_{im} X_{ij}^{mnk}$

gives the use (and also the requirement) of commodity k in industry n in zone j. All flows will be measured by weight, and refer to some implicit time period.

3 The model structure

The model uses an entropy-maximising approach and is an extension of the type given in Wilson (1970a, chapter 3; 1970b). Any known information about the flow of commodities between industries and/or zones is put in the form of constraints, and by maximising the entropy of the probability distribution associated with the flow variables, a solution may be found which represents the most probable distribution of materials between the industries and zones, given the known information. As more information becomes available, so the constraints may be adapted, and the model improved.

Before the particular constraints and associated details of the present model are outlined, some further preliminary comment is perhaps appropriate. Using entropy-maximising methods, Wilson explores a family of possible models that might be used to depict the interregional flow of commodities. It is assumed in all cases that these commodity flows must satisfy Leontief–Strout multiregional input–output relationships, but the input–output model that would result by including only such relationships is integrated with some type of gravity model behaviour by way of additional constraints. Thus we may derive an unconstrained gravity input–output model, a production- or attraction-constrained gravity input–output model, or a doubly constrained gravity input–output model. The nature of the gravity-type behaviour that can be incorporated depends on the information available for use with the model.

The model developed below builds on this foundation and introduces a clear distinction between industries, as producers and consumers of commodities, and the commodities themselves. This modifies the form of the constraint equations, and of the input–output relationships in particular. Further modifications are introduced via the incorporation of the materials-balance concept as a constraint in the model. This links the flow of manufactured goods normally associated with commodity flow models, with resource and residual flows for each industry. We may thus derive estimates for resource and residual flows based on the materials-balance constraints integrated with the more familiar input–output conditions. Endogenous model estimates for urban exports and imports arise naturally, given the inclusion of terms X_{io}^{mnk} and X_{oj}^{mnk} alongside the main model variable, where appropriate, in the constraints.

The following illustrate the type of constraint equations that would be suitable for the present kind of model.

3.1 A production constraint
The manufacture of goods in an industry may be assumed to be linearly related to the employment there. Information is available on total employment by industry by zone, so that this constraint may be taken as

$$\sum_{jnk} X_{ij}^{mnk} + \sum_{nk} X_{io}^{mnk} + \sum_{jk} Y_{ij}^{mk} = b^m E_i^m \,, \qquad k \in Q \,, \tag{1}$$

where in equation (1) Y_{ij}^{mk} represents the exogenous demand in zone j for product k from industry m in zone i; b^m is the output (by weight) per employee in industry m; and E_i^m is the total employment in industry m in zone i. Thus the left-hand side shows the outputs from industry m in zone i in terms of the model flow variables and flows to final consumers, and the right-hand side shows this output in terms of known industry employment and productivity data.

This constraint could be improved in two main ways; by replacing E_i^m by E_i^{mk} (that is the employment required per output of each commodity in each industry, by zone), in which case the flow of commodities rather than the more aggregate flow of total industry output would be constrained; or by obtaining data on output per employee by zone—as it stands equation (1) cannot allow for the productivity of labour, b^m, to vary in different zones of the city.

3.2 Input-output relationships
As mentioned above, we may appeal to the information available in input-output tables in estimating interindustry flows of materials. General familiarity with such tables and the relationships that may be derived from them will be assumed (see for example Isard, 1960; Stone and Brown, 1962) but some comment on their use in relation to the present model variables is appropriate.

3.2.1 *Industry requirement of intermediate products*
As indicated above, the Leontief–Strout assumption for multiregional input-output relationships will be adopted, namely that industries in one zone are not concerned about the origin or destination in space of their inputs or outputs; it does not matter whether they are demanded from or supplied to other zones in the city, or whether they imported or exported. Thus for industries n in zone j we may postulate the following interindustry relation:

$$\sum_{im} X_{ij}^{mnk} + \sum_m X_{oj}^{mnk} = a_j^{kn}\left(\sum_{imk'} X_{ji}^{nmk'} + \sum_{mk'} X_{jo}^{nmk'} + \sum_{ik'} Y_{ji}^{nk'}\right),$$
$$k, k' \in Q. \qquad (2)$$

This states that the amount of a given commodity k required by the industries in a given zone j (which can be met by flows from other industries elsewhere in the area and by imports, the terms on the left-hand side) is linearly related to the level of output of these industries (the terms in parentheses on the right-hand side). Coefficients a_j^{kn} give the input by weight of commodity k required per unit output of industry n in zone j[2].

It would, however, be very difficult to obtain technical coefficients at the urban zonal level as in many cases this would amount to knowing the production function of each establishment. It is therefore appropriate to sum this constraint over zones j to give an input-output relation for the

[2] The assumption of linearity that is required when using input-output accounts in this way is possibly less serious when applied to physical material flows (that is when the flows are measured by weight) than when applied to their monetary equivalents, as there is not as much scope for economies of scale in the former case.

whole urban area

$$\sum_{ijm} X_{ij}^{mnk} + \sum_{jm} X_{oj}^{mnk} = a^{kn}\left(\sum_{ijmk'} X_{ji}^{nmk'} + \sum_{jmk'} X_{jo}^{nmk'} + \sum_{ijk'} Y_{ji}^{nk'}\right) ,$$
$$k, k' \in Q . \qquad (3)$$

Thus we have a purely intersectoral input–output equation.

As an alternative to equation (3) it would be possible to consider separately the commodity inputs that are supplied from within the city, and those that have to be imported. Thus

$$\sum_{ijm} X_{ij}^{mnk} = g^{kn}\left(\sum_{ijmk'} X_{ji}^{nmk'} + \sum_{jmk'} X_{jo}^{nmk'} + \sum_{ijk'} Y_{ji}^{nk'}\right) , \qquad k, k' \in Q , \qquad (4)$$

$$\sum_{jm} X_{oj}^{mnk} = h^{kn}\left(\sum_{ijmk'} X_{ji}^{nmk'} + \sum_{jmk'} X_{jo}^{nmk'} + \sum_{ijk'} Y_{ji}^{nk'}\right) , \qquad k, k' \in Q . \qquad (5)$$

Equations (4) and (5) possibly make better use than equation (3) of local data (if available). The coefficients g^{kn} in equation (4) are those that would appear in the urban (or possibly regional) input–output table, and coefficients h^{kn} in equation (5) would be derived from the urban (or again, possibly regional) imports matrix.

3.2.2 *Resource requirements*
The requirement of resources from the environment may be assumed linearly related to industrial output.

$$\sum_{j} X_{jj}^{enk} = f^{kn}\left(\sum_{ijmk'} X_{ji}^{nmk'} + \sum_{jmk'} X_{jo}^{nmk'} + \sum_{ijk'} Y_{ji}^{nk'}\right) , \quad k \subset R , \quad k' \in Q . \quad (6)$$

Coefficients f^{kn} show the input of resource k required per unit output of industry n in the urban area. Note that in view of the restrictions on the definition of resources (that they are used where they are found), there is no transfer across space of this class of commodity. This is reflected in the term X_{jj}^{enk} on the left-hand side of equation (6). A similar restriction affects resource flows, see equation (10) below.

3.2.3 *Industry production of intermediate products*
The advantages of freely distinguishing between industries and commodities have already been mentioned, but this does mean that we need a constraint to tie particular commodities to particular industries—as yet there is nothing to show which commodities are produced by which industries, or how much of each commodity is in fact produced. To obtain data for the interindustry relationships derived in section 3.2.2, we would appeal to the so-called absorption and/or imports matrices (of the type given for example by the Central Statistical Office (1973, tables B and C, pages 38–53). We can resolve our new difficulty of needing to know something about the commodity production of each industry by turning to the so-called

make matrix (for example Central Statistical Office, 1973, table A, pages 30–37). However, as with equations in 3.2.2 above, an assumption of linearity is again required before the data can be used with this model, either (a) the commodity composition of an industry's output remains the same, regardless of the level of that output; or (b) each industry maintains its market share in the production of a given commodity. Thus case (a) gives (ignoring final-demand terms throughout this section):

$$\frac{X_{**}^{m*k} + X_{*o}^{m*k}}{X_{**}^{m**} + X_{*o}^{m**}} = D^{mk} \, ,$$

where D^{mk} is a constant. Thus the following may be taken as a constraint:

$$D^{mk}(X_{**}^{m**} + X_{*o}^{m**}) = X_{**}^{m*k} + X_{*o}^{m*k} \, , \qquad k \in Q \, . \tag{7}$$

In a similar way for case (b) we have

$$d^{mk}(X_{**}^{**k} + X_{*o}^{**k}) = X_{**}^{m*k} + X_{*o}^{m*k} \, , \qquad k \in Q \, , \tag{8}$$

where d^{mk} in equation (8) is industry m's market share in the production of commodity k.

Case (b) is possibly more appealing; market-share coefficients are probably more stable than the commodity composition of an industry's output, which is likely to fluctuate much more in response to changes in final demand for particular products. However, although equation (8) allows for the commodity composition of an industry's output to vary, the earlier input–output equations, for example equation (3), assume that industry input requirements for a particular commodity will not vary unless the total level of output (rather than the commodity composition) varies. This lends some weight in favour of choosing case (a) here, as this former case is more compatible with these earlier input–output assumptions.

3.2.4 An improved interindustry relation
Ideally, equations (3) [or (4) and (5)] and (7) or (8) should be combined into a single relationship, but this would require rather more detailed information. Thus it would be desirable to be able to use a coefficient $a^{kk'n}$ which gives the k input requirement per unit output of commodity k' in industry n. This would be more satisfactory for three main reasons:
(a) The use of this coefficient would avoid an unrealistic assumption, currently embodied in constraints (2), (3), and (4) or (5), that industry input requirements vary only with the level of output—that is, regardless of the commodity composition of that output [see the terms in parentheses in for example equation (2)]. This assumption is particularly serious if sectors are very highly aggregated.
(b) The use of the coefficient $a^{kk'n}$ automatically ties commodities to industries so that constraints (7) or (8) with their own strong linearity assumptions could be dropped.

(c) The term $a^{kk'n}$ is necessarily more satisfactory, because it is at a finer level than the original technical coefficient.

The corresponding interindustry relation [replacing equations (3) and (7) or (8)] would then be:

$$\sum_{ijm} X_{ij}^{mnk} + \sum_{jm} X_{oj}^{mnk} = \sum_{k'} a^{kk'n}\left(\sum_{ijm} X_{ji}^{nmk'} + \sum_{jm} X_{jo}^{nmk'} + \sum_{ij} Y_{ji}^{nk'}\right),$$

$$k, k' \in Q. \qquad (9)$$

3.2.5 Residuals flows

Following Leontief (1970) the usual input–output table may be extended to incorporate residual flows. Thus the output of any particular waste product from a sector is assumed linearly dependent on the production of useful goods. Again it is most likely that the relationship will have to be taken at the urban, rather than the zonal level. This gives

$$\sum_{i} X_{ii}^{mek} = A^{mk}\left(\sum_{ijnk'} X_{ij}^{mnk'} + \sum_{ink'} X_{io}^{mnk'} + \sum_{ijk'} Y_{ij}^{mk'}\right),$$

$$k \in W, \quad k' \in Q, \qquad (10)$$

where here, coefficients A^{mk} give waste k produced per unit output of industry m.

3.3 Materials balance

A model is being developed which takes account of the weight of all goods used or produced by industries in the city; that is, the weight of all material inputs must be accounted for as outputs. We may adopt this as a constraint in the model. This amounts to applying the law of conservation of mass to the industrial activities in the city.

Thus at the industry level the total mass inputs into each industry must equal the total mass outputs from each industry; at the zonal level the total mass inputs into any zone in the city must equal total mass outputs from that zone (apart from any stock increases in each case). Or we may combine these two conditions to give a materials balance relation for each industry in each zone. It is at this finer level of resolution that it is felt this relation may be most usefully be used. We may therefore take the following equation as a constraint:

total mass inputs to industry n in zone j = total mass outputs from industry n in zone j (including flows to final demand)[3] ,

$$\sum_{imk} X_{ij}^{mnk} + \sum_{k} X_{jj}^{enk} + \sum_{mk} X_{oj}^{mnk} = \sum_{imk} X_{ji}^{nmk} + \sum_{k} X_{jj}^{nek} + \sum_{mk} X_{jo}^{nmk} + \sum_{ik} Y_{ji}^{nk}$$

$$k \in Q \quad k \in R \quad k \in Q \quad\quad k \in Q \quad k \in W \quad k \in Q \quad k \in Q \qquad (11)$$

---

[3] Notice that any net stock changes are accounted for in the final demand term.

In principle it is possible to consider the materials balance equation at a much finer level of detail. It was mentioned above that it is theoretically possible to use any desired level of commodity classification. Thus at a very fine level—a level at which commodities are used, but are not transformed by the activities (for instance carbon and other elements)— the materials balance constraint may be stated as 'total inflows of each k into n in j must equal total outflows'. This latter possibility will not, however, be taken any further at this stage.

3.4 Cost constraint
We may form in the usual way a cost constraint that corresponds to the movement of manufactured goods. If C^{mnk} is the total amount spent on transporting commodity k between industries m and n and c_{ij}^{mnk} is the unit cost of transporting k between industry m in i and industry n in j, then the following equation may be taken as a cost constraint:

$$\sum_{ij} X_{ij}^{mnk} c_{ij}^{mnk} + \sum_i (X_{io}^{mnk} c_{io}^{mnk} + X_{oi}^{mnk} c_{oi}^{mnk}) = C^{mnk} , \qquad k \in Q . \tag{12}$$

The adoption of the Leontief–Strout multiregional input–output assumption did in effect, avoid the need for a zonally disaggregated input–output table (which would have, for example, coefficients a_{ij}^{kn} showing the input of commodity k from zone i required per unit output of industry n in zone j). However, in this model, we do wish to use information, and to produce model estimates, for the flow of commodities between spatially separated industries. Rather than rely on a spatially disaggregated input–output table we turn to the cost constraint to account for impedance, due to spatial separation, for the flow of commodities between a given pair of industries.

This completes the summary of the kind of relationships that are considered important in determining the flow of materials for the type of model outlined here.

4 The model estimates for the flow variables
A solution to the system can be obtained by maximising the entropy of the probability distribution associated with the flow variables (X_{ij}^{mnk}, X_{io}^{mnk}, X_{oj}^{mnk}, $k \in Q$; X_{jj}^{enk}, $k \in R$; X_{ii}^{mek}, $k \in W$), subject to constraints given above.

The role of the objective function in using entropy-maximising methods here is to make a statistical average of the information in the constraints, thus producing model estimates which are the most probable, given what we have assumed. The results given below were derived by using constraints (1), (3), (6), (8), (10), (11), and (12).

This solution may be thought of as one of a family of models that could have been derived here; a different selection of constraints that would give rise to an alternative solution would be possible, and perhaps desirable.

Because of its cumbersome nature, the details of the solution have been given in the appendix.

For manufactured goods, the movement of some commodity k between industry m in zone i and industry n in zone j in some specified time period may be represented by

$$X_{ij}^{mnk} = M_i^m \epsilon^{nk} \theta^k \alpha^{mk} \xi_j^n \exp(-\mu^{mnk} c_{ij}^{mnk}) , \qquad k \in Q , \tag{13}$$

where M_i^m, ϵ^{nk}, θ^k, α^{mk}, and ξ_j^n are balancing factors which ensure that this solution does in fact satisfy constraints (1), (3), (8), and (11) respectively (the full expressions for these balancing factors may be found in the appendix); μ^{mnk} are the Lagrangian multipliers associated with constraint (12). They are usually left in this exponential form, to be estimated separately.

Brief comments on the results is perhaps worthwhile: $M_i^m \exp(-\mu^{mnk} c_{ij}^{mnk})$ is the entropy-maximising equivalent of a production-constrained gravity model, and the other balancing factors in equation (13) add more accuracy to this gravity-model prediction by incorporating the additional information from constraints (3), (8), and (11), that is the known interindustry technology, and the fact that the weight of an industry's inputs and outputs must balance.

Of particular interest are the ξ_j^n and ϵ^{nk} terms, that is those associated with the materials balance and the interindustry relations. Reference has already been made to the difficulty in finding technical input coefficients a_j^{kn} [cf constraint (2)] at a zonal level, so that coefficients for the whole area will usually have to be used. This in effect means that we assume the same technology throughout the city for a given industry. However, the inaccuracies caused by using such an aggregate assumption may, in this model, be partially offset by the ξ_j^n term. This incorporates information about an individual industry's inputs and outputs at the zonal level, but in terms of data that should be much easier to find than individual zonal technical-input coefficients[4]. This follows because the only exogenous terms to estimate in the materials balance constraint, equation (11) above, are the final-demand terms, that is the total output from a given industry in a given zone destined for final consumers (which for present purposes are taken as households; local and central governments, excluding their industrial establishments; and investment in stocks and capital equipment).

Export and import flows are given by

$$X_{io}^{mnk} = M_i^m \theta^k \alpha^{mk} \exp(-\mu^{mnk} c_{io}^{mnk}) , \qquad k \in Q , \tag{14}$$

$$X_{oj}^{mnk} = \epsilon^{nk} \xi_j^n \exp(-\mu^{mnk} c_{oj}^{mnk}) , \qquad k \in Q , \tag{15}$$

and it can be seen that these include the same sort of terms as the intraurban flows given above. Exports are determined by productive

---

[4] The ultimate success of using the materials balance concept in this way will only become apparent after much empirical work.

capacity in each industry by zone in the city, and by market-share relationships; imports are determined by industrial technical relationships and materials balance. (Export flows from industries in the area must also, of course, satisfy the materials balance constraint, but reference to the appendix will show how the materials balance constraint on export flows may be absorbed into the mass term M_i^m.)

It is thus evident that we may assume exports and imports to be determined only by the relationships used to derive the local flows of goods. It is an interesting point whether exports should be determined in this way by the model, or whether they should be supplied as exogenous estimates. Substitution for exogenous export/import terms in the above model causes no difficulty in principle, it merely involves the replacement of the existing endogenous export/import terms in the constraints by their exogenous equivalents, but in practice disadvantages arise in relying on exogenous export estimates—because they are difficult to predict accurately.

The same argument could apply to import flows, though in this case it may be worthwhile to distinguish between competing imports (that is goods that are imported, but also made in the area) and noncompeting imports (goods which have no home-produced equivalent). In the latter case, imports could be determined by the model as before, but in the former case some exogenous estimate could perhaps be used.

Note that in the present model, the mechanism for determining the import of commodities works via the production constraint, equation (1). This determines the capacity of industries within the city to produce their own commodities, and hence the proportion of home demand for given goods which can be met by home production. This in turn determines how much needs to be imported.

The three results given so far are equivalent to the flows normally associated with interregional commodity-flow models. Most of these flows of goods will have to be accommodated on the transport networks. With this in mind, the estimates of the flows of goods will have to be translated from weight per month or year to truck loads per day or week before they can make a major contribution to meeting the increasing demands, caused by goods movements, on the limited transport resources.

The 'other side' of the present model considers links between the economic system and the environment. Outputs of residuals as determined from the present model are here given by

$$X_{ii}^{mek} = \omega^{mk} \frac{1}{\xi_i^m}, \qquad k \in W, \tag{16}$$

and the requirement, by industries, of environmental resources is given by

$$X_{jj}^{enk} = \xi_j^n \rho^{nk}, \qquad k \in R. \tag{17}$$

Balancing factors ξ_j^n, ω^{mk}, and ρ^k arise from the materials balance [equation (11)], the residuals [equation (10)], and the resource input-output constraints [equation (6)]. Thus it is seen, equation (16), that residual outputs by industry, by zone, depend on the aggregate emission factors (absorbed into the ω^{mk} term) for the whole area, which, via the materials balance constraint, have been scaled down to the individual industrial–zonal level.

Similarly, the requirement of resources from the environment depends on the citywide technical input coefficients (absorbed into the ρ^k term) and the materials balance constraint. Thus constraint (11) has again been useful in weighting aggregate citywide information to the individual zonal-industrial level. Previous approaches to the quantification of 'environmental repercussions' (see for example Leontief, 1970; Wilen, 1973; and Isard, 1969) relied solely on waste emission factors, A^{kn}, and technical input coefficients, ξ^{kn}, to determine residual and resource flows. As already stated, these prove difficult to find at fine spatial levels of resolution, hence the preference for using aggregate citywide coefficients in conjunction with the zonal–sectoral materials balance condition to find expressions for resource and residual flows at the zonal level.

The immediate application of the residuals equation (16) in determining waste outputs is useful, though limited. In the case of air pollution, the overall effect on the environment will depend not only on the total flow of residuals, but also on the assimilative capacity of the environment, which is in turn influenced by several factors. Thus, the model as it stands provides only one component, but could be used as an input to existing air pollution diffusion models of the type, for example, given in Shefer and Guldmann (1973), in order to assess the overall pollution effects.

Further limitations are caused by the tight restrictions on the definition of residuals—thus the model would need some adaptation to adequately handle, for instance, the recycling or processing of wastes. More generally, static-equilibrium approaches, to which class the present model belongs, have been criticised (Norton and Parlour, 1972). However, despite these factors, it is felt that this type of model can made a positive contribution in approaching problems caused by industrial-waste output.

5 Further comments
Equation (17) completes the estimates from the present model of the flows of materials generated by industrial activity in an urban area. We have estimates for the flows of commodities between the spatially separated industries within the region, for the export and import of goods, and for the flows between the industries and the environment.

With a general distribution model of the type given here it is often not the flow estimates that are most interesting, but rather the aspects that will give rise to a *change* in any given distribution pattern. It is, of course, the exogenous estimates that will cause such change, that is they will drive the model. A change in any of the terms that have had to be found exogenously will achieve this. Probably the most important of the exogenous terms to be estimated in the present case are those for the final-demand sector. For this, and possibly also for other exogenous parameters in any of the constraint equations, it might be worthwhile constructing submodels, although no details of such possibilities are given here.

To conclude on a more general note, the type of model outlined here is felt to provide a useful foundation on which further approaches can build. The focus in the model given above has been on viewing urban industries as generators and transformers of a continual flow of materials—resources, intermediate products and wastes. One interesting and immediate development would be the extension of the meaning of the terms used. Thus the term industry would be made to cover all activities in the economy; commodity would embrace any of the activities' inputs or outputs; and the zonal subscripts would provide the spatial component of the activities. We would then aim to represent much of the functioning of the urban economy in terms of these three components. The addition of time as a fourth component would of course be necessary to make this a possibly more realistic, dynamic model. Finally, although conceived at the urban level, this type of model may find application at other levels of resolution—regional or national.

Acknowledgement. The author gratefully acknowledges financial support from the Science Research Council.

References

Artle, R., 1965, *The Structure of the Stockholm Economy*, 2nd edition (Cornell University Press, Ithaca, New York).

Carroll, Jr, J. D., 1971, "Problems and issues in urban goods movements", *Special Report 120*, Highway Research Board, Washington DC, USA.

Central Statistical Office, 1973, *Input–Output Tables for the United Kingdom 1968* (HMSO, London).

Chisholm, M., O'Sullivan, P., 1973, *Freight Flows and Spatial Aspects of the British Economy* (Cambridge University Press, Cambridge).

Dales, J. H., 1968, *Pollution, Property and Prices* (University of Toronto Press, Toronto).

French, A., Watson, P., 1971, "Demand forecasting and the development of a framework for analysis of urban commodity flow", *Special Report 120*, Highway Research Board, Washington DC, USA.

Isard, W., 1960, *Methods of Regional Analysis* (John Wiley, New York).

Isard, W., 1969, "Some notes on the linkage of the ecologic and economic systems", *Regional Science Association Papers*, **22**, 85–96.

Kneese, A. V., Ayres, R. U., d.Arge, R. C., 1970, *Economics of the Environment: A Materials Balance Approach* (Johns Hopkins University Press, Baltimore).

Leontief, W., 1970, "Environmental repercussions and the economic structure: an input–output approach", *Review of Economics and Statistics*, **52**, 252–271.

Leontief, W., Strout, A., 1963, "Multi-regional input-output analysis", in *Structural Interdependence and Economic Development*, ed. T. Barna (MacMillan, London).

Maltby, D., 1973, "Traffic models for goods, services and business movements to manufacturing establishments", *Transport Planning and Technology*, **2**, 21-39.

Meadows, D. H., Meadows, D. L., Randers, J., Behrens, W. W., 1972, *The Limits to Growth* (Universe Books, New York).

Morrison, W. I., 1973, "The development of an urban inter-industry model", *Environment and Planning*, **5**, 369-383, 433-460, 545-554.

Norton, G. A., Parlour, J. W., 1972, "The economic philosophy of pollution: a critique", *Environment and Planning*, **4**, 3-11.

Shefer, D., Guldmann, J. M., 1973, "Mathematical models of industrial location and pollution abatement strategies", *Environment and Planning*, **5**, 577-588.

Stone, J. R. N., Brown, A., 1962, "A computable model of economic growth" in *University of Cambridge, Department of Applied Economics, A Programme for Growth*, volume 1 (Chapman and Hall, London).

Victor, P. A., 1972, *Pollution: Economy and Environment* (Allen and Unwin, London).

Wilen, J. E., 1973, "A model of economic system-ecosystem interaction", *Environment and Planning*, **5**, 409-420.

Wilson, A. G., 1970a, *Entropy in Urban and Regional Modelling* (Pion, London).

Wilson, A. G., 1970b, "Interregional commodity flows—entropy maximising approaches", *Geographical Analysis*, **2**, 255-282.

Appendix

Solution

A solution to the model may be found by maximising the entropy of the probability distribution associated with flow variables X_{ij}^{mnk}, X_{oj}^{mnk}, X_{io}^{mnk}, $k \in Q$; X_{jj}^{enk}, $k \in R$; X_{ii}^{mek}, $k \in W$; subject to the constraints. The constraints chosen in this case are first summarised; others would of course be possible.

Production constraint [equation (1)]:

$$\sum_{jnk} X_{ij}^{mnk} + \sum_{nk} X_{io}^{mnk} + \sum_{k} Y_{i*}^{mk} = b^m E_i^m , \qquad k \in Q . \tag{A1}$$

Industry relation [equation (3)]:

$$\sum_{ijm} X_{ij}^{mnk} + \sum_{jm} X_{oj}^{mnk} = a^{kn} \left(\sum_{ijmk'} X_{ji}^{nmk'} + \sum_{jmk'} X_{jo}^{nmk'} + \sum_{jk} Y_{j*}^{nk'} \right) ,$$
$$k, k' \in Q . \tag{A2}$$

Resource requirements [equation (6)]:

$$\sum_{j} X_{jj}^{enk} = f^{kn} \left(\sum_{ijmk'} X_{ji}^{nmk'} + \sum_{jmk'} X_{jo}^{nmk'} + \sum_{jk} Y_{j*}^{nk'} \right) ,$$
$$k \in R , \quad k' \in Q . \tag{A3}$$

Industry production of a commodity [equation (8)]:

$$d^{mk} \left(\sum_{ijmn} X_{ij}^{mnk} + \sum_{imn} X_{io}^{mnk} \right) = \sum_{ijn} X_{ij}^{mnk} + \sum_{in} X_{io}^{mnk} , \qquad k \in Q . \tag{A4}$$

Residuals production [equation (10)]:

$$\sum_{i} X_{ii}^{mek} = A^{mk} \left(\sum_{ijnk'} X_{ij}^{mnk'} + \sum_{ink'} X_{io}^{mnk'} + \sum_{k} Y_{i*}^{mk'} \right) ,$$
$$k \in W , \quad k' \in Q . \tag{A5}$$

Materials balance [equation (11)]:

$$\sum_{imk} X_{ij}^{mnk} + \sum_{k} X_{jj}^{enk} + \sum_{mk} X_{oj}^{mnk} = \sum_{imk} X_{ji}^{nmk} + \sum_{k} X_{jj}^{nek} + \sum_{mk} X_{jo}^{nmk} + \sum_{k} Y_{j*}^{nk} .$$
$$k \in Q \quad k \in R \quad k \in Q \quad k \in Q \quad k \in W \quad k \in Q \quad k \in Q \tag{A6}$$

Cost constraint [equation (12)]:

$$\sum_{ij} X_{ij}^{mnk} c_{ij}^{mnk} + \sum_{i} (X_{io}^{mnk} c_{io}^{mnk} + X_{oi}^{mnk} c_{oi}^{mnk}) = C^{mnk} , \qquad k \in Q . \tag{A7}$$

We may substitute an equivalent of equation (A1) into equations (A2), (A3), (A5) and (A6) giving:

$$\sum_{ijm} X_{ij}^{mnk} + \sum_{jm} X_{oj}^{mnk} = a^{kn} \sum_{j} b^n E_j^n , \qquad k \in Q , \tag{A8}$$

$$\sum_{j} X_{jj}^{enk} = f^{kn} \sum_{j} b^n E_j^n , \qquad k \in R , \tag{A9}$$

and

$$\sum_i X_{ii}^{mek} = A^{mk} \sum_i b^m E_i^m , \qquad k \in W , \qquad (A10)$$

$$\sum_{imk} X_{ij}^{mnk} + \sum_k X_{jj}^{enk} + \sum_{mk} X_{oj}^{mnk} = b^n E_j^n + \sum_k X_{jj}^{nek} .$$
$$k \in Q \quad k \in R \quad k \in Q \qquad\qquad k \in W \qquad (A11)$$

Now we maximise

$$S = - \sum_{ijmnk} X_{ij}^{mnk} \ln X_{ij}^{mnk} - \sum_{imnk} X_{io}^{mnk} \ln X_{io}^{mnk} - \sum_{jmñk} X_{oj}^{mnk} \ln X_{oj}^{mnk}$$
$$k \in Q \qquad\qquad k \in Q \qquad\qquad k \in Q$$

$$- \sum_{jnk} X_{jj}^{enk} \ln X_{jj}^{enk} - \sum_{imk} X_{ii}^{mek} \ln X_{ii}^{mek} ,$$
$$k \in R \qquad\qquad k \in W$$

subject to constraints (A1), (A8), (A9), (A4), (A10), (A11), and (A6).
λ_i^m, γ^{nk}, δ^{nk}, τ^{mk}, σ^{mk}, ϕ_j^n, and μ^{mnk} are Lagrangian multipliers associated with these constraints.
Let

$$\mathcal{L} = S - \sum_{im} \lambda_i^m \left(\sum_{jnk} X_{ij}^{mnk} + \sum_{nk} X_{io}^{mnk} + \sum_k Y_{i*}^{mk} - b^m E_i^m \right)$$
$$k \in Q \quad k \in Q \quad k \in Q$$

$$- \sum_{nk} \gamma^{nk} \left(\sum_{ijm} X_{ij}^{mnk} + \sum_{jm} X_{oj}^{mnk} - \sum_i a^{kn} b^n E_i^n \right)$$
$$k \in Q$$

$$- \sum_{nk} \delta^{nk} \left(\sum_j X_{jj}^{enk} - \sum f^{kn} \sum_j b^n E_j^n \right)$$
$$k \in R$$

$$- \sum_{mk} \tau^{mk} \left[d^{mk} \left(\sum_{ijmn} X_{ij}^{mnk} + \sum_{ijmn} X_{io}^{mnk} \right) - \sum_{ijn} X_{ij}^{mnk} - \sum_{in} X_{io}^{mnk} \right]$$
$$k \in Q$$

$$- \sum_{mk} \sigma^{mk} \left(\sum_{ijn} X_{ij}^{mnk} - A^{km} \sum_i b^m E_i^m \right)$$
$$k \in W$$

$$- \sum_{nj} \phi_j^n \left(\sum_{imk} X_{ij}^{mnk} + \sum_k X_{jj}^{enk} + \sum_{mk} X_{oj}^{mnk} - \sum_k X_{jj}^{nek} - b^n E_j^n \right)$$
$$k \in Q \quad k \in R \quad k \in Q \quad k \in W$$

$$- \sum_{mnk} \mu^{mnk} \left[\sum_{ij} X_{ij}^{mnk} c_{ij}^{mnk} + \sum_i (X_{io}^{mnk} c_{io}^{mnk} + X_{oi}^{mnk} c_{oi}^{mnk}) - C^{mnk} \right] .$$
$$k \in Q$$

If we set the following equal to zero:

$$\frac{\delta\mathcal{L}}{\delta X_{ij}^{mnk}} \, , \qquad \frac{\delta\mathcal{L}}{\delta X_{oj}^{mnk}} \, , \qquad \frac{\delta\mathcal{L}}{\delta X_{io}^{mnk}}$$

where $k \in Q$, and

$$\frac{\delta\mathcal{L}}{\delta X_{jj}^{enk}} \, , \qquad \frac{\delta\mathcal{L}}{\delta X_{ii}^{mek}} \, ,$$

$$k \in R \qquad\qquad k \in W$$

we obtain

$$X_{ij}^{mnk} = \exp\left(-\lambda_i^m - \gamma^{nk} - \sum_m \tau^{mk} d^{mk} + \tau^{mk} - \phi_j^n - \mu^{mnk} c_{ij}^{mnk}\right) , \qquad k \in Q ,$$

$$X_{io}^{mnk} = \exp\left(-\lambda_i^m - \sum_m \tau^{mk} d^{mk} + \tau^{mk} - \mu^{mnk} c_{io}^{mnk}\right) , \qquad k \in Q ,$$

$$X_{oj}^{mnk} = \exp(-\gamma^{nk} - \phi_j^n - \mu^{mnk} c_{oj}^{mnk}) , \qquad k \in Q ,$$

$$X_{ii}^{mek} = \exp(-\sigma^{mk} + \phi_i^m) , \qquad k \in W ,$$

$$X_{jj}^{enk} = \exp(\delta^{nk} - \phi_j^n) , \qquad k \in R ,$$

(absorbing a 1 into the multipliers, without loss of generality).
Now let

$$\exp(-\lambda_i^m) = M_i^m \, , \qquad \exp(-\phi_j^n) = \xi_j^n \, , \qquad \text{therefore } \exp(+\phi_i^m) = 1/\xi_i^m \, ,$$

$$\exp(-\gamma^{nk}) = \epsilon^{nk} \, , \qquad \exp(-\sigma^{mk}) = \omega^{mk} \, , \qquad \exp(-\delta^{nk}) = \rho^{nk} \, ,$$

$$\exp\left(-\sum_m \tau^{mk} d^{mk}\right) = \theta^k \, , \qquad \exp \tau^{mk} = \alpha^{mk}$$

so that

$$\theta^k = \prod_m \left(\frac{1}{\alpha^{mk}}\right)^{d^{mk}} .$$

Applying these substitutions to the above results we obtain

$$X_{ij}^{mnk} = M_i^m \epsilon^{nk} \theta^k \alpha^{mk} \xi_j^n \exp(-\mu^{mnk} c_{ij}^{mnk}) , \qquad k \in Q , \qquad\qquad \text{(A12)}$$

$$X_{io}^{mnk} = M_i^m \theta^k \alpha^{mk} \exp(-\mu^{mnk} c_{io}^{mnk}) , \qquad k \in Q , \qquad\qquad \text{(A13)}$$

$$X_{oj}^{mnk} = \epsilon^{nk} \xi_j^n \exp(-\mu^{mnk} c_{oj}^{mnk}) , \qquad k \in Q , \qquad\qquad \text{(A14)}$$

$$X_{ii}^{mek} = \omega^{mk} \frac{1}{\xi_i^m} , \qquad k \in W , \qquad\qquad \text{(A15)}$$

$$X_{jj}^{enk} = \rho^{nk} \xi_j^n , \qquad k \in R . \qquad\qquad \text{(A16)}$$

These are the results quoted in the text.
The terms M_i^m, ξ_j^n, ϵ^{nk}, ω^{mk}, ρ^{nk}, and θ^k, are often called balancing factors. Expressions for each of them may be derived by substituting results (A12)–(A16) into each of the constraint equations in turn. Thus we have

from (A1)

$$M_i^m = \frac{b^m E_i^m - \sum_k Y_{i*}^{mk}}{\sum_{jnk} \epsilon^{nk}\theta^k\alpha^{mk}\xi_j^n \exp(-\mu^{mnk}c_{ij}^{mnk}) + \sum_{nk}\theta^k\alpha^{mk}\exp(-\mu^{mnk}c_{io}^{mnk})},$$

$$k \in Q \; ; \quad (A17)$$

from (A8)

$$\epsilon^{nk} = \frac{\sum_j a^{kn}b^n E_j^n}{\sum_{ijm} M_i^m\theta^k\alpha^{mk}\xi_i^n \exp(-\mu^{mnk}c_{ij}^{mnk}) + \sum_{jm}\xi_j^n\exp(-\mu^{mnk}c_{oj}^{mnk})} \; ; \quad (A18)$$

from (A9)

$$\rho^{nk} = \frac{\sum_j f^{kn}b^n E_j^n}{\sum_j \xi_j^n} \; ; \quad (A19)$$

from (A10)

$$\omega^{mk} = \frac{A^{mk}\sum_i b^m E_i^m}{\sum_i \frac{1}{\xi_i^m}} \; ; \quad (A20)$$

from (A4)

$$\alpha^{mk} = \frac{d^{mk}\left[\sum_{ijmn}M_i^m\epsilon^{nk}\alpha^{mk}\xi_j^n\exp(-\mu^{mnk}c_{ij}^{mnk}) + \sum_{imn}M_i^m\alpha^{mk}\exp(-\mu^{mnk}c_{io}^{mnk})\right]}{\sum_{ijn}M_i^m\epsilon^{nk}\xi_j^n\exp(-\mu^{mnk}c_{ij}^{mnk}) + \sum_{in}M_i^m\exp(-\mu^{mnk}c_{io}^{mnk})} ; \quad (A21)$$

and

$$\theta^k = \prod_m \left(\frac{1}{\alpha^{mk}}\right)^{d^{mk}} \; ; \quad (A22)$$

from (A11)

$$\xi_j^n\left[\underset{k \in Q}{\sum_{imk}M_i^m\epsilon^{nk}\theta^k\alpha^{mk}\exp(-\mu^{mnk}c_{ij}^{mnk})} + \underset{k \in Q}{\sum_{mk}\epsilon^{nk}\exp(-\mu^{mnk}c_{oj}^{mnk})} + \underset{k \in R}{\sum_k \rho^{nk}}\right]$$

$$\underset{k \in W}{- b^n E_j^n - \sum_k \omega^{mk}\frac{1}{\xi_i^m}} = 0 \; . \quad (A23)$$

These equations have to be solved iteratively rather than directly for values of the terms M_i^m, ϵ^{nk}, ρ^{nk}, ω^{mk}, α^{mk}, θ^k, and ξ_j^n. A suitable iterative procedure might be to guess initial values for α^{mk} and hence find a first approximation for θ^k from (A22). With these values for α^{mk} and θ^k and guessed initial values for ϵ^{nk} and ξ_j^n, calculate M_i^m from (A17), ρ^{nk} from

(A19), and ω^{mk} from (A20). ϵ^{nk} may be found from (A18), and α^{mk} will follow from (A21). With all the approximated values so far found and guessed initial values for ξ_i^m ($i \neq j$ when $m = n$, $m \neq n$ when $i = j$), equation (A23) may be searched for an approximation for ξ_j^n (this being the dominant term here).

First approximations for each of the required terms have now been found, so the process may be repeated until the difference between successively approximated values of each of the balancing factors is negligible.

Government Action and Manufacturing Employment in the Northern Region 1952–1971

M.E.FROST
King's College, London

1 Introduction

By now, in 1974, forty years have passed since the government first took explicit action in an attempt to modify patterns of industrial activity in Great Britain in order to satisfy its social and economic objectives. Successive attempts to change these patterns have been mainly focused upon the manufacturing sector where restrictions and inducements have been used to persuade individual firms to locate new productive facilities in areas of the country whose industrial structures have been thought to be poorly adapted to existing economic conditions. This interaction of public and private forces in secondary industry is of great interest, partly because the government has established itself as a powerful new locational factor in the economic landscape, and partly because of the social importance of the outcomes of government policies in the areas which benefit from them. However, a further and more general motive for the analysis of the spatial effects of government industrial policies is that it is only by understanding the effects of past policies that future policies may be improved to tackle the apparently persistent spatial problems of the British economy.

However, studies which have attempted to examine the effects of the government's policies on the distribution of industry have faced a number of difficulties. The most important of these is the fundamental problem that it is very difficult to isolate the effects of government policies from 'normal' evolutionary changes in the economy when such evolutionary changes cannot be examined in isolation. This difficulty is compounded by the fact that the legislative framework within which government activities are set has been subject to frequent and far-reaching changes. These changes are fully outlined elsewhere (McCrone, 1969; Hallett *et al.*, 1973) but, since 1945, they make it very difficult to find areas enjoying government assistance, and devices by which assistance has been given, that have remained fairly stable for more than a few years. This second difficulty is further worsened by the fact that successive governments have used the legislative possibilities open to them in a highly variable manner, thus making any accurate assessment of the extent of government commitment to spatially oriented industrial policies at particular times extremely difficult.

Against this background of operational problems there have been two main approaches towards gaining some insight into the effects of government policies. The first is the questionnaire approach where industrial firms or plants are asked their experience of government policies and what the important factors are in their existing or prospective locations (Cameron and Clark, 1966; Cameron and Reid, 1966; Townroe, 1970). The second method deals more with aggregates—the industrial performances of particular areas are compared to discover whether their relative rates of growth or decline reveal the possible effects of government influence (Brown, A. J., 1967; Thirlwall, 1967). The two approaches are fundamentally complementary in that the relative weaknesses of one approach are offset by the relative strengths of the other. Thus the practical restriction on most questionnaire surveys to study only a limited selection of firms, often when they are in the act of moving, can be set against the ability of a more aggregate approach to study the progress of all of the industry in an area over a fairly extensive time period. In addition to this, the difficulty of identifying the effects of individual policies in an aggregate approach is partially offset by the ability of individual-firm studies to question firms on the results of particular government actions. However, in recent years it appears that the contribution made to this dual approach by aggregate methods has been somewhat lacking. The reason for this scant contribution lies in the extensive use of the shift and share methods as a means of comparing relative rates of regional growth or decline. This technique has been widely criticised on a number of counts (Brown, H. J., 1969; Buck, 1970; Mackay, 1968) which concern the unreliability of its disaggregation of relative regional growths, whilst this technique is defended by its adherents as a simple data-ordering device (Stilwell, 1969). However, from the point of view of an analysis of the effects of government policies, its main fault seems to lie in the temptation to analyse only crude summary figures related to a region's industrial performance. In shift and share terms very little success has been achieved in the industrial disaggregation of the differential component of relative growth, and yet it is a knowledge of how a particular industry has fared in relative terms that would provide a suitable base from which to mount a questionnaire survey aimed at discovering the reasons for its growth or decline in relation to the rest of the country.

In the light of these criticisms one objective of this study is to experiment with an alternative method of examining relative rates of regional employment growth in a manner designed to highlight individual industries in the Northern region which have either gained or lost employment rapidly in relation to the rest of the country. The second objective is to use this method to attempt a study of the impact of government industrial policies on the region. In this respect, the variability of government commitment to these policies can be used as a positive advantage. Thus the relative lack of government activity during the 1950s can be contrasted with the rapidly increasing level of such activity during the 1960s. This difference can be used to generate a simple hypothesis, namely that most industries would be expected to grow faster, or decline more slowly, in relation to the rest of the country during the 1960s compared with their performance in the 1950s. In these terms the second objective of this paper is to identify those individual industries that have achieved significant relative gains or losses in employment when the national position of the region is compared between the two periods and, further, to examine the rate at which these gains or losses have accumulated.

2 Data sources
The data used in the regional studies to follow are the estimates of employees (both employed and unemployed) provided by the Department of Employment [1]. These are used in the knowledge that they possess considerable weaknesses for a study of regional growth or decline (Mackay and Buxton, 1965). Employment itself is only a poor indicator of economic progress, whilst the data themselves are only estimates and are subject to sampling error which may be quite considerable for industries employing small numbers of people. These data are used in spite of these problems because there are very few alternatives, and certainly none that record in such detail.

However, before a continuous series can be produced a number of difficulties have to be overcome. The first of these is the change in the Standard Industrial Classification (SIC) that took place in 1958. In order to obtain an industrial classification that is comparable from 1952 to 1968 the Minimum List Headings of both the 1948 and 1958 Standard Industrial Classifications require some amalgamation. A summary of the groupings is provided in the Appendix. In addition to these groupings, small correction factors are necessary to compensate for redistributed Minimum List Headings, these corrections being derived from the quantitative assessment of the changing SIC contained in the 1961 Census. However, in spite of these amalgamations producing a set of eighty-five industrial categories, a further substantial SIC change in 1968 means that a limited number of categories cannot be traced through to 1971 without far-reaching amalgamations. These are noted in the table.

One further difficulty has to be overcome before going on to an analysis of the employment estimates: the problem of the change of regional boundaries in the period from 1952 to 1968. In order to obtain

[1] These estimates are published annually in the Ministry of Labour Gazette, 1958–1967; Department of Employment and Productivity Gazette, 1968–1970; Department of Employment Gazette, 1970–1971. Prior to this they are available on special request to the Department of Employment.

comparability through time, some amalgamations are necessary and produce the eight regions shown in figure 1. Even with these enlarged regions, no full records are available for the West Midlands for the years 1962, 1963, and 1964 except at SIC Order level. A crude estimate of the employment structure for this region in 1964 is made by distributing the Order totals for that year according to the shares of the 1965 Minimum List Headings but the 2 year gap to 1963 was considered too long for similar treatment.

Thus these groupings leave an almost continuous employment series available from 1952 to 1968 for eighty-five categories, with an extension possible in most cases to 1971. This is the basis on which some investigation of the processes of relative regional employment growth and decline can be made.

Figure 1. Outline map of regions used in this study.

3 Preliminary tests on relative rates of regional growth

Before setting out to specify a model of relative employment change it is important to study the way in which such changes take place through time. For instance it must be known whether the process of relative employment gain is one of sudden bursts, where a single region rapidly gains an advantage over the remainder of the country, or whether the process is a slow accretionary one where sustained growth by one region gives it a marked advantage over the others. These preliminary studies are described in greater detail elsewhere (Frost, 1975), so that only a brief summary is presented here.

In order to examine differences of relative employment changes, the yearly changes in employment for the eighty-five individual categories in each of the eight regions used in this study were expressed as deviations around their respective national rates of change. The characteristic pattern of these deviations was one of great irregularity through time, where particular industries in specific regions showed periods of sustained above-average growth very rarely. This irregularity was compounded by the fact that the smaller industries appeared to show rather more than a directly proportional amount of variation around national rates of change, which suggested a possible effect of sampling error in the employment estimates. To minimise the possible disturbance resulting from sampling variations a group of the larger industries were selected for further tests.

The object of these tests was to examine the extent to which relative employment changes were predictable, and thus useful in some form of extrapolation or forecasting exercise. The first test was to treat each industry in each area of the country as a dependent variable in a linear

Table 1. Deviation series—results for categories greater than 10000 employees (Northern region as the dependent variable).

Category	Coefficients of independent variables[a]					r^2	Durbin-Watson
	Southeast	Southwest	Northwest	Scotland	Wales		
2	−0·078	−0·179	−0·103	0·049	0·325	0·283	0·786
	(0·210)	(0·153)	(0·143)	(0·027)	(0·164)		
12	−0·716	−0·869	−0·547	−1·520	−0·573	0·469	1·679
	(0·313)	(0·905)	(0·256)	(0·876)	(0·761)		
17	−0·977	−1·120	−0·768	−0·854	−0·981	0·945	2·030
	(0·218)	(1·600)	(0·235)	(0·164)	(0·114)		
25	0·067	−0·651	0·091	−0·387	0·744	0·567	1·739
	(0·167)	(0·434)	(0·443)	(0·357)	(0·615)		
26	0·005	−0·311	−0·077	0·318	−0·334	0·715	1·861
	(0·013)	(0·058)	(0·230)	(0·301)	(0·410)		
30	−0·266	−0·007	−0·154	0·081	−0·439	0·585	1·794
	(0·140)	(0·391)	(0·029)	(0·366)	(0·056)		
32	−0·603	−1·230	−0·597	−0·053	−0·299	0·964	2·437
	(0·073)	(1·487)	(0·210)	(0·125)	(0·244)		
33	−0·186	−0·237	0·103	−0·384	0·464	0·728	1·867
	(0·097)	(0·317)	(0·162)	(0·189)	(0·520)		
34	−0·8999	−0·043	−0·583	−1·108	−0·609)	0·878	1·721
	(0·157)	(0·315)	(0·217)	(0·286)	(0·592)		
44	0·027	0·154	0·053	−0·056	0·123	0·213	1·983
	(0·074)	(0·236)	(0·209)	(0·222)	(0·283)		
60	−0·181	0·192	−0·303	−0·329	0·250	0·525	2·037
	(0·143)	(0·220)	(0·203)	(0·204)	(0·248)		
61	0·005	−0·310	0·125	0·037	−0·344	0·459	1·899
	(0·103)	(0·588)	(0·235)	(0·024)	(0·430)		

[a] Standard errors in parentheses.

relationship where the independent variables consisted of the records of employment for the same industry in other regions of the country. These relationships were estimated using the sixteen yearly deviations for the industries in each region that have been described above. The results for industries employing more than 10000 people in the Northern region are shown in table 1. In reviewing the r^2 and Durbin–Watson statistics jointly for these equations it can be seen that the extent to which the deviations of one region may be explained by the relative movements of the other regions in the country varies considerably. At one extreme, the case of 'bread and flour confectionery' (category 2) shows a very low level of explanation with considerable coherence in the residuals, thus producing

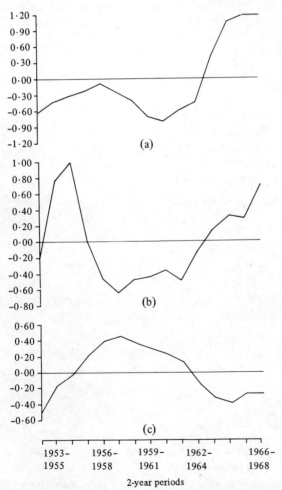

Figure 2. Selected residuals from smoothed employment series (Northern region as the dependent variable): (a) category 4; (b) category 8; (c) category 12.

a Durbin–Watson statistic as low as 0·786 while, at the other extreme, 'general iron and steel' (category 17) shows a high level of explanation with very little order in the residuals. In between these extremes, the bulk of industries show r^2 values of between 0·5 and 0·7, which indicate moderate but not particularly high levels of explanation.

These results are promising in the sense that they reveal some ordering in the deviations around national trends, but they are clearly not general enough to allow an analysis of all eighty-five categories. This lack of generality might result from the comparative absence of variation around national rates of employment change in several industries. In these circumstances the method of taking deviations accentuates the sampling error in the data, thus presenting a picture of disorder. To cure this

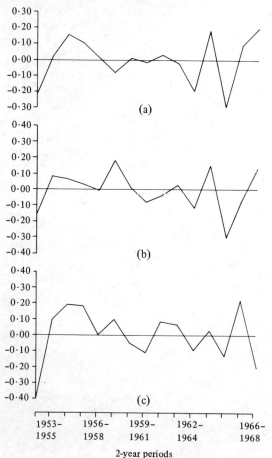

Figure 3. Selected residuals from smoothed employment series with national totals disaggregated into the relevant regional figures (Northern region as the dependent variable): (a) category 4; (b) category 8; (c) category 12.

failing, a second set of tests were made on the employment data without any transformation. Instead the data were smoothed using a 2 year moving average to subdue the effects of sampling error, and each industry was expressed as a function of the national level of employment using the sixteen-point series that remained after smoothing. The results of this exercise showed a distinct improvement on the levels of explanation achieved in the first test, with a substantial number of r^2 values of $>0 \cdot 8$. However, many of the results show a disturbing degree of coherence among the residuals, and produce very low Durbin–Watson values, thus indicating very incomplete explanation of regional employment levels by the relevant national totals. A selection of these residuals is shown in figure 2. Clearly this is not a basis for the building of any general model. The final form that was tried was a combination of the first two approaches. In this, the employment levels in all of the other regions were used as independent variables, once again a smoothed series being used for calibration. The effect of disaggregating the national totals into the relevant regional figures can be seen clearly if the residuals of figure 2 are compared with those for figure 3. The improvement highlights the importance of interregional relationships as a supplement to the substantial influence of general sectoral movements in explaining regional employment levels. Thus, after extensive tests on all of industrial categories of the Northern region, this seemed to be a suitable basis on which to specify a model of the Northern region's employment levels in comparison with the rest of the country.

4 Specification and calibration of a model of employment levels
Based on the experience of the tests carried out in the previous section, the form of relationships used to express the levels of employment in the Northern region in relation to the other regions of the country was as follows:

$$X_{1it} = \beta_{1i} + \beta_{2i} X_{2it} + \beta_{3i} X_{3it} \ldots + \beta_{8i} X_{8it} + u_{it}, \qquad \begin{aligned} i &= 1, 2, \ldots, 85, \\ t &= 1, 2, \ldots, n, \end{aligned}$$

where X_{1it} is the employment level in the Northern region at time t in the ith industrial category, X_2 to X_8 represent regions in the country other than the Northern region, u_{it} is a disturbance term, and β_i are coefficients to be estimated.

Once an expression of this type has been calibrated for a period in the 1950s, the second objective of the paper can be put into effect, namely to compare the position of individual industries in the Northern region between the 1950s and 1960s by using the expression to generate expected values of Northern employment levels from the performance of the other regions in the later period. However, before this can be done, the dates between which the calibration takes place must be set.

The opening date chosen was 1952. This was selected in order to avoid most of the immediate effects of government activity immediately after 1945 identified in Howard's evidence of firm movements (Howard, 1968). The closing date was rather more difficult to chose as there are no clear guidelines to indicate precisely when government interest in regional policies began to increase again. Legislatively, 1960 presents a clear divide (McCrone, 1969) but a recent study has set the starting date as late as 1963 (Moore and Rhodes, 1973). In this study a conservative estimate of 1960 is taken as the closing date in order to ensure, as far as possible, that the values of the coefficients remain constant over the calibration period.

The dates for calibration having been set, the problem then centres on the fact that there are only nine dates from which to estimate up to eight coefficients. In order to resolve this nearly indeterminate position, the individual industries were grouped according to their patterns of correlation with industries in other regions measured over the years 1950 to 1960. This was an attempt to find groups of individual categories with similar coefficients so that the data could be pooled for more efficient estimation. In this grouping procedure, eleven groups (A–K) were identified which ranged in contents from four categories to eleven (table 2). These encompassed all industries in the region except for a few very small categories whose employment showed no change over the period. These groups were used to calibrate the expression outlined above, with the intercept values for each category allowed to vary by the use of dummy variables. At this stage, three further categories, as noted in table 2, were lost owing to lack of variation in employment in other regions of the country—but each of these employed very few people in the Northern region as well. Thus estimates of the coefficients were obtained for seventy-five industrial categories. However, several problems were associated with the estimates. In the first place, a substantial reduction in the number of independent variables was required to eliminate some high intercorrelations amongst the independent variables, in some cases this

Table 2. Northern 'relationship' groups.

Group	Categories	Group	Categories
A	1, 12, 19, 25, 31, 47, 55, 65, 76, 78	G	4, 42[a], 64, 83
B	13, 20, 32, 40, 46, 49, 56[a], 57, 59, 73, 74	H	23, 38, 61, 66, 80
C	3, 14, 15, 33, 35, 37, 63	I	5, 6, 8, 11, 58
D	2, 18, 26, 44, 70, 77, 79, 82, 84, 85	J	41, 45, 60, 72
E	16, 17, 21, 24, 27, 50, 51, 52, 54, 67	K	9, 28, 30, 34, 68, 71[a], 75
F	7, 10, 22, 36, 69		

[a] Categories omitted from final calibration.

meant reducing the number of regions included in the equations to only two or three. More serious than this, however, were the problems of heteroscedastic and autocorrelated disturbances in the equations. Some heteroscedasticity would be expected to result from grouping the industries irrespective of size, particularly if the absolute size of the sampling error in the employment estimates were in any way related positively to the number of people employed within each category. From an inspection of the regression residuals, there was some evidence of unequal variance but this rarely seemed to be serious in isolation and so, in this study, the risk of a slightly inefficient estimation resulting from heteroscedastic disturbances was accepted as a consequence of the calibration procedures, without which no estimation would have been possible at all.

However, where heteroscedastic disturbances did appear to be of great significance was where such faults were accompanied by autocorrelation as well. Unfortunately, because of the pooling procedures involved in the calibration, there is no single reliable test for all forms of autocorrelation within the regression residuals. Durbin–Watson statistics can only be used as very crude guides, this places considerable emphasis on visual inspection of the residual values. In spite of this difficulty it was clear that three groups could be isolated where the patterns of the residuals caused concern. These were groups A, D, and K. Within these groups five categories—2, 12, 34, 55, and 85—showed clear signs of ordering in the residual values. There was no obvious cause for this other than misspecification of the model form. Since it would scarcely be worth changing the model form to suit five out of seventy-five industries, the groups containing those industries were reestimated with the offending categories excluded, the autocorrelated estimates of the coefficients and variances being accepted for those five.

Having calibrated the eleven equations to obtain the forms shown in table 3, we can use them to produce estimates of the employment within the Northern region based on the experiences of other regions during the 1960s, assuming that the Northern region maintained an identical relative position to those regions to that identified in the years from 1952 to 1960. In addition, a 99% confidence limit can be set around these expected values to obtain a range of expected values that makes allowance for the degree of randomness affecting employment levels which is estimated by the variance of the disturbance term in the regressions. These limits may be calculated for employment levels by using the standard formula (Johnston, 1963):

$$\text{confidence limit} = \text{expected level} \pm \tfrac{1}{2} t \hat{s} [C'(X'X)^{-1}C]^{\frac{1}{2}},$$

where X is the original matrix of independent variables, and C is a vector of values for the independent variables in each year of the 1960s, $\hat{s}$ is the

Table 3. Calibration results for eleven relationship groups.
(a) The Northern region's relationships with other regions.

Group	Coefficients of independent variables (and t values)						
	Southeast	Southwest	Wales	Yorkshire Humberside	Northwest	Scotland	Wales
A	−0·09 (3·45)		0·16 (1·74)		0·54 (5·60)		
A[a]		−0·46 (13·72)	0·09 (6·22)		0·59 (60·76)		
B	0·04 (14·87)		0·07 (4·16)		0·01 (15·21)		
C	0·11 (12·27)	−0·20 (3·40)	−0·04 (4·31)				
D	0·09 (5·46)		−0·03 (2·08)		−0·13 (2·22)	0·50 (9·08)	
D[b]	0·08 (3·86)		0·06 (2·29)	−0·26 (3·08)	0·14 (2·16)	0·21 (3·87)	
E	0·12 (6·96)		0·24 (3·74)		0·05 (3·37)	−0·15 (2·10)	
F	−0·01 (2·10)		0·04 (1·78)				−0·74 (6·37)
G		0·30 (9·36)	0·57 (5·87)			0·81 (4·67)	
H	0·03 (1·80)		0·03 (6·78)	0·20 (5·66)			
I	0·09 (9·41)						0·76 (8·97)
J	0·15 (2·00)						
K	−0·03 (2·49)		0·25 (12·38)	−0·13 (4·51)	0·12 (5·81)	0·10 (2·24)	
K[c]	−0·06 (1·70)		0·26 (4·65)	−0·18 (2·25)	0·16 (2·46)	0·26 (3·43)	

[a] Including categories 55, 12. [b] Including categories 2, 85. [c] Including category 34.

(b) Dummy structures of calibrated equations, industries measured in 10^3 of employees.

Group	Intercept term	Coefficients of dummy variables (and t values)								
		1	2	3	4	5	6	7	8	9
A	−1·26 (1·54)	−2·19 (1·09)	7·24 (1·46)	−4·80 (4·63)	1·57 (2·70)	1·85 (1·70)	−0·69 (1·74)	2·47 (1·60)		
A[a]	−1·31 (4·18)					−8·26 (14·91)	3·08 (5·30)	−21·60 (35·31)		−3·06 (5·51)
B	−0·12 (1·40)	−1·61 (1·98)	2·56 (14·94)			2·17 (19·32)	1·37 (13·41)			0·60 (6·00)

Table 3 (b) continued

Group	Intercept term	1	2	3	4	5	6	7	8	9
		Coefficients of dummy variables (and *t* values)								
C	2·17	−1·39	−0·75	−8·30	−7·94	5·05	−2·07			
	(13·69)	(5·06)	(4·14)	(6·51)	(6·39)	(8·18)	(6·83)			
D	−2·16	9·61	2·56			−10·13	2·03	1·50		
	(4·57)	(17·70)	(1·81)			(11·14)	(4·45)	(3·64)		
D^b	2·29	−2·87	10·10	−7·38		−5·24	−7·00	−2·59	−2·71	
	(2·12)	(2·69)	(28·80)	(3·59)		(6·09)	(4·60)	(2·43)	(2·50)	
E	−1·01	43·79			3·43	3·39	1·20	0·65		1·72
	(1·85)	(32·50)			(8·53)	(3·00)	(2·40)	(1·50)		(3·91)
F	3·61	3·85	−1·26		3·60					
	(12·80)	(14·10)	(1·80)		(18·35)					
G	1·18									
	(2·45)									
H	−2·30	3·43	3·57							
	(5·82)	(7·24)	(4·95)							
I	−0·69		0·89	−3·01						
	(3·20)		(4·40)	(16·03)						
J		0·42	15·46							
		(2·70)	(6·84)							
K	1·47					1·69				
	(1·98)					(2·60)				
K^c		2·67	42·25							
		(2·63)	(7·78)							

^a Including categories 55, 12.   ^b Including categories 2, 85.   ^c Including category 34.

(c) Statistics .

Group	σ^2	R^2	Durbin–Watson
A	0·70	0·98	1·89
A^a	2·13	0·97	0·80
B	0·06	0·96	1·61
C	0·14	0·98	1·66
D	0·09	0·99	1·84
D^b	0·19	0·97	1·27
E	0·63	0·98	2·04
F	0·21	0·95	1·64
G	0·06	0·97	1·98
H	0·17	0·98	1·62
I	0·19	0·94	1·68
J	0·19	0·97	1·51
K	0·04	0·98	1·93
K^c	0·45	0·97	1·10

^a Including categories 55, 12.   ^b Including categories 2, 85.   ^c Including category 34.

estimated standard deviation of the error term, and t is an appropriate value from the t distribution specific to the degrees of freedom of each calibration group. The change occurring in the Northern region's position for each industry can now be measured by calculating the amount by which the actual employment records of the region exceed or fall short of the expected range of values.

5 Deviations of employment levels in industries in the Northern region around expected levels of employment

In order to summarise the results of calculating the deviations of the Northern region's actual performance from the expected ranges, the industries that remain (some further categories are lost in 1965 when no data were published for industries employing less than 1000 people) are classified into five classes. This classification is a fairly crude, subjective one based primarily on visual inspection of the graphs of expected and actual employment levels. These graphs are presented elsewhere (Frost, 1974; 1975) but a numerical summary of the results is shown in table 4.

Class one consists of those industries which have not necessarily made the greatest relative gain in employment, but they are those which have shown the clearest and sharpest rise in employment away from the expected totals. In some cases these are also those industries making the largest relative gains as well. There are ten categories in this class. They are 'bread and flour confectionery'; 'food, meat, and vegetable products'; 'tube manufacture'; 'telegraph and telephone apparatus'; 'car and cycle manufacture'; 'spinning and weaving of cotton and linen'; 'manufacture of shirts, dresses, and underwear'; 'manufacture of glass products'; 'building materials and abrasives'; and 'rubber manufacture'. Of these ten industries the outstanding case of relative gain is that of 'telegraph and telephone apparatus'. From a comparatively insignificant national position in 1961 this industry almost trebled in size within the region, thus establishing the area as one of the four main producing areas in the country. However, on examining the class as a whole, it is difficult to find any common thread which might relate so varied a group of industries. The one factor that is fairly uniform is a tendency for very rapid relative growth around the years 1966 and 1967. Many of the industries first started rapid growth in this period, while those whose relative gains started before this all show acceleration in these years. By 1968 these relative gains amounted to 31100 jobs for the industries in class one alone, this indicates the importance of these rapidly growing industries to the region as a whole.

Class two contains those industries which have made substantial relative gains of about 500 jobs or more by 1968, but which do not show the same break with expected levels as those of class one. In many cases this is because they are larger industries, rather than the fairly new and rapidly growing elements of the regional economy identified in the previous class.

However, some make substantial relative gains in employment. There are twelve categories within this class which are listed in table 4. They range from the very large nonelectrical 'machinery and engineering' category through the 'manufacture of electrical machinery', 'timber production', and 'other printing and publishing'. In common with class one, the nature of the industries is very mixed as is their experience of relative gains through time. However, in spite of this variability, many of the industries

Table 4. Deviations around expected levels of employment (10^3 employees). Positive unless otherwise indicated.

Category	Deviation from expected employment level (10^3 employees)								
	1961	1964	1965	1966	1967	1968	1969	1970	1971
Class one									
2	0·3	0·4	0·4	0·7	2·0	2·4	1·9	2·1	2·6
9	0·5	1·4	1·4	1·6	2·7	3·8	4·6	6·4	6·4
18		1·2	1·1	0·8	1·6	2·2	2·7	3·1	2·9
32	0·6	2·1	4·4	7·6	8·4	9·4	8·8	10·3	9·9
35	−0·5	−0·4	−0·5		1·9	2·8	4·0	5·2	5·5
46		0·4	0·1	0·1		1·1	2·7	3·9	4·3
61	0·2		0·4	1·3	0·7	2·3	2·6	2·0	2·6
67	0·1			0·2	1·0	0·8	0·6	1·2	1·3
69	0·2	1·0	2·0	1·4	3·2	4·6	4·4	4·5	4·0
80	0·2	0·3			0·9	1·5	1·0	2·0	2·4
Class two									
6		0·2	0·3	0·6	0·6	0·8	0·7	0·6	0·6
12[a]	2·9	2·1	2·6	4·0	5·3	4·3			
20		0·5	0·3			0·3	0·4	0·3	0·6
72	1·3	1·7	1·4	1·2	1·1	0·4	1·0	1·4	1·4
25	−2·4		0·2	0·6	−0·3	3·2	2·5	2·0	6·4
30	−1·0	2·2	3·2	3·0	4·2	4·5	4·8	4·5	3·8
44	0·2	1·0	2·0	2·3	3·1	3·0	2·6	2·9	
50	1·6	0·7	0·4	0·9	0·6	0·4	0·7	1·0	1·3
60	0·6	1·1	1·0	1·6	2·6	2·4	1·8	2·1	2·1
64		−0·5	−0·8	−0·5		−0·3	1·0	0·9	1·1
70	0·3	1·3	1·7	1·1	1·9	1·0	1·7	1·3	1·0
79	−0·4	0·2	0·2	0·6	0·6	0·1	0·9	1·1	1·4
Class four									
3	−0·3	−0·5	−0·7	−0·9	−0·8	−0·8	−0·5	−0·4	−0·6
8		−0·1	0·1	−0·2	0·2			−0·4	−0·6
10	−0·2	−1·1	−0·9	−0·9	1·2	−1·4	−1·1	−1·0	−0·6
19	0·6	1·4	0·7	1·4	1·3	0·8		−0·3	−1·8
47	0·4	0·8	0·1			−0·2	−0·4	−0·7	−0·6
76[a]	0·4	−1·1	−0·3	−1·1	−0·9	−1·0			
78	−0·7	−0·6	−0·8	−0·8	−0·5	−0·7	−1·2	−1·2	−0·8
Class five									
17	2·0			−2·8	−4·6	−5·0	−7·8	−2·9	−8·4
34	−3·5	−8·4	−9·6	−10·2	−10·2	−13·4	−14·8	−12·4	−15·2

[a]Record ceases at 1968.

in this class show a tendency to rather more rapid relative gains in the years around 1966–1967, similar to that shown in the industries in the previous class. By 1968 these industries had shown a relative gain of 18000 jobs.

Class three consists of those industries that have not deviated a great deal from their expected ranges, the limit being set at about ±500 jobs. It is interesting that this class is by far the largest one, containing twenty-one categories. This indicates the fairly strong tendency to interregional stability of employment changes even in a period of very positive government intervention in the economy. However, in overall terms, the performance of industries in this class does not affect the region as a whole very much since, by 1968, they register a small net relative gain of 4600 jobs. For this reason they are not listed in table 4.

The final two classes contain the industries which registered significant relative losses of employment during the 1960s. The division is fairly clear between a fairly small group of seven categories which, between them, have a relative loss of 4200 jobs, and the three very large relative losers of employment: 'shipbuilding', 'iron and steel production', and 'locomotive production'. Once again, in class four with seven industries, the range of industry is quite wide from the 'manufacture of tobacco' and the 'manufacture of biscuits' to 'coke ovens and castings' and 'foundry work'. In general there are no industries which have lost a great deal of employment, rather, most of the industries just fail to reach the expected levels of employment fairly consistently throughout the period. This performance contrasts sharply with the fifth and final class which contains only three industries. The 'manufacture of locomotives and railway equipment' started the period with 4800 employees but declined rapidly until after 1965 no record is available of its employment since it fell below the 1000 employee cut-off point. The final two industries are, not surprisingly, 'general iron and steel' and 'shipbuilding and marine engineering'. By 1968 these two categories had between them accumulated a relative loss of 18400 jobs, 13400 of them coming from the shipbuilding category. By 1971 this relative loss had risen to 15000 jobs, which goes a long way towards wiping out a large part of the relative increases registered by the gaining categories. The main conclusion to be drawn from these figures is the marked preponderance of relative gains over relative losses of employment. Clearly, many manufacturing industries in the region fared much better in relation to the rest of the country during the 1960s than they did in the 1950s. If all classes are combined together then, by 1968, there is a total crude relative gain of employment amounting to 54000 jobs against which must be set a relative loss of 22600, giving a net gain of 31400 jobs. If some results are traced through to 1971 then the industries of class one accumulated a further gain of 10800 jobs, whilst the relative losses of the two remaining industries in class five rose by a further 5200 jobs, thus maintaining a very similar pattern to that seen in the earlier period.

6 Investigation of the rate of relative employment gains

However, in addition to these general conclusions, one interesting question remains. This concerns the tendency of the gaining categories to show a fairly general acceleration in relative growth around 1965 to 1967. In order to investigate the rate at which the gains were made, a new set of expected figures were derived using the yearly changes of employment in the country, thus generating a set of expected changes in the Northern region's employment. By using a slight modification of the previous formula to avoid problems of autocorrelation, a 99% confidence limit was set around these expected changes, and then the deviations of the North's actual performances were calculated. (For fuller details see Frost, 1974.) If these deviations are summed for those industries in classes one and two, then an interesting pattern emerges which is shown in figure 4. This graph confirms the impression of the previous section, and shows a clear peak of gains in the year 1967–1968, which falls away rapidly in the following year. This is interesting because practically every indicator of government

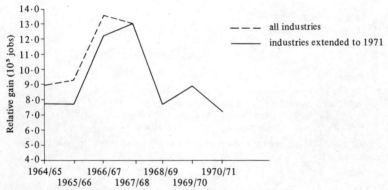

Figure 4. Total relative gains in classes one and two.

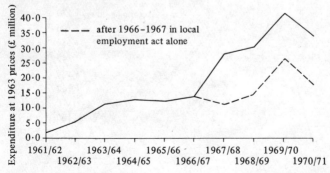

Source: Annual reports on the Local Employment Acts and Industrial Development Act, 1961–1971 (HMSO, London).

Figure 5. Expenditure in Northern region under Local Employment Act 1960 and 1966, together with the Industrial Development Act 1966.

spending on incentives and general investment in the region show rises towards the end of the period. The expenditure in the region under the Local Employment Acts and the Industrial Development Act shows a marked rise towards the end of the period (figure 5) as does the Northern region's share of total public investments in new building and construction (figure 6). In addition to this, the first payments of the Regional Employment Premium were made in 1968, bringing approximately another £30 million per year of government money into the region. However, in spite of this, the rate at which relative gains of employment were made by the region falls sharply after the peak of 1967–1968. Clearly, even on

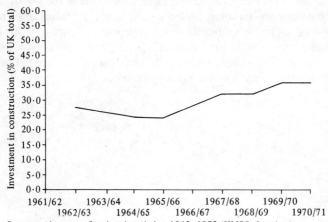

Source: Abstracts of regional statistics, 1965–1972 (HMSO, London).

Figure 6. Northern region's share of total public investment in new building and construction.

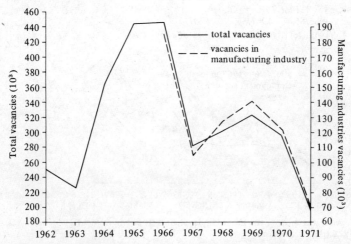

Source: British labour statistics year book, 1972 (HMSO, London)

Figure 7. United Kingdom national totals of unfilled vacancies.

the evidence of a few years available to this study, there appears to be no direct relationship between the rate of relative employment gain and the quantity of government assistance being provided to the region. The question then becomes one of finding other possible explanatory factors in the economy. In this respect the series which shows by far the greatest similarity to the pattern of relative gains is that of the number of unfilled vacancies in the economy (figure 7). Obviously very firm conclusions cannot be drawn on the evidence of seven observations, but the correspondence is very close, suggesting that some relationship must exist relating the rate of relative employment gains made by the Northern region to the level of demand for labour in the economy as a whole, the effects of the latter being lagged by about $1\frac{1}{2}$ years.

7 Conclusions
It is appropriate to draw two sets of conclusions from this work. The first set relate to the method that has been used to analyse the changing national position of manufacturing industry in the Northern region. This has proved to be moderately successful, with only five categories where the quality of estimation was open to serious doubt. It has facilitated the measurement of relative change in the Northern region on a yearly basis and has allowed some recognition to be made of the known randomness in the Department of Employment estimates of employees. Furthermore, as it has been shown elsewhere (Frost, 1975) that considerable complementarity between regions' employment changes exists even after the effects of national changes have been allowed for; this method has the advantage of taking such complementarity into account in a way that would not be possible using any modification of conventional shift and share methods.

The second set of conclusions relate to the evidence of regional change that has been produced in this study. It is clear that manufacturing industry in the Northern region employed many more people by 1968 and 1971 than would be expected from its performance as identified during the 1950s. In fact it can be seen that the region was some 30000 jobs better off by 1968, and the excess over the expected total was nearer 40000 jobs in 1971. The scale of this relative improvement largely reinforces the type of growth identified by Moore and Rhodes in their study of development areas as a whole (Moore and Rhodes, 1973). In addition to this general result the distribution of relative growth can be seen to be spread across a wide range of industries. The most rapid growth has clearly occurred in light industries that are new to the region, but this has been reinforced by substantial relative gains of employment made by some of the larger, well-established industries within the region.

However, in spite of the broad industrial base on which relative gains have been made, their distribution through time has been seen to be rather more concentrated. This uneven distribution suggests that the supply of labour in the economy as a whole is a critical factor in determining the rate at which the region experiences relative gains of employment, these gains appearing to result, in part, from a shortage of labour in the remainder of the country. This distribution of gains has also highlighted the decline in the relative improvement of the region in spite of an increase in government expenditure towards the end of the study period. This shows that the relationship between the level of government expenditure on regional problems and the resultant effects on the pattern of regional employment is by no means a simple one, depending very heavily, even after 40 years of government efforts, on the influence of general factors in the economy.

The evidence that has been presented above makes it very difficult to draw any general conclusions concerning the overall effectiveness of government regional policies. Superficially, it might be suggested that the apparently strong relationship between relative employment gains by the Northern region and the demand for labour in the economy is evidence of the ineffectiveness of government activity. However, it must be remembered that similar shortages of labour have occurred before, around 1955–1956 and 1961, without producing corresponding structural changes in manufacturing industry in the region. On this evidence it seems likely that it is the combination of government activity and economic conditions conducive to industrial change that is the critical factor lying behind the record of the North's performances during the 1960s. In terms of research into regional problems, this highlights the fact that great care must be taken not to interpret apparent relative gains of employment as resulting purely from the effects of government activity; whilst in the field of government policy these results show that the government cannot expect a direct return to the injection of more and more money into the 'problem' regions of the country. Instead, the key to the solution of regional problems lies more in managing the national economy in a way that will enable 'free market' economic forces to reinforce the effects of government policies.

References
Brown, A. J., 1967, "The 'green paper' on the development areas", *National Institute Economic Review*, **40**, 26-33.
Brown, H. J., 1969, "Shift and share projections of regional economic growth: an empirical test", *Journal of Regional Science*, **19**, 1-18.
Buck, T. W., 1970, "Shift and share analysis—a guide to regional policy?", *Regional Studies*, **4**, 445-450.
Cameron, G. C., Clark, B. D., 1966, *Industrial Movement and the Regional Problem*, Occasional Paper 5, Social and Economic Studies, University of Glasgow (Oliver and Boyd, Edinburgh).
Cameron, G. C., Reid, G. L., 1966, *Scottish Economic Planning and the Attraction of Industry*, Occasional Paper 6, Social and Economic Studies, University of Glasgow (Oliver and Boyd, Edinburgh).

Frost, M. E., 1974, "Regional employment change in Great Britain 1952-1968, with special reference to the influence of government policy on the Northern region", unpublished Ph. D. thesis, University of London.

Frost, M. E., 1975, *The Impact of Government Policy: A Case Study of Manufacturing Employment in the Northern Region* (Pergamon Press, Oxford).

Hallett, G., Randall, P., West, E. G., 1973, *Regional Policy for Ever?* (Institute of Economic Affairs, London).

Howard, R. S., 1968, *The Movement of Manufacturing Industry in the UK 1945-1965* (HMSO, London).

Johnston, J., 1963, *Econometric Methods* (McGraw-Hill, New York).

McCrone, G., 1969, *Regional Policy in Britain* (George Allen and Unwin, London).

Mackay, D. I., 1968, "Industrial structure and regional growth: a methodological problem", *Scottish Journal of Political Economy*, **15**, 129-143.

Mackay, D. I., Buxton, N. K., 1965, "A view of regional labour statistics", *Journal of the Royal Statistical Society, Series A*, **128** (part 2), 267-284.

Moore, B., Rhodes, J., 1973, "Evaluating the effects of British regional economic policy", *Economic Journal*, **83**, 87-110.

Stilwell, F. J. B., 1969, "Regional growth and structural adaptation", *Urban Studies*, **6**, 162-178.

Thirlwall, A. P., 1967, "A measure of the 'proper distribution of industry'", *Oxford Economic Papers*, **19**, 46-58.

Townroe, P. M., 1970, "Industrial location decisions", Occasional Paper 15, Centre for Urban and Regional Studies, University of Birmingham, UK.

Appendix

Relationship between industrial categories and the 1958 and 1948 Standard Industrial Classifications.

New industrial category		Minimum list heading	
		1958	1948
1	Grain milling	211	150
2	Bread and flour confectionery	212	151
3	Biscuits	213	152
4	Milk products	215	154
5	Cocoa and chocolate	217	156
6	Brewing and malting	231	163
7[a]	Other drinks	239	168
8	Tobacco	240	169
9	Food, meat, and vegetable products	214, 216, 218, 219, 229	153, 155, 157, 162
10	Coke ovens	261	30
11	Mineral oil refining	262	36
12[a]	Chemicals, dyes, and synthetic resins	271, 276	31
13[a]	Pharmaceutical products	272	32
14	Explosives and fireworks	273	33
15[a]	Paints and printing inks	274	34
16[a]	Light chemical products	275, 263, 277	35, 39
17	General iron and steel	311	40, 41, 43(i), 43(ii)
18	Tube manufacture	312	44
19	Castings and foundry work	313	42
20	Nonferrous metals	321, 322	49
21	Agricultural machinery	331	52
22	Small tools	332, 333	54
23	Industrial engines	334	55
24	Textile machinery	335	56
25	Other nonelectrical machinery	336-339, 349	69
26	Factory plant	341	52, 58
27	Ordnance	342	57
28	Scientific and surgical instruments	351	100
29	Watches and clocks	352	101
30	Electrical machinery	361	70
31	Insulated wires and cables	362	71
32	Telegraph and telephone apparatus	363	72
33	Radios, domestic, and other electrical goods	364, 365, 369	73-75, 79
34	Shipbuilding and marine engineering	370	50, 51
35	Car and cycle manufacture	381, 382	80
36[a]	Aircraft manufacture	383	82
37	Locomotives and railway equipment	384	84, 85
38	Railway carriages and wagons	385	86
39	Prams and hand trucks	389	89
40	Tools, implements, and cutlery	391, 392	90

Appendix (continued)

New industrial category		Minimum list	
		1958	1948
41	Bolts, nuts and screws	393	91
42	Wire and wire products	394	93
43	Jewellery and plate	396	102
44	Other light metals	395, 399	94, 95, 99
45	Manmade fibres	411	113
46	Spinning and weaving	412, 413	110, 111, 114, 115
47	Woollen and worsted manufacture	414	112
48	Jute	415	116
49[a]	Ropes, twines, and nets	416	117
50	Hosiery and other knitted goods	417	118
51	Lace	418	119
52[a]	Carpets	419	120
53	Narrow fabrics	421	121
54	Made-up textiles	422	122
55	Textile finishing	423	123
56	Other textile industries	429	129
57	Leather production	431	130
58	Leather goods	432	131
59	Fur goods	433	132
60	Production of outerwear	441–443	140
61	Shirts, dresses, and underwear	444, 445	141, 142
62	Hats and caps	446	143
63	Dresses, not elsewhere specified	449	147
64	Footwear	461	20
65	Bricks and fireclay goods	461	20
66	Pottery	462	21
67	Glass and glass products	463	22, 23
68	Cement production	464	24
69	Building materials and abrasives	469	29
70	Timber production	471	170
71	Furniture and upholstered goods	472, 473	171
72	Wooden containers and baskets	475	173
74	Wood and cork products, not elsewhere specified	479	179
75	Paper and board manufacture	481	180
76[a]	Cardboard boxes and cartons	482	182
77[a]	Other paper and board goods	483	181, 183
78	Printing and publishing of newspapers and magazines	486	186
79	Other printing and publishing	489	189
80	Rubber manufacture	491	190
81	Linoleum and leather cloth	492	191
82	Brushes and brooms	493	192
83	Toys and games	494	193
84	Miscellaneous stationers' goods	495	194
85	Other manufacturing industries	49, 499	199

[a] Records cease in 1968 owing to SIC changes.